Dr Beeching's Axe
50 YEARS ON

Dr Beeching's Axe 50 YEARS ON

ILLUSTRATED MEMORIES OF BRITAIN'S LOST RAILWAYS

JULIAN HOLLAND

Langstone bridge which carried the Hayling Island branch between Langston and North Hayling was a wonderful position for photography especially in the late afternoon. At the beginning of November 1963 just before the line closed, a 'Terrier' 0-6-0T makes its way towards Hayling Island against the background of a superb sunset.

D&C
David and Charles

ABOVE On 5 March 1966 the Locomotive Club of Great Britain (LCGB) ran a farewell tour over the Somerset & Dorset line to mark its closure two days later. Whilst the sunny weather was in contrast to the sadness of the occasion, 'West Country' and 'Battle of Britain' Bulleid pacifics Nos 34006 'Bude' and 34057 'Biggin Hill' make a glorious sight as they emerge from the twin bore Chilcompton tunnel on their way south from Bath to Bournemouth.

RIGHT In an idyllic setting near Bala, a BR Standard '4MT' 4-6-0 is heading east with a Dolgelly to Ruabon train in the summer of 1964 at a time when there were few trains per day over the 54 miles between the two towns.

OPPOSITE Baynards station on the Guildford to Cranleigh line was built to serve the nearby Baynards Park and was hidden away in the then remote countryside between Cranleigh and Rudgwick. It became quite famous for its display of dahlias which in the late summer and autumn adorned the flower beds on both platforms. Here, seen from the northbound platform, is the southbound platform after the station closed in June 1965, it heyday years past. However the story has a happy ending since the station was bought and restored by its new owner and is now kept in beautiful condition.

CONTENTS

INTRODUCTION

Wednesday 27 March 1963 was not a good day for me. As far as I can recall it was double physics followed by PE before disappearing off down to the art room for a bit of skiving – my art master Bernie Jones didn't seem to mind as I was probably helping out with the scenery for the school's next blockbuster Shakespearean production. Out of the corner of my eye I kept a lookout for the daily train of coal empties that used to struggle up from Gloucester's Bristol Road gasworks to Tuffley Junction – the regular loco was usually Fowler '4F' 0-6-0 No. 44123 and if the track was wet then we were treated to some wheelspin, stalling and sanding. With O-levels looming my trainspotting had been limited to a few local trips: on the previous weekend hanging around Gloucester on the Saturday – two 'Jubilees' Nos 45739 and 45575 – and visiting Horton Road and Barnwood sheds on the Sunday. Even by this date it was still virtually all steam, with the highlight on the Sunday being Class '9F' 2-10-0 No. 92000 in ex-works condition. Little did I know that within a few years this and countless other wondrous railway scenes would be swept away forever.

The page from my notebook for the week preceding the publication of the 'Beeching Report'. All of the sightings, mostly steam, were recorded in the Gloucester and Cheltenham area.

On the same day a hundred or so miles away to the east, in the Charing Cross Hotel, the Chairman of the British Railways Board, Dr Richard Beeching, was giving a news conference on the publication that day of his report on the future of Britain's railways. Titled *The Reshaping of British Railways* it was available from Her Majesty's Stationery Office for the princely sum of one shilling (5p).

Now, the closure of uneconomic railway lines was not a new phenomenon and had been gathering pace since 1948 when the rundown post-war railways were nationalised – around 3,000 miles had already been closed by the time of the 'Beeching Report'. The 1955 *Modernisation and Re-equipment of British Railways* was a worthy attempt to bring Britain's railways into the modern age over a period of 15 years but the implementation of it left a lot to be desired – untried and unreliable diesels were hurriedly introduced while modern and efficient steam locomotives, sometimes no more than five years old, were being sent to the scrapheap.

had been appointed by the then Minister of Transport, Ernest Marples, to the Stedeford Committee which was set up to look into modern management practices for the railways. So impressed was Marples with Beeching's ideas about drastically pruning the railway network that in 1961 he asked him to join the

British Transport Commission (BTC) as chairman-designate of the new British Railways Board. His brief was to reorganize Britain's railway system. Beeching became chairman of British Railways at the beginning of 1963 and within three months his infamous 'Report' had been published. Drastic surgery was not far away.

Britain's railways had been a steady drain on the taxpayer since nationalisation in 1948

Of course, Britain's railways had been a steady drain on the taxpayer since nationalisation in 1948 – but so had the Armed Forces, the Police and the NHS, except they are not expected to make a profit. Although the '1955 Modernisation Plan' had attempted to bring the railways into the twentieth century the steady drip, drip of passengers and freight to road transport coupled with a worn-out system, out-of-date working practices, over-manning and strikes had by 1961 brought about a staggering £87 million annual working deficit for British Railways – £1.65 billion at today's figures. The Government had to stem these ever-increasing losses to the public purse. Enter Dr Beeching.

In 1960 Dr Richard Beeching, then Technical Director at ICI,

The Modernisation and Re-equipment of British Railways was published in 1955 and foresaw a fifteen-year implementation period costing £1.24 billion. After eight years it was stopped in its tracks by the notorious 'Beeching Report'.

MODERNISATION
AND
RE-EQUIPMENT
OF
BRITISH
RAILWAYS

NOT FOR PUBLICATION, BROADCAST OR USE ON CLUB TAPES
BEFORE 00.30 HOURS G.M.T. TUESDAY, JANUARY 25TH, 1955.
ANY MESSAGES SENT IN ADVANCE TO ADDRESSES OVERSEAS
SHOULD BE PREFACED WITH THIS EMBARGO.

THE BEECHING REPORT

The 'Beeching Report', as it became known, consisted of two parts: Part 1 was made up of 148 pages of statistics and analysis and a 42-page Appendix listing stations and lines that were proposed for closure; Part 2 had 13 fold-out maps that illustrated the statistical information gathered in Part 1. In short the 'Report' recommended the closure of around 5,000 route miles of railway and the closing of a third of stations. Hidden away on page ten of Part 1 was the staggering piece of information that all of the statistics used in the report were gathered from a survey that took place in just one week, 17–23 April 1961. According to these figures a third of the route mileage carried only one per cent of passenger and freight traffic. And thus was the fate of our railways sealed.

With motorway-loving Ernest Marples as Conservative Minister of Transport the destruction of Britain's railways moved into top gear following the publication of the 'Report'. A change of Government on 16 October 1964 saw no end to the slaughter, especially in rural areas, even though the Labour

Western Region

British Railways Board

Transport Act 1962

Withdrawal of railway passenger services

The Minister of Transport has given his consent to the Board's proposals to discontinue the passenger train services between WEST DRAYTON & YIEWSLEY and STAINES WEST

and from the following stations and halts
Colnbrook Estate Halt
Colnbrook
Poyle Estate Halt
Poyle, for Stanwell Moor Halt
Staines West

These services will be withdrawn on Monday 29 March 1965

The terms of the Minister's consent can be inspected at local booking offices

Death sentence. Closure notices like this were being pasted up at thousands of stations up and down the country.

In total around 4,500 route miles, over 2,000 stations and 67,700 jobs were lost

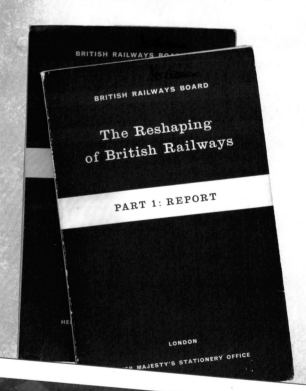

Party had previously pledged to halt the closures if elected – you just can't trust politicians, although to be fair there were a few reprieves under Labour's Barbara Castle. By August 1968 standard gauge steam traction had been eradicated from British Railways and another 3,500 route miles had been closed. Closures, albeit at a much slower rate, continued until the mid-1970s when the system stabilized to more or less what exists today. In total around 4,500 route miles, over 2,000 stations and 67,700 jobs were lost. In more recent and enlightened times – with gridlock imminent on Britain's road network – a few of these closed railways have been reopened but we will never be able to regain all that was destroyed in the frenzied destruction that took place following the publication of the 'Beeching Report'. What is even more maddening is that today's 'privatised' railways cost more in real terms to the taxpayer than poor old BR did in 1961!

BEECHING'S LIMITED EDITION TEAM

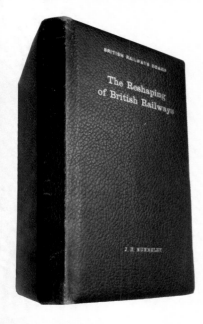

One of only three copies of the 'Beeching Report' which were bound in leather and stamped in gold with the names of Richard Beeching, F C Margetts and J H Nunneley respectively.

Leather-bound and gold-blocked copies of the 'Beeching Report' were presented to Dr Beeching and his two-man team by the British Railways Board. The team consisted of John Nunneley, formerly Deputy Director of Publicity and Promotions at Beaverbrook Newspapers, who joined the British Railways Board as Chief Publicity Officer; and Frederick Margetts, formerly General Manager of the North Eastern Region of BR, who was responsible for obtaining required railway data. Two 'Reports' were produced: a restricted issue for Government, printed in-house; and a copy for general sale to be printed and published by HMSO.

John Nunneley recruited ten highly skilled typists from outside the Railways, each working in shifts of ten hours in conditions of great secrecy. The media, knowing the 'Report' was in hand, went to great but unsuccessful lengths to obtain advance information of Dr Beeching's proposals, particularly those relating to overall network size reduction, withdrawal of passenger train services, and line and station closures.

John Nunneley's leather bound copy of the 'Report' was signed in 1984 by Lord Beeching and Mr Margetts. In his letter to John, 'Dick' Beeching mentioned that he had forgotten that it was the 21st anniversary of the 'Report' and went on to say 'that some of the recommendations in both it and in the second Report on "Rationalisation of the Trunk Routes" are still being rediscovered! Such is the refusal to collaborate with the inevitable.'

THE HOUSE OF LORDS HAS ITS SAY

Labour peer Lord Stonham made a speech in the House of Lords on 2 May 1963 on 'The Economic and Social Aspects of the "Beeching Plan".' Here are a few of his more interesting and wry observations:

'My Lords, on Monday in another place the right honourable gentleman the Minister of Transport said categorically that 25,726 jobs would disappear, and I think that illustrates the whole trouble that we are in to-day. It brings me into immediate disagreement with the noble Viscount with regard to his right honourable friend the Minister of Transport, who he said had been the subject of ungenerous attacks. Indeed, the noble Leader of the House paid such fervent tribute to his right

honourable friend, that I begin to wonder if this was a preliminary to his canonisation as St Ernest and his transfer to another sphere.'

'Then, dealing with the very reasonable request made by Lord Morrison of Lambeth for a cost analysis, a full inquiry into the roads on the same lines as we have now had from Dr. Beeching on the railways, he said, "We cannot possibly wait for such an inquiry".'

On the cost of roads to the tax payer:

'That is a total of £1,210 million a year, apart from the cost to the Health Services arising from noise, fumes and so on. And if you deduct the receipts from fuel duties and vehicle taxes, it reveals a net subsidy to road transport

of over £600 million a year that is, four times the railway deficit.'

'Everything in the Beeching Plan is in this book [*The 1955 Modernisation and Re-equipment of British Railways*], and it has been in increasingly large-scale operation for eight years. In fact we are now half-way through the fifteen-year plan which was adumbrated when this Report was published. Everything is in it except for some of the figures; and many of these figures in the Beeching Report are known to be wrong, although unfortunately none of them can be really checked...'

'In fact, the only pleasant comment I have heard on the Plan is the advice to use Dr. Beeching's face cream because it removes all lines.'

THE SECOND BEECHING REPORT

If implemented, the second Beeching report would have seen a further 4,500 miles of railways closed across Britain. The darker lines on the map show the few railways that would have remained.

Published on 16 February 1965, *The Development of the Major Railway Trunk Routes* was Dr Beeching's second Report which proposed investment in just nine main lines serving only major centres of population. By implication there would have been further swingeing closures of another 4,500 miles of railway, in many cases major trunk routes. This was all too much for the new union-sponsored Labour government to stomach who promptly rejected the report. Three months later Dr Beeching resigned as Chairman of the British Railways Board and returned to his old job at ICI.

RICHARD BEECHING

Richard Beeching was born in Sheerness, Kent, on 21 April 1913 and educated at Maidstone Grammar School and the Imperial College of Science and Technology, London, where he gained a first in physics. In 1936 he went to work at the Fuel Research Station and in the following year joined the Mond Nickel Company. During the Second World War he was loaned to the Ministry of Supply where he became deputy chief engineer of Armaments Design in 1946. In 1948 he went to ICI where he was a leading light in the development of 'terylene' and in 1953 was appointed as vice-

president of ICI in Canada.

In 1960 Beeching was appointed to the Stedeford Committee which was set up to look into modern management practices for the railways. A year later he was asked to join the British Transport Commission as chairman-designate of the new British Railways Board. In 1963, the year of his now infamous 'Report', Beeching was appointed Chairman of British Railways, a position he held until 1965 when he fell out with the newly incumbent Labour Minister of Transport, Tom Fraser, soon after the publication of his second report, *The*

Development of the Major Railway Trunk Routes. Soon after leaving BR Beeching was made a life peer.

Beeching then returned to ICI and was appointed deputy chairman. He retired in 1977 and died in East Grinstead, West Sussex, on 23 March 1985. While Beeching's name will always be linked with railway closures, some of his more positive recommendations such as liner trains and merry-go-round coal trains can be seen in action on Britain's railways today.

ABOUT THIS BOOK

This book is simply a memorial to all that was lost following the publication of the 'Beeching Report' 50 years ago. Across the land railways were ripped up and communities were broken apart. Vast regions of England, Scotland and Wales were left without a railway link to the outside world. Skilled railwaymen, who for generations had loyally given their all to the 'company', were tossed aside for the sake of a politically motivated love affair with road transport.

TOP With only a few weeks to go before closure of the line, Ivatt Class '2' 2-6-2T No. 41241 (now preserved) approaches Drws-y-nant station with a Barmouth to Corwen train on 19 December 1964.

ABOVE The end of a main line – Stanier 'Black 5' 4-6-0 No. 45292 halts at Woodford Halse station with a down train on the last day of services on the Great Central line, 3 September 1966.

Across the land railways were ripped up and communities were broken apart

There was never any joined-up thinking, it was never properly thought through and our country has suffered ever since – witness the near gridlock on our motorways. Thanks a lot Mr Marples for it is you who should shoulder most of the blame for this senseless destruction of our railway network – let's face it, Dr Beeching was only doing his job, albeit with a very handsome salary – and shame on all of the other politicians (of both parties) who followed in the coat tails of your dastardly plan.

With under four months to go before closure of this route '2251' Class 0-6-0 No. 3201 calls at Talybont-on-Usk with a Brecon to Newport train on 10 September 1962.

Author's note: I have tried to include every railway line that was closed as a result of the 'Beeching Report'. They are all shown on Maps 9 and 9A in Part 2 of the 'Report' and have been annotated for clarity at the beginning of each regional chapter in this book. Needless to say it is not plain sailing and there may well be some omissions: there are lines that were marked for closure on the maps which were actually closed before publication of the 'Report'; there are lines that were not originally on Beeching's original hit list but which were closed anyway; there are lines that were originally marked down for closure but which were reprieved; there are even one or two which seem to have not existed at all. I have tried to include them all.

THE CASUALTIES

1. Taunton to Chard and Chard Junction –
   10 September 1962
2. Gwinear Road to Helston – 3 November 1962
3. Plymouth to Launceston (GWR) – 31 December 1962
4. Chacewater to Newquay – 4 February 1963
5. Churston to Brixham – 13 May 1963
6. Witham to Yatton via Cheddar – 9 September 1963
7. Tiverton Junction to Hemyock – 9 September 1963
8. Brent to Kingsbridge – 16 September 1963
9. Stoke Canon (Exeter) to Dulverton via Tiverton –
   7 October 1963
10. Yeovil Town to Taunton – 15 June 1964
11. Bristol to Portishead – 7 September 1964
12. Tiverton Junction to Tiverton – 5 October 1964
13. Avonmouth to Filton Junction – 23 November 1964
14. Lostwithiel to Fowey – 4 January 1965
14A. Torrington to Halwill Junction – 1 March 1965
15. Chippenham to Calne – 20 September 1965
16. Barnstaple to Torrington – 4 October 1965
17. Axminster to Lyme Regis – 29 November 1965
18. Yeovil Town to Yeovil Pen Mill – 29 November 1965
19. Evercreech Junction to Highbridge – 7 March 1966
20. Bath Green Park to Bournemouth Central –
    7 March 1966
21. Mangotsfield to Bath Green Park – 7 March 1966
22. Seaton Junction to Seaton – 7 March 1966
23. Holt Junction to Patney & Chirton via Devizes –
    18 April 1966
24. Yeovil Town to Yeovil Junction – 3 October 1966
25. Yatton to Clevedon – 3 October 1966
26. Taunton to Barnstaple – 3 October 1966
27. Halwill Junction to Bude – 3 October 1966
28. Meldon Junction to Wadebridge – 3 October 1966
29. Gunnislake to Callington – 7 November 1966
30. Bodmin Road to Bodmin, Wadebridge and Padstow –
    30 January 1967
31. Sidmouth Junction to Sidmouth and Exmouth –
    6 March 1967
32. Okehampton to Bere Alston – 6 May 1968
33. Barnstaple to Ilfracombe – 5 October 1970
34. Taunton to Minehead – 4 January 1971
35. Wareham to Swanage – 3 January 1972*
36. Coleford Junction to Okehampton – 5 June 1972*
37. Maiden Newton to Bridport – 5 May 1975

Note: Dates give are for withdrawal of passenger services
* = not listed for closure in the 'Beeching Report'

THE SURVIVORS

A. St Erth to St Ives
B. Liskeard to Looe
C. Plymouth to Gunnislake
D. Exeter (Central) to Exmouth
E. Bristol (Temple Meads) to Severn Beach

Complete with wreath and large headboard ex-GWR '4575' Class 2-6-2T No. 5564 waits in deep snow at Yelverton station on the last day of service on the Plymouth to Launceston line on 29 December 1962.

Bristol Barrow Road's '2251' Class 0-6-0 No. 3218 is given a final touch up at Witham station while working the last day of passenger services on the Cheddar Valley Line on 7 September 1963.

Ivatt Class 2 2-6-2Ts Nos. 41307 and 41249 head through West Pennard station with the Locomotive Club of Great Britain's 'Somerset & Dorset Rail Tour' on the former S&DJR line from Highbridge to Evercreech Junction on 5 March 1966 – the final day of scheduled services on this line.

WEST COUNTRY

CARDIFF

BRISTOL

BOURNEMOUTH

EXETER

PLYMOUTH

13
15
11 E
21
23
25
6
20
19
34
10
20
33
26
1
18
24
16
12
7
9
37
14A
17
22
31
27
36
D
28
3
32
29
3
C
5
14 B
8

KEY TO BEECHING REPORT MAPS

▬▬▬	All passenger services to be withdrawn
▪▪▪▪	All stopping passenger services to be withdrawn
▬▬▬	No closure proposals

Taunton to Chard and Chard Junction

The town of Chard in Somerset was unfortunate as it was bypassed by the London & South Western Railway's main line between Salisbury and Exeter when it opened in 1860. An earlier proposal to convert the Chard Canal between Creech St Michael, near Taunton, and Chard into a railway came to nothing and it was only on 8 May 1863 that the town became rail connected when a 3¼-mile branch line from Chard Road (later renamed Chard Junction), on the LSWR main line, to Chard Town was opened by the Chard Railway Company. The following year the company was taken over by the LSWR.

Meanwhile the Chard & Taunton Railway had been authorised in 1861 to build a 12¾-mile line from Creech St Michael to Chard alongside the existing canal. This scheme was taken over by the broad gauge Bristol & Exeter Railway (later to form part of the Great Western Railway) in 1862 – the B&ER also purchased and closed the canal in the same year. The line opened to a new joint station in Chard on 11 September 1866. Here there was a change of gauge, thus preventing through running, and LSWR trains which still called at Chard Town station were forced to reverse out of their terminus before continuing the short journey to the joint station. Here the two companies led separate existences with their own signal boxes and staff and it wasn't until 1891 that the GWR converted the Taunton line to standard gauge – the delay in conversion was due to GWR paranoia that the LSWR would obtain running powers into Taunton. Chard Town station closed in 1917 when the GWR took over operating the line to Chard Junction – the joint station at Chard was also renamed Chard Central. Chard Town station remained open for goods until 1966 (see below).

Although from 1917 train services were operated by the GWR and later, following nationalisation, by the Western Region, there were very few through trains timetabled between Taunton and Chard Junction – the normal pattern of weekday service in the late 1950s was five return journeys between Taunton and Chard Central and seven shuttle trains from Chard Central to Chard Junction. Services were suspended for four months in 1951 due to the national shortage of coal. Listed for closure in the 'Beeching Report', the end actually came on 10 September 1962, over six months before its publication, when both lines were closed to passengers. Freight services continued between Creech St Michael and Chard until 1964 and between Chard Junction and Chard Town until 1966 – the last steam-hauled goods train ran on 12 June 1965 behind Class '4MT' 4-6-0 No. 75005 after which NBL 'D63XX' diesel hydraulics were used.

Labour peer Lord Stonham, in his speech to the House of Lords on 2 May 1963, chose to point out that 'The Mayor of Chard last week set out the true position in the West Country in these words: "To annihilate the unprofitable, but extremely safe, railway system by increasing the lethal propensities of our ridiculous and costly road system will transfer the price to be paid in money to an account which will be paid for in blood." We shall also have to pay a lot in money.'

The section of trackbed between Chard, Donyatt and Ilminster is now a footpath and cycleway (National Cycle Route 33) while the former station buildings at Hatch, Ilminster and Chard Central have all survived.

With only just over a month before closure, '5700' Class 0-6-0PT No. 3787 waits at Chard Central station with a train from Taunton on 4 August 1962.

'4500' Class 2-6-2T No. 4570 leaves Nancegollan station with a train for Helston on 23 July 1958.

Seen here on 15 August 1960, deserted Coryton station lay deep in rural Devon on the Plymouth to Launceston branch.

CLOSED
NOVEMBER
3
1962

Gwinear Road to Helston

The Helston Railway was opened as a standard gauge branch line from Gwinear Road, on the Great Western Railway's Plymouth to Penzance main line, to Helston on 9 May 1887. Later taken over by the GWR, the 8¾-mile line became famous for the groundbreaking railway feeder bus service from Helston to The Lizard which began operating in 1903 – an authorised light railway along this route had previously failed to materialise due to lack of funds.

The frequent passenger service on the line normally amounted to seven journeys each weekday between Helston and Gwinear Road and eight in the opposite direction with some trains passing at intermediate Nancegollan station. Goods traffic was heavy, particularly during the Second World War when the Royal Naval Air Station was being built at nearby Culdrose, but also for seasonal traffic such as broccoli and flowers.

Although the line was listed for closure in the 'Beeching Report', the end actually came over five months earlier on 3 November 1962 when passenger services, by then dieselised, ceased. Goods traffic continued until 3 October 1964 when NBL Type 2 diesel locomotive D6324 hauled the last official goods train on the branch. Any remaining wagons were collected by the same loco on 9 October and by mid-1965 the rails had been lifted.

Despite closure nearly 50 years ago much of the infrastructure of the line remains intact. Most of the bridges and the viaduct over the River Cober north of Helston still stand while the new Helston Railway Preservation Company is currently relaying track at the southern end of the line between Truthall and Trevarno.

CLOSED
DECEMBER
31
1962

Plymouth to Launceston (GWR)

The broad gauge South Devon & Tavistock Railway opened from Tavistock Junction, on the South Devon Railway near Marsh Mills, to Tavistock in 1859 and amalgamated with the latter railway shortly afterwards. It was extended to Launceston by the Launceston & South Devon Railway in 1865 and was amalgamated with the SDR in 1873. The entire route became part of the GWR in 1876.

In the same year the standard gauge London & South Western Railway had reached Lydford from Okehampton and had obtained running powers over mixed gauge track on the GWR's line from Launceston to Plymouth. This arrangement ended in 1890 when LSWR trains began to travel over the Plymouth, Devonport & South Western Junction Railway between Lydford and Devonport. The GWR's line to Tavistock and Launceston was converted to standard gauge in 1892. This meant that both Tavistock and Launceston were served by two stations and the duplication of routes was never a recipe for financial success. To reduce costs the GWR terminus at Launceston was closed in 1952 with trains from Tavistock South diverted into the ex-LSWR station.

Listed for closure in the 'Beeching Report', passenger services were withdrawn on 31 December 1962. Goods services continued between Lydford and Tavistock South until 25 September 1964, Lydford and Launceston until 28 February 1966 and china clay traffic from Tavistock Junction to Marsh Mills until 2008. Much of the line's infrastructure such as viaducts and tunnels survives today. The Plym Valley Cycle Path follows the trackbed between Marsh Mills and Yelverton while the section from Marsh Mills to Plym Bridge has been reopened by the Plym Valley Railway.

CLOSED FEBRUARY 4 1963

Chacewater to Newquay

The single track railway from Blackwater Junction, a quarter of a mile west of Chacewater, to Newquay via Perranporth was one of the last new railways of any importance to be built in Cornwall. It was opened between Chacewater and Perranporth on 6 July 1903 and to Newquay on 2 January 1905. The section between Shepherds station and Tolcarn Junction, near Newquay, was built along the course of a former mineral railway that served East Wheal Rose Mine. On the Cornish main line, Blackwater Junction was originally built as a triangular junction complete with three signal boxes but this was taken out of use in 1924 and trains from Perranporth and Newquay continued along a new parallel single track before joining the main line at Chacewater.

By the 1950s weekday passenger services usually consisted of between seven and nine return trains, the majority starting or finishing their journey at Truro. Journey times for the 18¾ miles between Newquay and Chacewater were around an hour with trains passing at St Agnes or Perranporth. Despite being well patronised during the summer months this scenic railway with tantalising glimpses of the sea was closed completely on 4 February 1963 – less than two months before it was listed for closure in the 'Beeching Report'.

Today, a 1½-mile section of the trackbed of the line near the site of Mitchell & Newlyn Halt is used by the 15 inch gauge Lappa Valley Railway between its stations of Benny Halt and East Wheal Rose. Some infrastructure has survived including the St Agnes station building, Goonbell Viaduct and Cox Viaduct near Perranporth.

CLOSED MAY 13 1963

Churston to Brixham

The two-mile broad gauge Torbay & Brixham Railway opened between Churston, on the Paignton to Dartmouth line, to the fishing port of Brixham on 28 February 1868. The station here was inconveniently located high on a hill some distance from the harbour. More or less entirely financed by Brixham solicitor Richard Wolston, the cost of building the railway led to his bankruptcy two years later but the company continued to be run by his family. The line was worked by the South Devon Railway until 1876 when that company became part of the Great Western Railway. From then until 1883, when the GWR bought the company, the Brixham branch was totally independent – however, the struggle to survive eventually led to the sale of the railway. The line was converted to standard gauge in 1892.

Outgoing fish traffic from Brixham was the mainstay of the line right up until closure although passenger traffic for the seven-minute journey seriously declined in the 1950s following a cutback in services due to a shortage of coal and competition from a Devon General bus service which linked Churston station with a more conveniently located stop in Brixham. Steam auto trains were replaced by diesel multiple units in 1961 but it was all too late. According to BR, closure would save £4,800 each year and over £13,000 in maintenance costs spread over the next five years. Listed for closure in the 'Beeching Report', the Brixham branch succumbed on 13 May 1963, less than two months after the publication of the infamous report. A year later the rusting railway came back to life for a short time during the making of a film but the track was lifted shortly afterwards.

'4575' Class 2-6-2T No. 5526 leaves Perranporth station with a train for Newquay on 14 September 1958.

'1400' Class 0-4-2T No. 1470 waits in the bay platform at Churston station with the 11.07am train to Brixham on 15 August 1960.

Smartly turned out by Bristol Barrow Road shed, '2251' Class 0-6-0 No. 3218 gets ready to leave Shepton Mallet station on the last day of passenger services on the Cheddar Valley line, 7 September 1963. Judging by the black smoke fireman David Sheppard appears to be using up some slack he found in the tender!

CLOSED
SEPTEMBER
9
1963

Witham to Yatton via Cheddar

The first part of what became known as the Strawberry Line opened in 1858 between Witham, on the Bristol to Weymouth line, and Shepton Mallet. Known as the East Somerset Railway, the broad gauge line was extended westwards to the small city of Wells in 1862. The terminus here was named Wells East. From the west the broad gauge Cheddar Valley & Yatton Railway opened between Yatton, on the Bristol & Exeter Railway's main line, to Wells in 1870. Operated from the outset by the B&ER, the city terminus was named Tucker Street. Between these two stations was a third terminus: the by-then standard gauge Somerset & Dorset Railway station of Priory Road at the end of their branch line from Glastonbury. The 200 yards of standard gauge track prevented through running between Witham and Yatton until 1875 when both the East Somerset (bought by the Great Western Railway in 1874) and the Bristol & Exeter's Cheddar Valley railways were converted to standard gauge. A year later the B&ER was amalgamated with the GWR.

With popular tourist destinations such as Cheddar, Wookey and Wells and important goods traffic such as strawberries and milk, the 'Strawberry Line' was kept fairly busy until the Second World War.

Journey time for the 31¾-mile journey was around a leisurely 1½-hours. However, increased competition from road transport brought a serious decline in traffic after the war and this delightful rural railway was listed for closure in the 'Beeching Report'. Apparently the line had working expenses of £60,000 per year as against receipts of £9,500 and a third of the passengers using it were schoolchildren. Closure soon followed on 9 September 1963 although goods traffic continued between Yatton and Cranmore until July 1964, with bitumen traffic from Ellesmere Port continuing to Cranmore via Witham until 1985.

However this was definitely not the end for the Strawberry Line. Now a footpath and cycleway with the same name utilises the trackbed from Yatton station through to Cheddar via Shute Shelve Tunnel. An extension eastwards to Wells and Shepton Mallet is currently being planned. At the eastern end of the line the East Somerset Railway based at Cranmore station runs steam trains along 2½ miles of track to Mendip Vale on the eastern outskirts of Shepton Mallet. Modern Foster Yeoman stone trains continue to use the eastern end of the line between Merehead Quarry and the main line at Witham.

CLOSED SEPTEMBER 9 1963

Tiverton Junction to Hemyock

The independent Culm Valley Light Railway was financed by local farmers and land owners and opened between Tiverton Junction, on the Great Western Railway's Bristol to Exeter main line, and Hemyock on 29 May 1876. The promised profits never materialised so the shareholders cut their losses and sold the railway to GWR in 1880.

Despite the earlier failure of the light railway company, the 7½-mile meandering branch line saw better times under GWR ownership. Several industries were attracted to the valley along with an enormous rail-connected creamery that was built at Hemyock. Passenger traffic was never heavy – in the 1950s only three or four return trips each day – and was catered for by a couple of antiquated former Barry Railway gas-lit coaches hauled by Class '14XX' 0-4-2Ts into the British Railways era. Getting rid of steam haulage and the veteran coaches was reckoned by BR to save them £1,500 each year. Listed for closure in the 'Beeching Report', this delightful little line lost its passenger service on 9 September 1963 but goods, in particular milk traffic from the creamery, continued with diesel haulage until 31 October 1975.

Since closure, the route of the line has been severed by the M5 motorway near Tiverton Junction but several stretches of the trackbed are now footpaths alongside the River Culm.

A busy scene at Kingsbridge station, looking towards the buffers with a Brent-bound diesel railcar waiting to depart, circa 1963.

CLOSED SEPTEMBER 16 1963

Brent to Kingsbridge

The railway was slow in coming to the South Hams district of South Devon, adequately served as it was by horse-drawn coach services. Late in the day the Kingsbridge & Salcombe Railway was authorised in 1882 but was taken over by the Great Western Railway before its opening on 19 December 1893.

The scenic 12½-mile single track line from Brent, on the GWR's Exeter to Plymouth main line, followed the twists and turns of the Avon Valley and crossed the river at numerous points – the only passing place was at Gara Bridge. In the 1930s camping coaches were stationed at stations along the line which was also served by a through coach from Paddington on the 'Cornish Riviera Express'. In the Second World War the line was exceptionally busy during the build-up to the D-Day landings in June 1944.

Steam was replaced by diesel multiple units in 1962 but by then the writing was on the wall and the line was listed for closure in the 'Beeching Report'. Despite a last-minute upsurge in traffic, complete closure came on 16 September 1963 – the prospect of reopening it as a heritage line soon came to nothing thanks to the machinations of British Railways. Glad to see the back of the line, BR had lifted all of the track within eight months of closure.

Although the goods shed still survives at Kingsbridge, sadly the station building was demolished in 2009. Intermediate stations at Avonwick, Gara Bridge and Loddiswell have been restored as private residences. Many of the bridges also survive.

'1400' Class 0-4-2T No. 1450 has just arrived at Hemyock from Tiverton Junction with the Locomotive Club of Great Britain's 'West Countryman Rail Tour' on 24 February 1963. The well-dressed enthusiasts were carried in an ex-Barry Railway coach and brake vans.

Stoke Canon (Exeter) to Morebath Junction via Tiverton

CLOSED
OCTOBER
7
1963

The 19½-mile Exe Valley line between Morebath Junction, on the Devon & Somerset Railway's Taunton to Barnstaple line, and Stoke Canon, on the GWR's main line north of Exeter, was built in two sections, both to the standard gauge. The northerly section between Tiverton and Morebath was authorised as the Tiverton & North Devon Railway in 1875 and opened on 1 August 1884. The southerly section from Stoke Canon to Tiverton was authorised as the Exe Valley Railway in 1874 but was built by the GWR and opened on 1 May 1885.

Morebath Junction signal box became famous in the 1890s and early twentieth century as having the only signalwoman employed on Britain's railways. As a through route the Exe Valley line was lightly used and for many years until closure passenger services were normally catered for by two-coach auto trains pushed or pulled by a '14XX' Class 0-4-2T. Most trains ran between Exeter St David's and Dulverton, where they connected with trains on the Taunton to Barnstaple line – journey times for the 24¾-mile journey took around a leisurely 1hr 10min.

Listed for closure in the 'Beeching Report', the inevitable came on 7 October 1963 when all passenger and goods services were withdrawn, though the short branch line from Tiverton Junction to Tiverton lasted another year (see Tiverton Junction to Tiverton). The only exception was goods traffic which continued to be carried between Stoke Canon and Thorverton until May 1964.

Despite closure 50 years ago some railway infrastructure remains. The station buildings at Brampford Speke Halt, Thorverton and Up Exe Halt still survive as private houses while the level crossing keeper's cottage and signal cabin can be seen at the site of Cove Halt station. The station building and goods shed at Cadeleigh & Bickleigh is now the home of the Devon Railway Centre. Much of the railway route around Tiverton has disappeared beneath asphalt.

An English country railway about to be swept away forever – '5700' Class 0-6-0PT No. 3659 calls at Thorverton station with the 3.20pm Bampton to Exeter train in May 1963.

CLOSED JUNE 15 1964 Yeovil Town to Taunton

The single track railway from Taunton to Yeovil was originally built as a broad gauge line by the Bristol & Exeter Railway. Leaving the B&ER's main line north of Taunton at Durston Junction the line struck off in a southeasterly direction across the Somerset Levels through Athelney, Langport, Martock and Montacute before ending at Hendford terminus to the west of Yeovil. The line opened throughout on 1 October 1853. The following year it was extended to the Wilts, Somerset & Weymouth Railway's station at Pen Mill. After the standard gauge Salisbury & Yeovil Railway reached Yeovil from Yeovil Junction a new joint station, Yeovil Town, was opened on 1 June 1861 and the B&ER's Hendford station became a goods depot. Dual gauge track was laid between Bridgwater and Yeovil in 1867 but the broad gauge was dispensed with in 1879.

The northern end of the line between Athelney and Langport was incorporated in the GWR's new cut-off between Castle Cary and Taunton which opened in 1905 – however this main line took a shorter route from Athelney to a new flyover junction at Cogload, north of Taunton. Trains to Yeovil continued to use the original route from Durston Junction until closure.

The railway was often prone to flooding in the winter but, despite much local support, the service was listed for closure in the 'Beeching Report'. Closure came on 15 June 1964 although the double track section between Athelney and Langport remains open for main line trains between Castle Cary and Taunton via Cogload Junction.

Today, a 1½-mile section of the trackbed from the site of Langport West station towards Martock is now a footpath and cycleway on the Parrett Trail. The railway's route between the A303, southeast of Martock, and the outskirts of Yeovil has been utilised for the A3088 road.

'4575' Class 2-6-2T No. 5548 arrives at Martock station on the Taunton to Yeovil line during the 'big freeze' of 30 April 1959.

CLOSED SEPTEMBER 7 1964 Bristol to Portishead

The 9¾-mile broad gauge branch line from Parson Street Junction in Bristol to Portishead was built by the Bristol & Portishead Pier & Railway and opened in 1867. An extension to Portishead Pier was opened in 1879. The line was converted to standard gauge in 1880 and purchased by the Great Western Railway in 1885.

Even up to the late 1950s passenger services through the Avon Gorge from Bristol Temple Meads to Portishead were fairly frequent, with up to 16 return journeys each weekday throughout the year and five on Sundays from April to September.

A new, resited, station was built at Portishead in 1954 but the passenger service, by now operated by diesel multiple units, was listed for closure in the 'Beeching Report'. Closure came on 7 September 1964 with goods services lasting until 1981.

However, unlike other closed branch lines the single track along the scenic Avon Gorge was never lifted, gradually being overtaken by nature. It was reopened in 2002 as far as Pill with a new extension to a coal terminal and a car loading terminal at Royal Portbury Dock. A proposal to reopen a further three miles to the site of Portishead station and recommence passenger services is currently being considered.

The driver of a Class '118' diesel multiple unit (DMU) from Portishead accepts the single-line tablet (and has a chat) from the signalman at Clifton Bridge station only a few days before closure of the line to passengers in September 1964. Note the splendid Triumph combination on the down platform.

Deep snow at Tiverton station in February 1963 – on the left '1400' Class 0-4-2T No. 1421 waits to depart with the 1.20pm for Tiverton Junction while No. 1450 waits to depart with the 12.30pm for Dulverton.

Hymek diesel-hydraulic D7031 pauses at Henbury station with a down local in August 1964.

CLOSED
OCTOBER
5
1964

Tiverton Junction to Tiverton

The 4¾-mile branch line between Tiverton Junction and Tiverton was opened by the Bristol & Exeter Railway on 12 June 1848. Originally built to a broad gauge it was later converted to standard gauge by the Great Western Railway in 1884 to coincide with the arrival of the standard gauge Exe Valley line at Tiverton where a new station was built.

Connecting with main line trains at Tiverton Junction, the regular shuttle service along the line was normally operated by Class '14XX' 0-4-2Ts pushing or pulling an auto coach. By the 1950s the service amounted to 13 return trips each day, taking 12 minutes in each direction, with all trains calling at the only intermediate station of Halberton Halt.

Listed for closure in the 'Beeching Report', the line closed to passengers on 5 October 1964 although goods trains continued to reach Tiverton until 1967. The last train, a brake van special organised by the University of Exeter Railway Society on 2 June 1967, was headed by 0-6-0 diesel shunter D2133.

Although much of the course of the railway can still be followed it has completely disappeared under new roads around Tiverton. The station at Tiverton Junction was closed on 12 May 1986 and replaced by a new Tiverton Parkway station resited two miles further north.

CLOSED
NOVEMBER
23
1964

Avonmouth to Filton Junction

Built primarily as a freight route for trains to and from Avonmouth Docks, the 7¼-mile double-track railway between Avonmouth and Filton Junction was opened by the Great Western Railway in 1910. Passenger services were introduced at the same time but were withdrawn in 1915. They were reinstated in 1922 as part of a circular service from Bristol Temple Meads via Avonmouth, Henbury, Filton Junction and back to Temple Meads. Regular passenger services were withdrawn on 23 November 1964 although an unadvertised workmen's train continued to use the route between Filton and North Filton Platform until 1 March 1965. Although the line was singled in 1965 the growth of rail freight traffic from Avonmouth Docks led to its redoubling in the 1990s. It is still open for freight today.

CLOSED
JANUARY 4 1965
Lostwithiel to Fowey

On 1 June 1869 the broad gauge Lostwithiel & Fowey Railway was opened to carry china clay to Fowey. However, the rival Cornwall Minerals Railway opened a separate and shorter line from Par to Fowey in 1874 – the ensuing price war between the two railways to carry the china clay eventually led to the initial closure of the line from Lostwithiel in 1880.

The redundant line remained unused until 1892 when it was bought by the Cornwall Minerals Railway and rebuilt to standard gauge, opening throughout to Fowey for both goods and passengers on 16 September 1895. The CMR was amalgamated with the Great Western Railway in 1896.

Although the Par to Fowey line lost its passenger service as early as 1929, the 5½-mile scenic line, hugging the west bank of the River Fowey from Lostwithiel, retained its passenger service of eight return trains each weekday until being listed for closure in the 'Beeching Report'. Closure to passengers came on 4 January 1965 but the line remained open as far as Carne Point for china clay traffic, a service that still operates today.

Curiously, the Par to Fowey freight-only line through the 1,173 yard-long Pinnock Tunnel was converted into a private road for use by English China Clay lorries in 1968.

'1400' Class 0-4-2T No. 1434 at Fowey station with a train for Lostwithiel on 30 April 1959.

CLOSED
MARCH 1 1965
Torrington to Halwill Junction

The last standard gauge railway to be built in North Devon was the North Devon & Cornwall Junction Light Railway which partly replaced a 3-foot gauge tramway originally built in 1880 between Torrington and clay works at Marland. The light railway opened between Halwill Junction and Torrington in July 1925; passenger traffic on the line was minimal but clay traffic and bricks transhipped at Fremington Quay kept the line open.

Passenger services between Torrington and Halwill Junction were fairly minimal – by the early 1960s there were only two return journeys along the 20½-mile meandering line. Trains were usually mixed (i.e. also conveying goods wagons) and the journey time was an extremely leisurely 1 hour 25 minutes (an average speed of 14½ mph).

Listing for closure came in the 'Beeching Report'. The end came for passenger trains on 1 March 1965. However, the northern section from Torrington to Meeth was kept open for clay traffic until 1982. Today this section forms part of the picturesque Tarka Trail footpath and cycleway from Barnstaple.

BR staff and a passenger pose for the camera at Petrockstow station on 3 June 1963. Ivatt Class '2' No. 41313 is heading the 4pm Torrington to Halwill train.

'1400' Class 0-4-2T No. 1463 waits to depart from Chippenham with a train bound for Calne on 18 August 1957.

CLOSED
SEPTEMBER
20
1965

Chippenham to Calne

By the 1860s the Wilts & Berks Canal serving the Wiltshire town of Calne and its important Harris Bacon Factory had become stretched to capacity. An alternative method of transport was sought and so the Calne Railway Company was born. Operated from the outset by the Great Western Railway, the 5¼-mile broad gauge line opened between Chippenham and Calne on 3 November 1863. The line was converted to standard gauge in 1874 and absorbed by the GWR in 1892. The unusually named Black Dog Halt on the line was the private station of the Marquess of Lansdowne who also had a siding from which his racehorses could be taken to race meetings.

Traffic remained buoyant on the profitable line until after the Second World War – there was heavy usage by Royal Air Force personnel during the war and the output from the Harris Bacon Factory with its liveried goods vans heading out to destinations around the country kept the branch line very busy. The rot set in during the 1950s with increasing competition from road transport and despite dieselisation of passenger services as early as 1958 traffic continued to dwindle. Listed for closure in the 'Beeching Report', the branch line lost its goods services on 2 November 1964 with passenger services ceasing on 20 September 1965.

The last train to run was the normally empty-stock DMU working which left Calne crowded with passengers at 11.20pm on Saturday 18 September. The train had been greeted by the local mayor and a crowd of local residents and left to the sound of a bugler playing the 'Last Post'. At Black Dog Halt the train, now fitted with a wreath, ran over 100 fog detonators that had been fixed to the line.

Today, while Calne station has long disappeared beneath an industrial estate, almost the entire trackbed of the line has been reopened as a footpath and cycleway known as the Chippenham to Calne Railway Path (National Cycle Route 11).

CLOSED

OCTOBER 4 1965

Barnstaple to Torrington

The first railway to open in North Devon was a horse-drawn tramway that opened between Barnstaple and Fremington Quay in 1848. By 1854 the North Devon Railway (later to become part of the London & South Western Railway) had opened its broad gauge line from Crediton to Barnstaple. The Fremington line became steam hauled and was extended west to Bideford in 1855 and to Torrington in 1872. The GWR reached Barnstaple from Taunton in 1873 and the following year the LSWR opened its line to Ilfracombe.

The passenger service on the 14¼ miles between Barnstaple Junction and Torrington was fairly frequent with ten return trains each weekday until the early 1960s. Journey time was just over 30 minutes. A through coach from Waterloo to Torrington was also conveyed on the 'Atlantic Coast Express' on summer Saturdays until 1964.

Despite strong local opposition with appeals to retain the Barnstaple to Bideford passenger service, the line was listed for closure in the 'Beeching Report'. Closure came on 4 October 1965 although the line remained opened for creamery traffic from Torrington until 1980 and clay traffic from Meeth until 1982. Today the trackbed, the north section hugging the shore of the Taw Estuary and the southern section along the meandering valley of the River Torridge, forms part of the popular Tarka Trail footpath and cycleway. Much railway infrastructure remains, including Instow station and signal box, Bideford station with its old BR coach now a café, and Torrington station – the latter housing the Puffing Billy pub. The Trail continues from Torrington as far as Meeth along the trackbed of the light railway.

Torrington station on a sunny 10 June 1964 – Ivatt Class '2' 2-6-2T No. 41248 does a spot of shunting while a train departs for Barnstaple.

'6400' Class 0-6-0PT No. 6430 waits to depart from Yeovil Pen Mill with an auto train for Yeovil Town station on 17 September 1964.

CLOSED

NOVEMBER 29 1965

Yeovil Town to Yeovil Pen Mill

The Bristol & Exeter Railway's broad gauge line from Taunton to Yeovil (Hendford) was opened on 1 October 1853 (see Yeovil Town to Taunton) and was extended to the new Wilts, Somerset & Weymouth Railway's station at Pen Mill in 1854. After the standard gauge Salisbury & Yeovil Railway reached Yeovil from Yeovil Junction a new joint station, Yeovil Town, was opened on 1 June 1861 and the B&ER's Hendford station became a goods station. The broad gauge was dispensed with by the GWR in 1879.

As part of the programme of widespread Beeching closures in the southwest the ½-mile spur from Town station to Pen Mill station was closed on 29 November 1965 – until that date it had been served by an auto train shuttle service for the two-minute journey. The site of Town station is now a cinema and car park but the road overbridge to the south of the station site still survives. Pen Mill is still served by trains between Bristol and Weymouth.

CLOSED
NOVEMBER
29
1965

Axminster to Lyme Regis

The railway came to the historic harbour town of Lyme Regis rather late in the day. While the London & South Western Railway's Yeovil to Exeter main line had opened through nearby Axminster in 1860 it took another 43 years before the Lyme Regis branch was opened. Built as a Light Railway, the 6¾-mile branch opened between Axminster and the resort on 24 August 1903. The steeply graded and winding line had one main engineering feature, the ten-arch viaduct at Cannington, and one intermediate station at Combpyne. However, Lyme Regis station was inconveniently set on a hill, 250 ft above sea level, necessitating a strenuous ¾-mile walk up from the town centre. Train services usually consisted of nine or ten return journeys each day but on summer Saturdays from 1953 to 1963 through coaches were also provided on two trains from Waterloo.

The branch was famous for its ancient steam motive power which consisted of three ex-LSWR Adams 4-4-2 radial tanks built in 1885. These were introduced in 1913 and remained in service until 1961, the branch loco being housed overnight in a diminutive engine shed at Lyme Regis. Steam gave way to diesel multiple units in November 1963 and

the goods service was withdrawn soon after. With increasing competition from Southern National Omnibuses it was inevitable that the branch would be listed for closure in the 'Beeching Report' – the end came on 29 November 1965. Attempts to reopen part of the line in 1970 came to nothing and now Cannington Viaduct with its unsightly jack arch is the only reminder of this quaint seaside railway. In the late 1970s the station building at Lyme Regis was dismantled and rebuilt at Alresford station on the Mid-Hants Watercress Line in Hampshire.

Deputising for a failed DMU, Ivatt Class '2' 2-6-2T and auto coach leaves Cannington Viaduct with the 3.35pm Lyme Regis to Axminster train in March 1965.

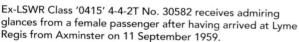

Ex-LSWR Class '0415' 4-4-2T No. 30582 receives admiring glances from a female passenger after having arrived at Lyme Regis from Axminster on 11 September 1959.

Evercreech Junction to Highbridge

The broad gauge Somerset Central Railway opened from Highbridge, on the Bristol & Exeter Railway's main line, to Glastonbury in 1854. The line was extended westwards to Burnham-on-Sea in 1858 and a branch from Glastonbury to Wells was opened in the following year. With the ambition of building a railway to link the Bristol and English channels, the SCR extended eastwards from Glastonbury to Cole in 1862 where it met the standard gauge Dorset Central Railway's line from Wimborne. Shortly afterwards the two railways were amalgamated as the Somerset & Dorset Railway and the broad gauge section converted to standard gauge.

An extension from Evercreech Junction to meet the Midland Railway at Bath was opened in 1874 (see Bath Green Park to Bournemouth) but the cost of the heavily engineered line left the S&DR in dire financial straits. In 1876 it was rescued by a coalition of two railway companies, the Midland Railway and the London & South Western Railway, to become the Somerset & Dorset Joint Railway. With the opening of the Bath extension the original S&DR 'main line' became a bit of a backwater – steamer traffic from Burnham never lived up to expectations and the line from Highbridge to the resort was closed to passengers in 1951. The S&DJR's workshops at Highbridge had already closed in 1930.

Changes to British Railways' regional boundaries in 1958 left the Highbridge to Evercreech Junction line under Western Region management and by 1962 the rot had set in and the whole S&DJR system was listed for closure in the 1963 'Beeching Report'.

Closure was scheduled for 3 January 1966 but a last-minute hitch with alternative bus arrangements gave the railway a short reprieve, From then until closure on 7 March a skeleton passenger service was operated – the Highbridge branch had only two return trains each day. A final enthusiasts' 'last train' was run along the branch on Sunday 6 March behind Ivatt 2-6-2Ts Nos 41283 and 41249 and the following day the much-loved S&DJR was no more.

On the Highbridge branch only the section from Highbridge to Bason Bridge was left open, for milk trains, until 3 October 1972. Today, the trackbed of the former Somerset Central Railway's main line can be walked or cycled from the western outskirts of Glastonbury for a distance of five miles through the Shapwick Heath National Nature Reserve.

Ivatt Class '2' 2-6-2T No. 41290 gets ready to leave Glastonbury & Street station with a train for Highbridge on 1 January 1966 – this was originally planned to be the last day of services on the S&D until a local replacement bus operator pulled out at the last minute.

An unusual sight on this route was this Swindon-built three-car Cross-Country DMU operating the 5.55pm Bath Green Park to Bristol Temple Meads service north of Oldlands Common station on 13 May 1964.

A well-cleaned BR Standard Class '4' 2-6-4T No. 80041 pauses at Colyton station on the Seaton branch with the LCGB's 'East Devon Rail Tour' on 28 February 1965.

CLOSED
MARCH 7 1966
Mangotsfield to Bath Green Park

The broad gauge Bristol & Gloucester Railway opened in 1844. It was taken over by the Midland Railway in 1845 and converted to standard gauge in 1854. An eight-mile double-track branch line opened in 1869 running from Mangotsfield, north of Bristol, to a temporary terminus at Queen Square, Bath. A year later the MR opened its permanent terminus at Bath – known as the Midland Station, it was renamed Green Park in 1951.

The line had two uses – the first for MR local traffic between Bristol and Bath (the intermediate stations between Mangotsfield and Bath were Warmley, Oldland Common and Bitton); the second for through trains between the North and the Midlands and Bournemouth via the Somerset & Dorset Joint Railway (see Bath Green to Bournemouth). The branch closed to passenger traffic on 7 March 1966 although goods trains continued to serve Bath gas works until 1971. Nearly the entire route was reopened as the Bristol & Bath Railway Path by Sustrans in 1984 while the three miles of the line between Oldland Common, Bitton and Avon Riverside is now a heritage railway known as the Avon Valley Railway.

CLOSED
MARCH 7 1966
Seaton Junction to Seaton

The 4¼-mile branch line from Seaton Junction (originally named 'Colyton for Seaton'), on the London & South Western Railway's main line, to the seaside town of Seaton was opened by the Seaton & Beer Railway on 16 March 1868. It was taken over by the LSWR in 1885. With intermediate stations at Colyton and Colyford the line sprang into life on summer Saturdays when holidaymakers descended on the town from London – even until 1963 there were through coaches carried on three separate trains from Waterloo. To cope with this seasonal traffic the Southern Railway had extended the platforms at Seaton in 1937. After being listed for closure in the 'Beeching Report' diesel multiple units were belatedly drafted in to work on the line but to no avail – after already losing its goods service the line closed along with Seaton Junction station on 7 March 1966.

Today, the 2ft 9in gauge Seaton Tramway carries holidaymakers in miniature electric trams from its terminus at Seaton along the trackbed of the line beside the peaceful estuary of the River Axe to Colyton. The station (now a private house), down platform and footbridge still survive at Seaton Junction.

CLOSED

MARCH

7

1966

Bath Green Park to Bournemouth Central

The Somerset & Dorset Railway was formed in 1862 by the amalgamation of the Somerset Central Railway and the Dorset Central Railway (see Evercreech Junction to Highbridge). With its numerous viaducts and tunnels the S&DR's steeply graded extension northwards across the Mendip Hills from Evercreech Junction to Bath left the company in a poor financial position. The line was opened in 1874 – two years later the ailing company was rescued by the Midland Railway and the London & South Western Railway and became the Somerset & Dorset Joint Railway. At the southern end the opening of the important Corfe Mullen Junction to Broadstone line in 1885 speeded up trains heading for Poole and Bournemouth. Increased traffic soon led to the doubling of the single line between Blandford and Corfe Mullen and between Midford and Templecombe. At the latter station all stopping trains had to reverse up or down a linking spur to the LSWR station, an archaic working that lasted until closure.

Working heavy trains over the Mendips inevitably led to double-heading of trains and until the early 1960s some fascinating combinations of locos could be seen heading the North-South 'expresses' – of which the 'Pines Express' was the most famous – between Bath and Evercreech Junction with underpowered ex-MR 0-6-0s or 4-4-0s often teamed up with ex-SR light Pacifics or BR Standard 4-6-0s. The introduction of BR Class '9F' 2-10-0s in 1962 able to haul these trains without assistance came too late as all through trains were withdrawn at the end of that summer season.

Farewell to the Former Somerset and Dorset Joint Railway

Photo: I. Peters.
53807, the (then) sole survivor of the S.D.J.R. class 7F 2-8-0s at Masbury summit with the 8.55 a.m. down freight from Bath on the last day of its service, 5th September, 1962.
Block Courtesy: Railway Magazine.

Photographic Souvenir
in connection with
LAST PASSENGER TRAIN
on the
Bath — Templecombe — Bournemouth Section
SUNDAY, 6th MARCH, 1966
Organised by the STEPHENSON LOCOMOTIVE SOCIETY
(Midland Area)

The Stephenson Locomotive Society's enthusiasts special along the S&DJR was one of two 'last trains' run on this route on 6 March 1966. This one was headed by Stanier '8F' 2-8-0 No. 48706 and BR Standard Class '4MT' 2-6-4T No. 80043.

With the northern part of the line in the hands of the Western Region, the S&DJR was now living on borrowed time. Train services were reduced and through ticketing to other parts of British Railways was withdrawn. BR made it quite clear that they wanted rid of the line and it was inevitably listed for closure in the 'Beeching Report' – the Secretary of the Templecombe Labour Party even resigned in disgust over the government's broken pre-election pledge to halt rail closures. However, due to a last minute problem with organising replacement bus services, the planned closure of 3 January 1966 was postponed until 7 March. As a mark of protest against the 'vicious attitude' of BR, a signalman at Binegar stopped an LCGB 'last' train on Saturday 1 January – he issued a statement to the crew and apologised to the passengers. For the next two months the S&DJR held out against the odds as the last bastion of steam in the West Country.

The S&DJR in all its glory – the southbound 'Pines Express' leaves Bath Green Park headed by newly-allocated BR Standard Class '4' 4-6-0 No. 75023 and unrebuilt 'West Country' Class 4-6-2 No. 34041 'Wilton' on 9 September 1961.

The very last day on the S&DJR and an end of an era. Watched from the lineside by local people and railway photographers, one of the enthusiasts last trains run over the route on 6 March 1966 was double-headed by 'West Country' Class 4-6-2 No. 34006 'Bude' and 'Battle of Britain' Class 4-6-2 No. 34057 'Biggin Hill'.

Filled with enthusiasts and local mourners, the last regular trains ran on the Saturday 5 March but two enthusiasts' last trains ran the length of the line on the Sunday – their mournful whistles echoing over the Mendip Hills signalling the end of an era. Organised by the Stephenson Locomotive Society and the Locomotive Club of Great Britain, these trains were double-headed by Class '8F' 2-8-0 No. 48706 and 2-6-4T No. 80043, and Bulleid Light Pacifics Nos. 34006 'Bude' and 34057 'Biggin Hill'.

Today, there is surprisingly much activity along the line. Bath Green Park station with its overall roof survives as a car park and covered space for markets. South of Bath a new cycleway is being built through Devonshire Tunnel, Combe Down Tunnel and across Tucking Mill Viaduct and Midford Viaduct – it will be known as the Two Tunnels Greenway (National Cycle Route 24 from Bath to Frome). Midsomer Norton station has been restored by the Somerset & Dorset Railway Heritage Trust who are also relaying track southwards towards Masbury. The magnificent 27-arch Charlton Viaduct now forms a backdrop to Kilver Court Gardens in Shepton Mallet. At Yentson, two miles south of Templecombe, the 2ft gauge Gartell Light Railway runs along part of the old trackbed. At Shillingstone the station has been restored and is open to the public.

Holt Junction to Patney & Chirton via Devizes

Yeovil Town to Yeovil Junction

Missing out as part of the route of Brunel's GWR main line from Paddington to Bristol, the eight-mile branch line from Holt Junction, north of Trowbridge, to the town of Devizes was opened in 1857. As a through route it came into its own on the opening of the Berks & Hants Extension from Hungerford to Devizes in 1862. This extension effectively robbed the Kennet & Avon Canal of most of its commercial traffic. GWR trains could now also travel from Paddington to Bristol via Reading, Newbury, Hungerford and Devizes and also to Weymouth via the same route to Holt Junction and then via Westbury and Castle Cary. However, the opening of the Lavington cut-off between Patney & Chirton and Westbury in 1900 effectively relegated the Devizes line to secondary status. A few through trains still ran through Devizes from Paddington – even in 1959 there were still three return trains each weekday from Paddington to Trowbridge via Devizes and one from Paddington to Bristol along the same route.

The 13-mile Devizes line was also useful as a diversionary route during times of engineering work on the main line to the north but by the early 1960s the through trains had stopped running and local train services had been dieselised. Listed for closure in the 'Beeching Report', this useful route was closed on 18 April 1966. Today, all that remains at Patney & Chirton is the long footbridge over the main line while the single line tunnel under Devizes Castle is now bricked up.

Backed by the London & South Western Railway, the Salisbury & Yeovil Railway reached Yeovil Junction in 1860. At great speed the Exeter & Yeovil Railway (also backed by the LSWR) was opened from Yeovil Junction to Exeter later that year. However, the junction station was some distance from the town of Yeovil which was already served by trains at Pen Mill station. To link Yeovil Junction with the town a 1¾-mile spur was opened via the Wilts, Somerset & Weymouth's line to a new joint station, Yeovil Town, on 1 June 1861. Here, the Exeter & Yeovil built its engine shed which remained in use until June 1965. A turntable was also installed more conveniently at the Junction station and this survives today in working order as part of the Yeovil Railway Centre. Under Western Region management, a regular steam auto train service connected Junction station with Town station until it was replaced by a four-wheel diesel railbus on 28 December 1965.

As part of the programme of widespread Beeching closures in the southwest, the spur from Junction station to Town station was closed to passengers on 3 October 1966. Yeovil Junction station, with its delightful privately-run station buffet, is still open for business on the Salisbury to Exeter main line. Opposite the station is the Yeovil Railway Centre with its short steam-hauled line and which, with its 70ft turntable, is also a servicing centre for visiting main line steam locomotives. The spur from Junction station down to Pen Mill station (still semaphore signalled in 2011), on the Castle Cary to Weymouth line, is kept open as a diversionary route.

The first of the 4-6-0 'Modified Halls', No. 6959 'Peatling Hall, arrives at Devizes with the 3.15pm Westbury to Reading train on 21 March 1964.

Now under Western Region control, an auto train from Yeovil Town enters Yeovil Junction behind '6400' Class 0-6-0PT No. 6430 on 17 September 1964.

With only three months to go before closure of this branch line, a two-car Gloucester R C & W Co-built DMU leaves Yatton with the 5.46pm to Clevedon on 2 July 1966.

CLOSED
OCTOBER
3
1966

Yatton to Clevedon

The broad gauge 3½-mile branch line from Yatton, on the Bristol & Exeter Railway's main line, to the small resort town of Clevedon opened on 28 July 1847. Despite the coming of the railway the town never developed to the extent of its southerly neighbour, Weston-super-Mare. The branch was converted to standard gauge by the GWR in 1879.

A fairly frequent return shuttle service of 30 trains operated on the line each weekday until the early 1960s when the line was dieselised. However, by then, increasing competition from car ownership and road buses led to a serious decline in passenger numbers and the line was listed for closure in the 'Beeching Report'. Goods traffic ceased on 10 June 1963 with passenger services ending on 3 October 1966, a date which marked the closure of many other lines in the region. Today, little remains of Clevedon station which was demolished in 1968; a set of railway points erected as a memorial stands upright in the town's Queen's Square shopping centre. Yatton station is still open and is served by stopping trains between Bristol and Weston-super-Mare.

'4300' Class 2-6-0 No. 6372 waits to leave Dulverton with a train for Barnstaple Junction on 25 August 1962.

Taunton to Barnstaple

The broad gauge single track Devon & Somerset Railway opened between Norton Fitzwarren, on the Bristol & Exeter Railway's main line south of Taunton, to Barnstaple in 1873. Worked from the outset by the B&ER and from 1876 by the Great Western Railway, the line's first years were marked by a poor service, a shortage of passing loops and disputes over the carrying of mail and coal. However, the 1880s saw a marked improvement in the line – it was converted to standard gauge in 1881 when more crossing loops were installed and in 1887 a new connecting line from its Barnstaple station to the LSWR's Barnstaple Junction station saw the first through services from the GWR to Ilfracombe via this route. Despite this, trains still had to reverse in or out of Barnstaple (renamed Victoria Road in 1940) before continuing their journey, an operating problem that was not solved until a direct spur line bypassing the station was added in 1905.

Following the First World War the line increasingly became used by holiday trains from all parts of the GWR system during the summer months. To cope with this increased traffic the GWR doubled the line between Norton Fitzwarren and Milverton in the 1930s and lengthened the passing loops. These trains continued to run until the early 1960s when this delightful rural line was listed for closure in the 'Beeching Report'. By then the all-important cattle and milk traffic had been lost to road transport and any remaining goods traffic between Taunton and Barnstaple was diverted via Exeter. Steam working ceased in 1964 after which the slimmed-down passenger service was handled by single-car diesel units until total closure on 3 October 1966.

Today much of the course of the railway can still be followed, although both the B3227 Milverton bypass and part of the A361 North Devon Link Road between South Molton and Barnstaple have swallowed up large sections. Occasional glimpses of the railway can still be seen at Exebridge (embankment and remaining bridge arch), Brushford (restored Dulverton station buildings, platform and goods shed) and Barnstaple (Victoria Road goods shed).

CLOSED
OCTOBER

3
1966

Halwill Junction to Bude

The railway came late in the day to the North Cornish seaside resort of Bude. In 1872 the London & South Western Railway opened a 20½-mile branch line from Okehampton to Holsworthy. In 1886, Halwill & Beaworthy (later named Halwill Junction), 12½ miles along the branch from Okehampton, became a junction when the first section of the LSWR's North Cornwall Railway to Wadebridge opened as far as Launceston. The Holsworthy branch was extended over the splendid Holsworthy Viaduct to Bude in 1898. Although the station was inconveniently located on the outskirts of the town, the townsfolk were delighted and Bude soon became a popular holiday destination for Londoners

during the summer months, with through carriages carried on expresses from Waterloo. Up until September 1964 the 10.35am summer Saturday departure from Waterloo – the famous 'Atlantic Coast Express' – carried through carriages to Padstow and Bude, with the train being split at Halwill Junction. Other passenger services on the line were provided by trains from either Halwill Junction or from Okehampton. Cattle traffic was a very important source of revenue for the railway until this was increasingly taken over by road transport after the Second World War.

Along with the rest of the ex-LSWR's 'Withered Arm' network in North Cornwall the Bude branch was listed for closure in

the 'Beeching Report'. Despite dieselisation and staff reductions in the autumn of 1964, closure was inevitable and came on 3 October 1966. Today, at Holsworthy, a footpath and cycleway crosses the resurfaced Derriton Viaduct (built in 1879 and the first concrete viaduct to be built in Britain), proudly standing as a memorial to this short-lived seaside branch line.

BR Standard Class '3' 2-6-2T No. 82018 arrives at Whitstone & Bridgerule station with a Bude to Halwill Junction train in 1963.

Meldon Junction to Wadebridge

Despite the London & South Western Railway reaching the village of Halwill in 1872, the next stage in the company's tenuous 44-mile single track route to Wadebridge was slow in coming. Meandering through sparsely populated rolling farmland, the LSWR-sponsored North Cornwall Railway opened from Halwill Junction to Launceston in 1886 and to Wadebridge in 1895. It was later extended along the side of the Camel Estuary to Padstow in 1899 (see page Bodmin Road to Bodmin, Wadebridge and Padstow).

The coming of the railway to this isolated part of North Cornwall brought enormous benefits to farmers who could quickly transport their cattle and milk by rail to markets and bottling plants in London. Vast quantities of slate were also carried by rail from the giant quarry at Delabole along with fish from Padstow. Up to the early 1960s there was a passenger service of four return trains each day running along the route from Okehampton to Padstow plus through coaches from Waterloo on the 'Atlantic Coast Express'. Summer Saturdays saw extra trains from Waterloo including an overnight service that left Waterloo at 12.45am, an early morning train that left at 7.28am and two portions of the 'ACE' – all hauled along the North Cornwall line by Bulleid Light Pacifics. In 1963 the Western Region took control of all ex-SR routes west of Exeter and the rot soon set in with all through trains including the 'ACE' being withdrawn on 7 September 1964. On 5 September 1964 the very last down 'ACE' arrived at Halwill Junction from Exeter behind 'N' Class 2-6-0 No. 31845. The train was then split with the Bude portion heading off behind 2-6-4T No. 80037 while 31845 headed off for the last time to Padstow. Remaining local services were dieselised in 1965, with stations becoming unmanned.

Serving a small local population and unable to compete with road transport the line, much loved by Poet Laureate John Betjeman, was listed for closure in the 'Beeching Report'. The end came on 3 October 1966 when it closed completely.

Today, the Launceston Steam Railway runs for 2½ miles westwards along the former trackbed of the line from its new station at Launceston to Newmills. Apart from the original stations at Launceston and Tower Hill all of the other station buildings along the line have survived in different guises.

BR Standard Class 2-6-4T No. 80039 heads a short train away from Port Isaac Road station on the North Cornwall line on 25 July 1964.

Class 'O2' 0-4-4T No. 30225 blows off steam impatiently as it waits to leave the overall-roof station at Callington with a train for Calstock and Bere Alston in the summer of 1958.

CLOSED
NOVEMBER
7
1966

Gunnislake to Callington

One of the last railways to be built in Cornwall, the 9½-mile branch line from Bere Alston to Callington on the Plymouth, Devonport & South Western Junction Railway's main line between Plymouth and Lydford, opened as late as 2 March 1908. However, the 3ft 6in gauge East Cornwall Mineral Railway had opened along most of this route from Calstock Quay on the banks of the River Tamar to Callington as early as 1872. Serving local mines and quarries, the mineral railway fell on hard times and was taken over by the PD&SWJR in 1891 and rebuilt as a standard gauge Light Railway. The steeply-graded line was linked to the junction at Bere Alston via a new viaduct across the Tamar at Calstock.

In a region where other forms of transport were (and still are) much slower due to the difficult local geography, the scenic Callington branch was a highly successful operation. While passenger traffic remained buoyant, the output from the mines and quarries had dwindled by the Second World War although this loss was more than made up for by the growth in the conveyance of fruit and flowers which continued until the mid-1960s.

The Callington branch along with the rest of the former LSWR main line north of Plymouth was listed for closure in the 'Beeching Report'. Eventually common sense prevailed as closure would have caused much hardship to the communities west of the Tamar such as Gunnislake due to their poor road connections. In the end the steeply graded section from Gunnislake to Callington was closed on 7 November 1966 while the LSWR main line north of Bere Alston was closed on 7 September 1968. From that date the remaining local train services from Plymouth to Gunnislake have had to reverse at Bere Alston with the guard of the train operating the points.

Bodmin Road to Bodmin, Wadebridge and Padstow

The railway between Bodmin Road, on the GWR main line between Plymouth and Penzance, and Padstow was built in four distinctly separate stages over a period of 65 years.

One of the earliest railways in Britain, the Bodmin & Wadebridge Railway opened between Wadebridge Quay, Bodmin and Wenford Bridge in 1834. Built primarily to carry sand, stone and agricultural goods, it was the first steam-operated line in Cornwall. Although taken over by the London & South Western Railway in 1846, it remained isolated from the rest of the expanding national rail network until as late as 1888 when the Great Western Railway opened its branch line from Bodmin Road to Bodmin General with a link to the B&WR at Boscarne Junction.

However, the B&WR was only connected to its parent company, the LSWR, in 1895 when the line from Halwill and Delabole opened to Wadebridge. In the same year the LSWR realigned the approaches to the old B&W station at Bodmin and opened a new terminus here – it was renamed Bodmin North in 1949. To complete the railway picture in the area the LSWR opened its line from Wadebridge along the south shore of the Camel Estuary to Padstow in 1899.

Until the 1960s, railway operations in the Bodmin area were fairly complicated. There was a shuttle service from the GWR main line at Bodmin Road to Bodmin General with some trains reversing here and continuing on to Wadebridge and Padstow via Boscarne Junction. Other services operated between the LSWR terminus at Bodmin North, Wadebridge and Padstow. As a railway junction Wadebridge was a busy place, not only with the comings and goings of trains between Bodmin and Padstow but also via the North Cornwall line to and from Okehampton and Exeter. Hauled by Bulleid Light Pacifics after the Second World War there were also through coaches to and from Waterloo on the 'Atlantic Coast Express'.

China clay traffic along the Wenfordbridge branch from Dunmere Junction was in the hands of ancient Beattie 0-4-2 well-tanks, based at Wadebridge, until as late as 1962 when ex-GWR 0-6-0PTs took over. These were replaced by diesel shunters in 1964 until closure of the branch in 1983.

As with all of Cornwall's branch lines, except Falmouth and Newquay, the Bodmin Road to Padstow passenger service was listed for closure in the 'Beeching Report'. While Wadebridge had already lost its service from the North Cornwall line in 1966, the end came for the rest of the railway on 30 January 1967.

Four-wheel railbus W79977, carrying a wreath, operated the final service between Bodmin North and Wadebridge in the evening of 28 January. On the same day there were so many passengers wanting to travel that single-car diesel unit W55014 had to be replaced by D6309 and three coaches for the Bodmin Road to Wadebridge service.

Goods traffic from Bodmin Road to Wadebridge lingered on until 1978 and china clay traffic from Wenfordbridge to Bodmin Road via Boscarne Junction continued until 1983.

Today, the whole route between Bodmin Parkway (originally Bodmin Road) and Padstow has a new lease of life. The section between Bodmin Parkway, Bodmin General and Boscarne Junction is now operated as the Bodmin & Wenford Railway while the trackbed from Wenfordbridge and Bodmin to Padstow via Boscarne Junction and Wadebridge is a popular footpath and cycleway known as the Camel Trail. Wadebridge station is now a day care centre (named after local poet John Betjeman) for elderly people while that at Padstow is now a council office, café and cycle-hire centre.

All aboard! A pram is hoisted on board four-wheel railbus W79977 at Boscarne Junction station in July 1964.

BR Standard Class '3' 2-6-2T No. 82023 enters Sidmouth station with a train from Sidmouth Junction on 26 June 1960.

CLOSED
MARCH
6
1967

Sidmouth Junction to Sidmouth and Exmouth

Built as a narrow gauge line to aid in the construction of a new harbour, the first railway at the select resort of Sidmouth opened in 1836. However both the railway and the harbour project were soon abandoned and quickly forgotten. Further west along the coast at the seaside town of Exmouth, the Exeter & Exmouth Railway had opened from the London & South Western Railway's Exeter Queen Street station (later renamed Central) on 1 May 1861. A year later the Sidmouth Railway was authorised to build an 8¼-mile branch line along the valley of the River Otter from Sidmouth Junction, on the LSWR's main line east of Exeter, to Sidmouth via Tipton St John's in 1862. Financial and engineering problems were encountered and the line opened on 6 July 1874 – although worked by the LSWR, the Sidmouth Railway remained independent until the Big Four Grouping of 1923.

The Budleigh Salterton Railway opened from its junction with the Sidmouth Railway at Tipton St John's to Budleigh Salterton on 15 May 1897. It was worked by the LSWR and was taken over by that company in 1912. In the meantime the LSWR had extended its branch line from Exmouth to Budleigh Salterton as late as 1 June 1903, thus providing an alternative coastal route from Exeter to Sidmouth Junction.

The Exmouth and Sidmouth branch line from Sidmouth Junction saw a fairly frequent service of passenger trains – the majority ran from the junction to Sidmouth with passengers changing trains for Budleigh Salterton and Exmouth at Tipton St John's. However, on summer Saturdays until September 1964 through coaches to both Sidmouth and Exmouth were provided on three trains from Waterloo, the train dividing at busy Tipton St John's. In addition to this a very curious working between Cleethorpes and Exmouth (via an extremely convoluted route which included the Somerset & Dorset Joint Railway) also used the line during summer Saturdays up until 1962.

The entire route from Exeter to Exmouth, Budleigh Salterton, and Sidmouth Junction plus the Sidmouth branch was listed for closure in the 1963 'Beeching Report'. Belatedly some economies were made in the same year when diesel multiple units replaced steam but the inevitable, apart from the reprieved Exeter to Exmouth branch, came on 6 March 1967. Goods traffic continued from Sidmouth Junction to Sidmouth until complete closure in May of that year. Sidmouth Junction station also closed at the same time but was reopened as Feniton station in 1971.

Today, the station buildings at Ottery St Mary, Tipton St John, Sidmouth and East Budleigh still survive albeit with different uses.

Okehampton to Bere Alston

What was to eventually become part of the London & South Western Railway's main line between Exeter and Plymouth was opened by the LSWR-backed Devon & Cornwall Railway from Coleford Junction to Okehampton in 1871.

With the completion of Meldon Viaduct west of Okehampton, the D&SR was extended to Lydford in 1874 where it met the broad gauge Launceston & South Devon Railway (an extension of the South Devon & Tavistock Railway). Initially LSWR trains ran through to Plymouth via Lydford and then along mixed gauge track of the South Devon & Tavistock Railway's line to Tavistock Junction near Plymouth. The first trains along this route arrived in Plymouth in 1876 with the LSWR terminus at Devonport being reached over GWR metals through the city. This arrangement was highly unsatisfactory for the LSWR but an independent company soon came to its rescue: authorised in 1883, the Plymouth, Devonport & South Western Junction Railway opened between Lydford and along the Tamar Valley to the LSWR terminus in Devonport in 1890. The 22½-mile line involved the building of many bridges and tunnels and was worked from the outset by the LSWR. The PD&SWJR remained prosperous and independent until 1922 when it was absorbed by the LSWR.

Soon after its opening, the LSWR's through route from Plymouth to Waterloo saw the progress of 'Ocean Liner' trains that competed with the rival GWR route for the fastest route for embarked transatlantic passengers and mail to London. This all came to an end after the GWR opened its shorter route via Castle Cary and Westbury in 1904 and the derailment of a fast-moving LSWR boat train, along with the death of 28 passengers, at Salisbury in 1906 which finally put an end to the racing.

In 1927 the LSWR introduced the famous 'Atlantic Coast Express' which ran from Waterloo with through coaches to seaside resorts in Devon and North Cornwall. Also included in the train and its extra summer portions until the early 1960s were carriages for Plymouth, which after the Second World War were all hauled west of Exeter by Bulleid's new Light Pacifics. While the 'ACE' and other Waterloo to Plymouth overnight and restaurant car expresses continued to run until September 1964, a more short-lived named Pullman train, the 'Devon Belle', also operated between Waterloo and Exeter from 1947. Running only during summer months, the train was split at Exeter Central where one half left for Ilfracombe and the other half left for Plymouth. The Plymouth destination was dropped in 1949 while the Ilfracombe train complete with observation car continued until 1954. One oddity on this route during the BR period was the through restaurant car express from Plymouth to Brighton which took around 6½ hours to complete its tortuous journey.

Sadly this wonderful steam railway odyssey around Dartmoor was soon to come to an end when, apart from the section from Coleford Junction to Okehampton and Exeter to Barnstaple, all of the former LSWR lines in North Devon and North Cornwall were listed for closure in the 'Beeching Report'. Closure between Okehampton and Bere Alston came on 6 May 1968 and the line's use as a through route ended; the section south to Devonport was reprieved and kept open for trains to the Gunnislake branch.

Today, rail travellers between Devonport and Gunnislake can enjoy a superb scenic journey including highlights such as the curving bow string girder bridge over the River Tavy and the magnificent viaduct over the Tamar at Calstock. The trackbed, bridges and tunnels between Bere Alston and Tavistock remain intact and a scheme to reopen the main line between these two points is under consideration. Brentor station survives while the substantial station building at Tavistock North is now 5-star self-catering accommodation. The trackbed between Lydford and Meldon Viaduct is now a footpath and cycleway known as the Granite Way.

Unusual motive power for this ex-SR route, former GWR '4300' Class 2-6-0 No. 7335 arrives at Bere Alston with a Plymouth to Exeter train in the summer of 1958. 'O2' Class 0-4-4T No. 30225 waits in the bay platform with a connecting train for Calstock and Callington.

The last day of services on the Ilfracombe branch – the Exmoor Belle Rail Tour calls at Mortehoe & Woolacombe station on 3 October 1970.

A very long Inter-City DMU passes through Crowcombe with the 1pm (SO) Minehead to Paddington train on 18 July 1970; less than six months later the line closed and Butlin's at Minehead lost its important rail link with the outside world.

CLOSED OCTOBER 5 1970

Barnstaple to Ilfracombe

Backed by the London & South Western Railway, the Barnstaple & Ilfracombe Railway opened its 15-mile single track line in 1874. While the major engineering feature on the line was the curving steel bridge over the River Taw at Barnstaple, trains also encountered a gradient of 1-in-40 up Braunton Bank and then down 1-in-36 to Ilfracombe. Until the end of steam most trains needed double heading and/or banking up these fearsome gradients.

The line was doubled by 1891 and soon trains from far flung departure stations on the LSWR (via Exeter) and the GWR (via the Taunton to Barnstaple line) were bringing holidaymakers to Ilfracombe. Introduced in 1927, the 'Atlantic Coast Express' conveyed through carriages from Waterloo to Ilfracombe until 1964 while the post-war 'Devon Belle' Pullman train also terminated at Ilfracombe until 1954.

Transferred from the Southern to the Western Region in 1963, most of the former LSWR lines west of Exeter were effectively given a death sentence and the Ilfracombe branch was listed for closure in the 'Beeching Report'. Goods and through trains ceased to run on 7 September 1964 when diesel multiple units were introduced, then the line was singled in 1967. The end came on 5 October 1970 when it was completely closed while an attempt to reopen it by a preservation association in the early 1970s came to nothing. The bridge over the Taw was dismantled in 1977. Today, the trackbed between Barnstaple Quay and Braunton and between Mortehoe & Woolacombe station and Ilfracombe is a footpath and cycleway forming part of the Tarka Trail. The station buildings at Barnstaple Town, Wrafton, Braunton and Mortehoe & Woolacombe still survive.

CLOSED JANUARY 4 1971

Taunton to Minehead

The 14¾-mile broad gauge West Somerset Railway opened in 1862 with trains being worked by the Bristol & Exeter Railway. An eight-mile extension from Watchet to the small harbour village of Minehead was opened by the Minehead Railway in 1874 with trains being worked throughout from Taunton by the B&ER and from 1876 by the GWR. The entire branch was converted to standard gauge in 1882 and the Minehead Railway was taken over by the GWR in 1897 although the WSR remained independent until 1922.

Minehead soon became a popular resort and to cope with increased demand the GWR quadrupled the main line between Taunton and Norton Fitzwarren and doubled the sections from the latter junction to Bishops Lydeard and from Dunster to Minehead. Camping coaches were also installed at various stations along the line but the Second World War brought an end to this summer traffic.

Despite cost saving measures in the post-war years, the line was listed for closure in the 'Beeching Report'. Minehead station was featured in the filming of the Beatles' 'A Hard Day's Night' in early March 1964! Goods traffic ceased in the same year but despite strong local opposition to closure the end came on 4 January 1971.

The overgrown line was purchased by Somerset County Council in 1973 and reopened in stages by the newly formed West Somerset Railway Company between 1976 and 1979. With a physical connection with the national rail network at Norton Fitzwarren, the reborn West Somerset Railway from Bishops Lydeard to Minehead is currently Britain's longest standard gauge heritage railway.

CLOSED

JANUARY

3
1972

Wareham to Swanage

Operated from the outset by the London & South Western Railway, the Swanage Railway opened between Worgret Junction, just over a mile to the west of Wareham station, to Swanage in 1885. The 10¼-mile railway was subsequently taken over by the LSWR in 1886.

The arrival of the railway led to the former village of Swanage developing into a thriving seaside town while the clay extraction industry around Furzebrook provided the majority of goods traffic. Passenger services normally consisted of a push-pull service to and from Wareham with some trains being extended to and from Bournemouth Central. Several through trains to and from Waterloo also ran on summer Saturdays until September 1964.

Although the railway was not listed for closure in the 'Beeching Report' this did not guarantee its continuing survival. Steam haulage was replaced by diesel electric multiple units in 1967 but the line was seen as surplus to requirements and closure was announced for 1968. A reprieve followed but the line was closed on 3 January 1972. BR lifted the track with indecent haste, leaving only clay traffic from Furzebrook and, from 1978, oil traffic from a new terminal at Wytch Farm. Once this traffic eventually ended, the line from the Wytch Farm terminal to Worgret Junction was mothballed.

Meanwhile the Swanage Railway Society started to reopen the line from Swanage with first trains running along a short section in 1979. By August 1995 the line had been extended to Corfe Castle and Norden. No regular trains currently run through to Wareham but the link at Worgret Junction is occasionally used by special trains from the national rail network.

Steam returns to the Swanage branch – the 'Dorset Coast Express' headed by unrebuilt 'West Country' Class 4-6-2 No. 34023 'Blackmore Vale' (now preserved) pauses at Corfe Castle en route to Swanage on 7 May 1967.

CLOSED

JUNE

5
1972

Coleford Junction to Okehampton

Financially backed by the London & South Western Railway, the Devon & Cornwall Railway opened from Coleford Junction, one mile north of Yeoford on the North Devon Railway's line to Barnstaple, to Okehampton in 1871. It was later extended by the LSWR over Meldon Viaduct to Lydford in 1874. The company also opened a branch from Okehampton to Holsworthy in 1879. By the end of the nineteenth century the LSWR's main line to North Cornwall was in place – known as the 'Withered Arm', its tentacles reached to Bude, Padstow and Plymouth by 1899. By 1968 this had all been swept away by Dr Beeching and Okehampton had become an unstaffed station at the end of a branch line, served only by trains from Exeter. Much to the relief of local people the 13½-mile Okehampton branch was not listed for closure in the 'Beeching Report' but this may well have been due to the continuing stone traffic from British Railway's Meldon Quarry and use of the line by trains carrying troops heading for training on the nearby Dartmoor military ranges. Despite this, the little-used passenger service ceased on 5 June 1972 and not too many tears were shed.

Since then the line has been kept open for stone traffic from Meldon Quarry and in 1997 the Dartmoor Railway started operating a diesel heritage railway between Meldon Quarry and Sampford Courtenay via Okehampton. Work is currently in hand to extend services to an interchange station at Yeoford on the Exeter to Barnstaple Tarka Line. In 2010 the Devon & Cornwall Railway Ltd (a subsidiary of Iowa Pacific Holdings which bought the Dartmoor Railway in 2008) announced plans to reinstate a through passenger service between Okehampton and Exeter.

Unrebuilt 'Battle of Britain' Class 4-6-2 No. 34080 '74 Squadron' leaves Okehampton with a train for Exeter Central in April 1960. The locomotive shed can be seen behind the train.

Far from the madding crowd - a rural scene that was soon to disappear for ever as a single-car diesel unit calls at Toller station with a Maiden Newton to Bridport train on 1 September 1964.

CLOSED
MAY
5
1975

Maiden Newton to Bridport

In the early years of railway building the town of Bridport failed to be put on the map only due to the proposed coastal railway from Southampton to Exeter running out of steam at Dorchester. Eventually the townsfolk had to be content with their own broad gauge branch line which was opened by the Bridport Railway from Maiden Newton, on the Great Western Railway's newly-opened line from Castle Cary to Dorchester, on 12 November 1857. Worked from the outset by the GWR, the 9¼-mile branch was converted to standard gauge in 1871 and, in 1884, extended a further two miles from Bridport station to Bridport Harbour, the latter being renamed West Bay. The extension was never a success as West Bay never developed as a hoped-for seaside resort and was closed to passengers on 22 September 1930. However, it remained open for goods until the end of 1962 and the track was lifted in 1965.

Connecting with trains on the Castle Cary to Weymouth line, passenger services on the Bridport branch remained fairly constant for well over 100 years with around 11 return trains on weekdays and four on Sundays. Despite the line being listed in the 'Beeching Report', its end was a long time coming. Goods services ceased in 1965 when steam traction was replaced by a diesel railcar and the fact that it survived so long until closure on 5 May 1975 was probably due to the poor roads in the area and a local council subsidy; the line was one of the last of Beeching's proposed closures to take place in Britain. With indecent haste British Rail had lifted the track by the end of that year.

Now, nearly 50 years later, there are plans to convert the trackbed of the Bridport branch into a footpath and cycleway. While Maiden Newton station is still fortunately open, the other station buildings along the line have had an interesting history since closure: Toller station was taken down and reconstructed at the South Devon Railway's Totnes station; Powerstock station is a private residence; part of Bridport station found a new home on the Beer Heights Light Railway near Seaton; while West Bay station has been restored to its former glory and now houses a café.

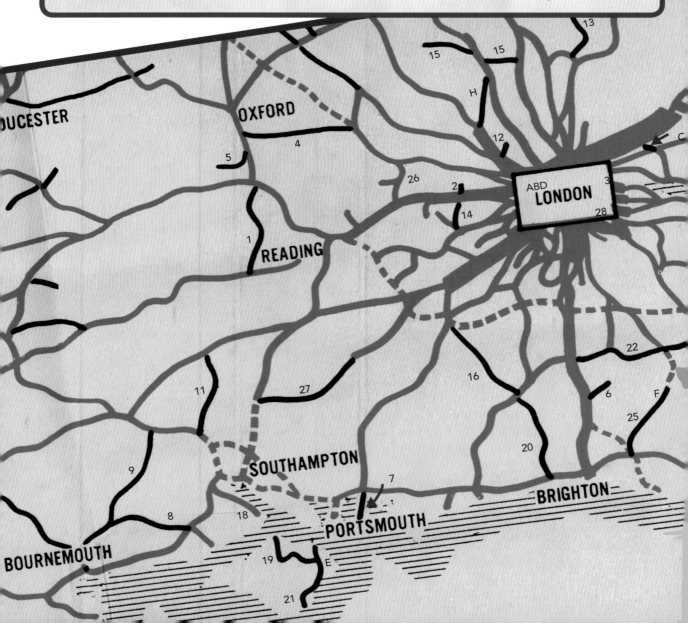

THE CASUALTIES

1. Didcot to Newbury – 10 September 1962
2. West Drayton to Uxbridge Vine Street – 10 September 1962
3. Seven Sisters to Palace Gates – 7 January 1963
4. Oxford to Princes Risborough – 7 January 1963
5. Radley to Abingdon – 9 September 1963
6. Haywards Heath to Horsted Keynes – 28 October 1963
7. Havant to Hayling Island – 4 November 1963
8. Brockenhurst to Broadstone – 4 May 1964
9. Salisbury (Alderbury Junction) to West Moors – 4 May 1964
10. Crowhurst to Bexhill West – 15 June 1964
11. Andover Junction to Kimbridge Junction (Romsey) – 7 September 1964
12. Harrow & Wealdstone to Belmont – 5 October 1964
13. St Margarets to Buntingford – 16 November 1964
14. West Drayton to Staines West – 29 March 1965
15. Dunstable to Hatfield – 26 April 1965
16. Guildford to Christ's Hospital – 14 June 1965
17. Eridge to Hailsham – 14 June 1965
18. Southampton (Totton) to Fawley – 14 February 1966*
19. Smallbrook Junction to Cowes (Isle of Wight) – 21 February 1966
20. Christ's Hospital to Shoreham – 7 March 1966
21. Shanklin to Ventnor (Isle of Wight) – 18 April 1966
22. Three Bridges to Tunbridge Wells – 2 January 1967
23. Appledore to New Romney – 6 March 1967
24. Polegate to Hailsham – 9 September 1968
25. Lewes to Uckfield – 24 February 1969
26. Bourne End to High Wycombe – 4 May 1970*
27. Winchester to Alton – 5 February 1973
28. Dalston Junction to Broad Street – 27 June 1986*

Note: Dates given are for withdrawal of passenger services
* = not listed for closure in the 'Beeching Report'

THE SURVIVORS

A. Clapham to Kensington Olympia
B. Richmond to Barking
C. Romford to Upminster
D. Watford Junction to Croxley Green
E. Ryde Pier Head to Shanklin
F. Crowborough to Uckfield
G. Ashford to Ore (Hastings)
H. Watford Junction to St Albans Abbey

SOUTHERN ENGLAND

HARWICH

SOUTHEND-ON-SEA

An ironic juxtapositioning of a closure notice at Havenstreet station on the Ryde to Cowes line in 1966. Good old British Rail!

The very last train to use the Hayling Island branch was the LCGB's 'Hayling Farewell' special on Sunday 3 November 1963. It is seen here leaving Langstone en route for Hayling Island behind Class 'A1X' 0-6-0T No. 32636 with sister engine No. 32670 bringing up the rear.

DOVER

G   23

Suitably inscribed in chalk on the smokebox, Ivatt Class '2' 2-6-2T No. 41287 arrives at Christ's Hospital with the last timetabled train between Guildford and Horsham on 12 June 1965.

CLOSED
SEPTEMBER
10
1962

Didcot to Newbury

Originally seen as part of a main north-south trunk railway running between Manchester and Southampton, the Didcot, Newbury & Southampton Railway was authorised in 1873. However, rivalry between the GWR (which worked the line) and the LSWR (which saw it as encroaching on their territory) eventually led to the southern section between Winchester and Southampton being cancelled. Didcot to Newbury opened in 1882 and Newbury to Winchester (Chesil) in 1885.

The DN&SR failed as an independent cross-country line although from 1891 its trains were allowed to run over the LSWR main line between Winchester and Southampton via the new 33-span Hockley Viaduct to Shawford Junction. For some years a few through trains ran between Paddington and Southampton via Newbury and the DN&SR but locally generated passenger traffic on this single-track route remained light. The independent DN&SR was amalgamated with the GWR in 1923. Nevertheless through goods traffic between the rest of the GWR system and Southampton Docks remained fairly heavy, especially during the World Wars – during the Second World War track was doubled between Didcot and Newbury and passing loops reinstated between Newbury and Winchester to cater for extra traffic. After the war the cross-country route reverted into a rural backwater.

The section from Newbury to Winchester closed on 7 March 1960 while that from Didcot to Newbury was listed for closure in the 'Beeching Report'. Despite dieselisation of passenger services the end came on 10 September 1962 although the line occasionally saw diverted services until complete closure in 1964. Track was lifted in 1967. Upton & Blewbury, Compton and Hermitage stations along the section from Didcot to Newbury have a new lease of life as private residences.

'6100' Class 2-6-2T No. 6167 carries out a spot of shunting with a couple of parcel vans at Uxbridge (Vine Street) in September 1962.

CLOSED
SEPTEMBER
10
1962

West Drayton to Uxbridge Vine Street

The 2½-mile single track broad gauge branch line from West Drayton, on the main line out of Paddington, to Uxbridge was opened by the Great Western Railway on 8 September 1856. It was later converted to standard gauge in 1871 and doubled in 1881. In 1884 a short section of the Uxbridge branch at West Drayton was joined by a new branch line meeting it from Staines (see West Drayton to Staines West). An intermediate station at Cowley was opened in 1904. Following the opening of two other lines to Uxbridge the original GWR station was renamed Uxbridge Vine Street in 1907. Commuter passenger traffic was inevitably lost to the quicker and more frequent Metropolitan and Piccadilly underground trains which also served Uxbridge and the line was listed for closure in the 'Beeching Report'. While still shown on Beeching's Map No. 9, passenger trains on this route had ceased over six months before on 10 September 1962. Goods services continued until July 1964. The track was lifted within 12 months and the site of Vine Street station has long disappeared under so-called road improvements, while that of Cowley has been covered by housing. Featuring a short length of broad gauge track, a short section of trackbed beside Cleveland Road in Cowley is now a nature reserve.

Restarting from a signal stop south of Didcot, '4300' Class 2-6-0 No. 6302 heads towards Newbury with a long freight train on 22 September 1961.

CLOSED JANUARY 7 1963 Seven Sisters to Palace Gates

The 2¼-mile branch line from Seven Sisters, on the Liverpool Street to Enfield Town line, to Palace Gates at Wood Green was opened by the Great Eastern Railway on 7 October 1878. It was originally planned to extend the line to connect with the Great Northern Railway's branch from Highgate at Alexandra Palace but in the event the steep gradient up to the Palace put paid to this proposal. Commuter trains ran from Palace Gates to Liverpool Street, Stratford or Fenchurch Street and in 1887 a service to North Woolwich was added. Although located close to the Great Northern Railway's main line out of King's Cross, Palace Gates remained isolated from that line, apart from a siding connection, until 1944 when a new spur was opened from the Hertford Loop line at Bounds Green.

Passenger traffic on the Palace Gates branch declined heavily following the opening of the Piccadilly underground line in the 1930s and commuter services to Liverpool Street were soon withdrawn. The Palace Gates to North Woolwich suburban commuter service remained steam hauled until replaced by diesel multiple units for the 12½-mile journey in 1962. Although listed for closure in the 'Beeching Report', the Palace Gates branch and its intermediate stations at West Green and Noel Park closed to passengers on 7 January 1963 – nearly three months before publication of the report. Goods traffic continued to use the line until the end of 1964 with the track being lifted two years later. The station buildings at Palace Gates, West Green and Noel Park have long since disappeared.

CLOSED JANUARY 7 1963 Oxford to Princes Risborough

The 18½-mile single-track railway between Princes Risborough and Kennington Junction, 2½ miles south of Oxford, was built by the broad gauge Wycombe Railway but was worked from the outset by the Great Western Railway. The section from High Wycombe to Thame via Princes Risborough opened on 1 August 1862 while that from Thame to Kennington Junction opened on 24 October 1864. The railway was converted to standard gauge in 1870. For some years it carried through trains between Oxford and Paddington but this declined with the 1910 opening of the GWR's Birmingham direct line through Princes Risborough.

In a bid to boost traffic, the GWR introduced steam railmotors on the line in 1908, at the same time opening additional halts at Garsington Bridge, Horspath and Towersey. This experiment ended in 1915 – along with the other halts Garsington Bridge was also closed but reopened as Morris Cowley to serve the nearby car factory in 1928. Despite this the line was listed for closure in the 'Beeching Report', although in the event it closed on 7 January 1963, nearly three months before the report's publication.

At the western end goods traffic continued (and still does) to operate Morris Cowley while at the eastern end oil trains continued to operate to Thame until 1991. New BMW Minis are now carried by rail in double-deck car transporters from the old Morris Cowley factory to south coast ports for export. A seven-mile footpath and cycleway known as the Phoenix Trail now runs along the trackbed of the old line between Princes Risborough and Thame.

Brush Type 3 diesel D5666 has just arrived at Palace Gates station with a train from Seven Sisters on the last day of passenger services on the branch, a snowy 5 January 1963.

'Castle' Class 4-6-0 No. 5089 'Westminster Abbey' passes through Wheatley on the Thame branch on Sunday 11 September 1960. The train was the diverted 2.10pm Paddington to Birkenhead.

A single car diesel unit waits to depart from Abingdon terminus with a train for Radley shortly before closure of the line to passengers in 1963.

CLOSED
OCTOBER
28
1963

Haywards Heath to Horsted Keynes

With an intermediate station at Ardingly, the 4½-mile double track line between Hayward's Heath, on the London to Brighton main line, and Horsted Keynes, on the newly-opened Lewes to East Grinstead line, was opened by the London, Brighton & South Coast Railway on 3 September 1883. The two major engineering features on the line were Sheriff Mill Viaduct (now demolished) and Lywood Tunnel. Trains ran along a dedicated track alongside the main line north of Haywards Heath until a connection was put in at Copyhold Junction in 1931. The line was electrified with the third-rail system by the Southern Railway in 1935.

The Lewes to East Grinstead line finally closed on 17 March 1958 but partly reopened in 1960 as the Bluebell Line, becoming the world's first standard gauge steam heritage railway to operate a public service. While goods traffic ceased in 1962, Horsted Keynes continued to be served by electric trains from Haywards Heath until 28 October 1963 when the line east of Ardingly closed, although it did see the passage of steam locomotives and stock destined for the Bluebell Railway for some months afterwards. The section from Copyhold Junction to Ardingly remains open today and is used by stone trains to and from a Hanson Aggregates depot. Apart from the demolished Sheriff Viaduct, the trackbed of the route between Ardingly and Horsted Keynes is now owned by the Bluebell Railway which has plans to reopen it in the future.

CLOSED
SEPTEMBER
9
1963

Radley to Abingdon

The 1¾-mile broad gauge branch line from Abingdon Junction, on the GWR line between Oxford and Didcot, and Abingdon opened on 2 June 1856 and was converted to standard gauge in 1872. In 1873 the eastern end of the line was extended a further ¾-mile northwards to a new junction station at Radley. For the last 30 years of its life train services on the branch were operated by a GWR Class '1400' and an auto coach with a journey time of five minutes. Listed for closure in the 'Beeching Report', passenger services ceased on 9 September 1963. Goods traffic, in particular to and from the MG car factory at Abingdon, continued until the 1980s when the track was lifted. Radley station is still served by trains between Oxford and Didcot.

Unrebuilt 'Battle of Britain' Class 4-6-2 No. 34068 'Kenley' heads out of Horsted Keynes with a Ramblers Excursion on 27 September 1959.

CLOSED
NOVEMBER
4
1963

Havant to Hayling Island

The 4½-mile branch line from Havant, on the Portsmouth to Brighton main line, to Hayling Island was opened by the Hayling Island Railway Company on 17 July 1867. The railway was taken over by the London, Brighton & South Coast Railway in 1872. The main engineering feature on the line was the timber viaduct across Langstone Harbour and the weight restrictions placed on this structure meant that motive power remained in the hands of Stroudley's diminutive 'Terrier' 0-6-0Ts until closure. The line came to life in the summer months when thousands of daytrippers would descend on the resort, carried there on the frequent railway service from Havant. The journey, with stops at the two intermediate stations of Langstone and North Hayling, took 13 minutes. During the peak periods on summer weekends trains would be full to bursting and usually needed two 'Terriers' to haul them. At other quieter times most trains were of the mixed variety, conveying a carriage and goods trucks.

While still profitable, the Hayling Island branch was listed for closure in the 'Beeching Report' – the reason given by British Railways was the prohibitive cost of replacing the timber bridge over Langstone Harbour. The line closed to all traffic on 4 November 1963 with the final timetabled trains on the previous Saturday being packed to capacity with locals and enthusiasts. An enthusiasts' special ran over the branch on the Sunday 3 November hauled by 'Terrier' 0-6-0Ts Nos 32670 and 32636.

Today, while the wooden viaduct across Langstone Harbour has long been dismantled, the trackbed of the rest of the railway between Havant station and Hayling Island is a footpath and cycleway known as the Hayling Billy Leisure Trail. Reached via the modern road bridge over the harbour, a lonely concrete signal post now stands guard over the surviving foundations of the old railway bridge. The goods shed on the site of Hayling Island station is now a theatre.

Ex-LB&SCR Class 'A1X' 0-6-0T No. 32662 crosses Langstone Bridge with the 4.05pm Havant to Hayling Island train on 2 November 1963, the last day of regular services on this delightful branch line.

Brockenhurst to Broadstone

The Southampton & Dorchester Railway was an early scheme to build a main line along the south coast from Southampton to Exeter. Promoted by a Mr Castleman, a Wimborne solicitor, the meandering single-track line had opened from Southampton to Dorchester across the New Forest via Brockenhurst, Ringwood, Wimborne and Broadstone in 1847. Nicknamed Castleman's Corkscrew because of its roundabout route, the railway was taken over by the London & South Western Railway in 1848.

The 25-mile railway was never a great success despite being doubled in later years and in 1888 it was bypassed to the south by a more direct main line from Brockenhurst to Hamworthy Junction via Christchurch, Bournemouth and Poole. From then until closure the former main line was relegated to a secondary route, only coming to life on summer Saturdays when it was used by Weymouth and Swanage-

bound trains bypassing congested Bournemouth. The western end of the line as far as West Moors was also used by Salisbury to Bournemouth trains. Up until closure a stopping train service of around eight return trains each weekday was provided between Brockenhurst and Bournemouth West – passenger traffic was never heavy and two coaches usually sufficed although motive power could range from Class 'M7' 0-4-4Ts to Bulleid Light Pacifics. Listed for closure in the 'Beeching Report', Castleman's Corkscrew between Brockenhurst and Broadstone closed on 4 May 1964 – the same day as the connecting line from Salisbury to West Moors. Goods trains continued to reach Ringwood from Broadstone until 1967 after which West Moors became the railhead until the 1970s.

Today, much of Castleman's Corkscrew can be enjoyed on foot, bike or horse. Apart from a few flooded cuttings the trackbed can be followed through the

BR Standard Class '3' 2-6-2T No. 82028 at the head of the last school train for Brockenhurst Grammar School over the Ringwood and Wimborne line, 2 May 1964.

New Forest National Park from a point one mile southwest of Brockenhurst to the outskirts of Ringwood. Holmsley station is now a popular tea room and restaurant – the trackbed for a mile east of here is now a road. To the west of Ringwood the 16½-mile Castleman Trailway follows the trackbed to Upton Country Park near Hamworthy. One mile west of Ringwood the SR concrete platform and nameboard still survive at Ashley Heath station.

Class 'M7' 0-4-4T No. 30031 arrives at Holmsley station with a Bournemouth West to Brockenhurst train on 21 July 1962.

A photo full of wonderful detail (spot the Lambretta scooter!) taken at Daggons Road station, circa 1961.

Salisbury (Alderbury Junction) to West Moors

Worked from the outset by the London & South Western Railway, the 19-mile Salisbury & Dorset Junction Railway opened from Alderbury Junction, on the Salisbury to Romsey line, to West Moors, on Castleman's Corkscrew on 20 December 1866. Running for most of its length along the valley of the River Avon, the single-track line led a fairly quiet existence although on summer Saturdays it was a useful route for holiday trains from the GWR system at Salisbury to south coast resorts. Even as late as 1963 it was used by such trains originating in Cardiff, Nottingham and Swansea but by then the writing was already on the wall as the line had been listed for closure in the 'Beeching Report'. The end came on 4 May 1964 on the same day as closure of Castleman's Corkscrew. The track had been lifted by 1965 and today, only the station building at Breamore survives although the road overbridge at the site of Verwood station provides an unusual backdrop to a garden.

BR Standard Class '4MT' 4-6-0 No. 75065 calls at Fordingbridge station with the 4.50pm Bournemouth West to Salisbury train on 23 May 1961.

Class 'H' 0-4-4T No. 31519 leaves Sidley station with a Bexhill West to Crowhurst train on 12 June 1957.

CLOSED
JUNE
15
1964

Crowhurst to Bexhill West

With an intermediate station at Sidley, the 4½-mile branch line from Crowhurst to Bexhill was opened by the Crowhurst, Sidley & Bexhill Railway in 1902. It was absorbed by the South Eastern & Chatham Railway in 1905. The line was closed to passengers in 1917 but reopened two years later. Steam push-pull trains were replaced by diesel-electric multiple units in 1958 but the line was listed for closure in the 'Beeching Report'. Closure to all traffic came on 15 June 1964 and the track had been lifted within a year. Once serving four platform faces, the impressive terminus building at Bexhill West is now home to an auctioneers, pub and restaurant.

CLOSED
SEPTEMBER
7
1964

Andover Junction to Kimbridge Junction (Romsey)

A railway linking Redbridge, on the Southampton to Dorchester line, and Andover was first authorised in 1847. The line was to be built by the London & South Western Railway along the course of the derelict Andover & Redbridge Canal which had opened in 1796. However this scheme came to nothing due to the severe financial problems brought on during the years of 'Railway Mania'. It was revived by the Andover & Redbridge Railway in 1858 which obtained authorisation for a broad gauge railway along the same route. However, that company went bankrupt soon after building had commenced and in the end the LSWR took over the unfinished line in 1863, opening it as a standard gauge single-track line on 6 March 1865. Running along the valley of the River Test the line abounded in sharp curves as it faithfully followed the course of the old canal – so bad were the curves that the line was realigned and doubled in 1885.

In addition to serving the villages along the Test Valley, the Sprat & Winkle Line as it became known was also used by Midland & South Western Junction Railway through trains from Cheltenham to Southampton which commenced operations in the late 1890s. This route was particularly busy during the First World War carrying troops from army camps on Salisbury Plain to Southampton Docks. The MSWJR ended operations in 1961 when this little-used cross-country route was closed between Andoversford Junction (near Cheltenham) and Andover Junction.

Seen here on 22 May 1957, Horsebridge station is now a finely restored private residence alongside the Test Way long distance footpath.

The LSWR also opened a six-mile double track line between Hurstbourne, northeast of Andover Junction, and the Sprat & Winkle Line at Fullerton Junction in 1885. Singled in 1913, the line was closed to passengers in 1931 and to goods from Fullerton Junction to Longparish in 1956.

Despite closure of the MSWJR in 1961, train services along the Sprat & Winkle continued for three more years – by 1963 all trains were timetabled to call at every station between Andover Junction and Portsmouth Harbour. Listed for closure in the 'Beeching Report', the line closed between Andover Junction and Kimbridge Junction, north of Romsey, on 7 September 1964 although the ¾-mile stub from Andover Junction to Andover Town was left open for goods traffic until 1967.

Today, the trackbed of the line from Fullerton Junction to beyond Mottisfont forms part of the 49-mile Test Way long distance footpath. Many railway bridges survive along this section while the highlight must surely be the beautifully restored station at Horsebridge.

Class 'T9' 4-4-0 No. 30726 leaves Horsebridge station with a train from Andover Junction to Romsey and Eastleigh in 1958.

Nicknamed the 'Belmont Belle', the last DMU service prepares to leave Belmont for Harrow & Wealdstone on 3 October 1964.

CLOSED
OCTOBER
5
1964

Harrow & Wealdstone to Belmont

The Harrow & Stanmore Railway was opened from Harrow, on the LNWR main line out of Euston, to Stanmore on 18 December 1890. It remained a popular route for commuters until the electric Metropolitan Railway opened to Stanmore in 1932. After this, traffic on the branch from Harrow declined to such a point that passenger services were cut back to the busier station of Belmont in 1952. Although still relatively busy during the rush hour periods the remaining 1¼-mile branch was listed for closure in the 'Beeching Report', the end coming despite much local protest on 5 October 1964. Goods traffic to Stanmore had already ended earlier that year and, despite local efforts to get it reopened, the entire branch had been lifted by 1966. The site of Belmont station now lies beneath a car park.

CLOSED NOVEMBER 16 1964

St Margarets to Buntingford

Authorised in 1858 as the Ware, Hadham & Buntingford Railway, the 13¾-mile branch line from St Margaret's, on the Great Eastern Railway's line from Broxbourne to Hertford East, to Buntingford was opened on 3 July 1863. The single-track line was extremely costly to build with numerous bridges and compensation to landowners nearly bankrupting the company before the line was completed. It was saved from oblivion by the Eastern Counties Railway, later to become part of the newly-formed Great Eastern Railway. The latter company took over operations from opening and bought the company in 1868.

For over 90 years the Buntingford branch was a profitable concern – up until the 1930s the line carried large volumes of goods traffic and through commuter services to Liverpool Street remained robust until the 1950s. However, by 1959 the rapid decline in passenger traffic led to the withdrawal of through trains and the introduction of single car diesel units between Buntingford and St Margaret's where passengers for Liverpool Street were forced to change. With rapidly declining receipts the branch was listed for closure in the 'Beeching Report'. Passenger services ceased on 16 November 1964, although goods trains continued to operate for another ten months. British Railways had lifted the track by early 1966.

Today, the station buildings at Buntingford and Braughing still survive – the latter has been fully restored complete with platform, a length of track and a railway carriage.

A Derby-built three-car DMU halts at Hadham station with the 9.55am Buntingford to St Margaret's train on 14 November 1964, the last day of services on this branch.

CLOSED MARCH 29 1965

West Drayton to Staines West

The single-track branch line between West Drayton, on the GWR main line out of Paddington, and Staines West opened on 2 November 1885. At West Drayton it diverged from the branch line to Uxbridge Vine Street and dived under the main line before heading out across farmland to Staines. Here, the hoped-for connection with the London & South Western Railway's lines to Reading and Waterloo failed to materialise until the Second World War when a temporary link was laid at Staines Moor Junction. The connection remained in use until 1947 when it was closed.

Although passenger traffic was never heavy the branch served industrial estates at Colnbrook and Poyle – wayside halts were opened to serve both of these in 1961 and 1954 respectively. Listed for closure in the 'Beeching Report', the single-car diesel unit service along the 6¼-mile branch ended on 29 March 1965. Goods traffic to Staines continued until 1981 when the branch was cut back to Colnbrook; today aviation fuel for Heathrow and bulk stone trains continue as far as this point but south of here the track has been lifted and the trackbed severed by the M25 motorway. At the southern end a new connection was laid in 1981 from the Windsor branch to Staines West to serve an oil depot. This closed in 1991.

A final special was run over the freight-only Staines West branch in 1981 and it carried the headboard from the last regular train which had run on 27 March 1965: 'The end is nigh, prepare to meet thy bus'!

A Stephenson Locomotive Society special, headed by preserved GNR 'J52' Class 0-6-0ST, pauses at the GNR pattern signal box at Ayot on 14 April 1962.

CLOSED
APRIL
26
1965

Dunstable to Hatfield

The town of Dunstable had already been reached by the London & North Western Railway's 6¾-mile branch line from Leighton Buzzard in 1848. However, the people of Luton were not happy as they had expected the line to continue eastwards to serve their growing town. Eventually the Luton, Dunstable & Welwyn Junction Railway came to their rescue although by the time the section from Dunstable to Luton had opened in 1858 this company had amalgamated with the Hertford & Welwyn Junction Railway to become the Hertford, Luton & Dunstable Railway. The rest of the single-track line eastwards from Luton to the GNR main line at Welwyn opened on 1 September 1860 and the following year the HL&DR was taken over by the Great Northern Railway.

For a few years GNR trains from Dunstable and Luton ran to Hatfield via a junction at Welwyn. However, in 1868 the branch was given its own parallel line alongside the GNR main line between Welwyn and Hatfield and the junction removed. From 1868 Luton was also served by the Midland Railway's main line but the two railways remained unconnected until 1965 when a spur was laid. While the majority of the 20¼-mile GNR branch was built as single-track,

the section from Luton to Dunstable was eventually doubled in 1899.

Although freight traffic remained fairly healthy on the Luton to Dunstable section, by the 1950s the rest of the branch had witnessed a fairly rapid decline in passenger usage and the Hatfield to Dunstable service was listed for closure in the 'Beeching Report' – the Leighton Buzzard to Dunstable branch had already closed on 2 July 1962. Planned for 6 January 1965, the closure of the branch got a temporary reprieve but all to no avail: the end came on 26 April. Goods traffic continued between a new spur at Luton and an oil terminal and cement works at Dunstable until 1989 when the line was mothballed.

Today, the trackbed of the branch line between Welwyn Garden City and Wheathampstead is now a three-mile footpath and cycleway known as the Ayot Greenway which forms part of National Cycle Network Route 57. The track between Luton and Dunstable has only recently been lifted to make way for a new concrete guided busway. To the west of Dunstable the trackbed of the line to Leighton Buzzard as far as Stanbridgeford is also a footpath and cycleway forming part of National Cycle Network Route 6.

Bulleid 'Charlies' (Class 'Q1' 0-6-0s) Nos 33027 and 33006 approach Baynards station en route from Horsham to London via Guildford, with the LCGB's 'The Wealdsman Rail Tour' on 13 June 1965. This was the last train to travel over the Christ's Hospital to Guildford line.

CLOSED
JUNE
14
1965

Guildford to Christ's Hospital

The Horsham & Guildford Direct Railway was authorised in 1860 to build a 15¼-mile single-track line from Peasmarsh Junction, 1¾ miles south of Guildford on the London & South Western Railway's main line to Portsmouth, to Stammerham Junction, on the London, Brighton & South Coast Railway's Mid-Sussex line some 2½ miles southwest of Horsham. The railway was eventually allowed running rights for its trains over the LSWR between Guildford and Peasmarsh Junction. With the railway incomplete the H&GDR was amalgamated with the LBSCR in June 1864. Exacerbated by the building of a tunnel at Baynards instead of a planned cutting, construction was painfully slow and the line eventually opened on 2 October 1865.

On opening, the single-track line had only one passing place, at Baynards. To increase traffic capacity passing loops were added at Bramley in 1876 and at Cranleigh in 1880. At the southern end of the line Stammerham Junction was given a station in 1902 – named Christ's Hospital (West Horsham), it was built in a grand style with seven platforms to serve the new Christ's Hospital School. Passengers from Guildford could then change here for the Mid-Sussex or Shoreham lines without having to first travel northwards to Horsham.

By the early 1960s both goods and passenger traffic was in serious decline, the former decimated by a national rail strike in 1955 and the latter not helped by inconvenient connections at Horsham. Listed for closure in the 'Beeching Report', the line was scheduled to shut on 11 November 1963 – goods trains had already ceased in 1962. By then it was only served on weekdays by two morning trains (the last from Horsham to Guildford leaving at 7.55am!) and four afternoon/early evening trains in each direction. However, numerous objections to the closure postponed the inevitable until 14 June 1965 – on that day it became the only railway in Surrey to be closed under the Beeching proposals.

Carrying 400 passengers (instead of the normal six), the final regular train left Guildford for Horsham at 7.34pm on Saturday 12 June headed by Ivatt 2-6-2T No. 41287. Chalked on the ribbon-bedecked smokebox were the words 'The End, Farewell, Farewell' and on the side tanks 'Last Day'. The last train to travel the line was the Locomotive Club of Great Britain's steam-hauled 'Wealdsman' special on Sunday 13 June.

Today, while there is a proposal to reopen the line between Cranleigh and Guildford, much of the trackbed forms a 37-mile footpath, cycleway and bridleway known as the Downs Link that runs from near Guildford to Shoreham-on-Sea. Along the route there is also still much to interest lovers of closed railways: at Bramley & Wonersh the platforms and level crossing gates have been restored; the attractive station building at Baynards has been restored to its original condition; and at Rudgwick the unusual bridge over a bridge can be seen from a viewing platform. However, the once impressive Christ's Hospital station has been reduced to two short platforms serving trains on the Horsham to Littlehampton line.

CLOSED
JUNE
14
1965

Eridge to Hailsham

What was later to become known as the Cuckoo Line, the railway between Eridge and Polegate was built by the London, Brighton & South Coast Railway in two sections. The southern section from Polegate to Hailsham opened in 1845. To the north of Hailsham an early scheme for a narrow gauge railway failed to materialise and it was not until 1876 that the LBSCR was authorised to build a single-track line from Hailsham to Eridge – the latter station had already been served by trains between Tunbridge Wells and Lewes since 1868. The line from Hailsham to Eridge opened in 1880 and the next year the junction at Polegate was rearranged to allow trains from the Cuckoo Line to continue to Eastbourne. In 1894 the junction with the Cuckoo Line at Eridge was moved one mile further south to a new location at Redbridge Mill.

Despite a frequent regular interval service introduced in the 1950s, the line was listed for closure in the 'Beeching Report' – the service between Eridge and Hailsham was withdrawn on 14 June 1965 although Heathfield continued to be served by goods trains until 1968. Carrying a wreath and headboard with the words 'Farewell Faithful Servant', the last regular train left Tunbridge Wells West for Eastbourne at 6pm on Saturday 12 June – it left Horam to the accompaniment of exploding detonators and Guy Fawkes rockets. The southern section from Polegate to Hailsham remained open for passengers until 8 September 1968. Today much of the trackbed of the Cuckoo Line south of Heathfield is a popular footpath and cycleway known as the Cuckoo Trail.

Class 'U' 2-6-0 No. 31803 and Class 'N' 2-6-0 No. 31411 approach Mayfield with the LCGB's 'The Wealdsman Rail Tour' on 13 June 1965 – this was the last passenger train to travel between Eridge and Hailsham.

'USA' Class 0-6-0Ts Nos 30064 and 30073 arrive at Fawley from Totton with an LCGB last special on 19 March 1966 – the branch had closed to passengers a month previously but today remains open for oil trains and military traffic.

CLOSED
FEBRUARY
14
1966

Southampton (Totton) to Fawley

Opened by the Southern Railway on 20 July 1925, the 4½-mile single-track branch line along the west shore of Southampton Water from Totton to Fawley was one of the last light railways to be built in Britain. With intermediate stations at Marchwood and Hythe its *raison d'etre* was the new oil refinery at Fawley. As a light railway, the stations were pretty basic and there were no level crossing gates along the line. It also served the Marchwood Military Port which had been established in 1943 to aid the following year's D-Day landings; with its internal railway system the port is currently home to ships of the Royal Fleet Auxiliary and has recently been expanded to deal with container ships.

In addition to the regular oil trains from Fawley Refinery and military traffic to Marchwood, the line also supported a spartan passenger service entirely for the benefit of shift workers at the refinery. The 1963 service consisted of one early morning and one late afternoon train each way to and from Southampton Central between Monday and Friday.

Strangely, the meagre passenger service on the line escaped the attention of the Beeching team and it was not listed for closure in the 'Report'. However this oversight did not save it and passenger services ceased on 14 February 1966 when the last train, the 4pm from Southampton and return, was operated by DMU No. 1128. Two enthusiasts' specials, double-headed by 'USA' Class 0-6-0Ts Nos 30064 and 30073, were run over the weekend of 19/20 March. The line is still used by military traffic to Marchwood and oil trains from Fawley Refinery to various parts of Britain.

21 1966 Smallbrook Junction to Cowes (Isle of Wight)

The first railway to be built on the Isle of Wight was the Cowes & Newport Railway which opened in 1862. However, it remained isolated from the island's other railways for some years. While the Isle of Wight (Newport Junction) Railway opened between Newport and Sandown in 1875 it was another four years before it was physically joined to the C&NR via a viaduct at Newport, by which time the company had gone bankrupt. A short goods-only branch line was opened to Medina Wharf near Cowes in 1875. To the east of Newport, the Ryde & Newport Railway opened its line from Smallbrook Junction, on the Isle of Wight (Eastern Section) Railway's line from Ryde to Shanklin, in 1875. All three railways (C&NR, the bankrupt IoW(NJ)R and IoW(ES)R) amalgamated to form the Isle of Wight Central Railway in 1887.

By 1900 the island's railway system was in place and remained so for another 52 years. In 1923 the island lines became part of the newly-formed Southern Railway which set about modernising the by-then antiquated Victorian system. With the exception of a few ex-LBSCR 'Terrier' tanks, all of the ancient steam locomotives and worn out coaching stock were replaced by modern carriages and newly-built Class '02' 0-4-4 tanks. Under SR management passenger traffic continued to grow, especially during the busy summer season when holidaymakers in their hundreds of thousands descended on the island each year. Apart from a lull during the war, this rosy picture continued until the early 1950s when competition from road transport started to make inroads into passenger traffic.

With new British Railways management looking to prune uneconomic branch lines the first closure on the island came in 1952 when the Merstone to Ventnor West line closed. A year later the Brading to Bembridge and Newport to Freshwater lines closed, followed in 1956 by the Newport to Sandown line. What was left (Ryde to Ventnor and Ryde to Cowes) struggled on with ageing locomotives and coaching stock but both lines were listed for closure in the 'Beeching Report'. Despite numerous objections, especially from islanders worried about more traffic clogging up their narrow roads, the end for virtually all the island's railways came in 1966. First to close was the Smallbrook Junction to Newport and Cowes line on 21 February 1966 while the Shanklin to Ventnor line went on 18 April; Ryde to Shanklin was reprieved and converted to third rail electrification.

Meanwhile, goods trains continued to operate to Newport and Cowes until May 1966 after which all of the island's withdrawn steam locomotives and coaching stock were stored awaiting disposal at Newport station. But this was not the end for the Smallbrook Junction to Newport line – in 1971 a group of preservationists moved in to Havenstreet Station and by 1991 had completely reopened the line as a heritage railway from a new station at Smallbrook Junction to Wootton, east of Newport. The line now sees passenger trains hauled by beautifully restored steam locomotives and vintage coaching stock. The trackbed of the line from Newport to Cowes now forms part of the 62-mile Round the Island Cycleway.

Class '02' 0-4-4T No. 22 'Brading' leaves Cowes with a train for Ryde on the last day of service over this line, 20 February 1966.

Rebuilt 'Battle of Britain' Class 4-6-2 No. 34050 'Royal Observer Corps' is the centre of attention at Steyning with the LCGB's much-travelled 'The Wealdsman Rail Tour' on 13 June 1965.

A liquid presentation is made to the crew of Class 'O2' 0-4-4T No. 14 (formerly named 'Fishbourne') at Wroxall, en route from Ventnor to Ryde on the last day of service, 17 April 1966.

CLOSED MARCH 7 1966 — Christ's Hospital to Shoreham

Faced with a proposal by their rival, the London & South Western Railway, to build a line through the North Downs to Shoreham, the London & Brighton Railway received authorisation in 1846 for its own line from Horsham to Shoreham. However, due to the withdrawal of the LSWR proposal and the economic woes of the time the line was not built. Following several other failed proposals the London, Brighton & South Coast Railway (the successor to the L&B) finally opened the 17½-mile Steyning Line between Shoreham and Itchingfield Junction, south of Stammerham Junction (later Christ's Hospital), in 1861. In addition to the regular passenger service between Brighton and Horsham as well as agricultural goods traffic the Steyning Line was a popular route for excursions trains from London and further afield.

The line was also heavily used during the Second World War and kept fairly busy until the 1950s – schools traffic, buoyant passenger numbers during the summer and large amounts of coal, cement and gypsum for factories at Beeding and Southwater all combined to paint a fairly rosy picture. However, by 1963 declining goods and passenger traffic led to the line being listed for closure in the 'Beeching Report'. Despite this threat a regular-interval service of 17 return trains each day still operated between Brighton, Shoreham and Horsham and steam made way for diesel-electric multiple units in 1964. Despite numerous objections the line finally closed on 7 March 1966 although the northern section as far as Southwater was retained for goods traffic until 1982.

Today, much of the trackbed between Christ's Hospital and Shoreham is a footpath, cycleway and bridleway forming the southern section of the Downs Link that runs from near Guildford to Shoreham.

CLOSED APRIL 18 1966 — Shanklin to Ventnor (Isle of Wight)

The Isle of Wight (Eastern Section) Railway opened from Ryde (St John's Road) to Shanklin in 1864 and was extended southwards to Ventnor through a ¾-mile tunnel under Boniface Down in 1866. The company was renamed the Isle of Wight Railway and went on to open a short branch line from Brading to Bembridge in 1882. In 1880 the main line was extended 1¼ miles northwards from Ryde St John's Road to Ryde Pier Head, where trains connected with paddle steamers from Portsmouth. St John's Road remained the hub of the railway system and it was here that the steam locomotive shed was located until the end of 1966.

By far the busiest railway on the island was the 8½-mile section from Ryde Pier Head to Shanklin which carried hundreds of thousands of holidaymakers during the summer months. The frequent service of steam trains started or ended their journeys at Ventnor, four miles south of Shanklin.

By the time of the publication of the 'Beeching Report' in 1963 there were only two lines left operating on the island and both were listed for closure. The Smallbrook Junction to Cowes lines was the first casualty but despite much opposition from islanders the Shanklin to Ventor section closed to passengers on 18 April 1966 – steam hauled to the end. Goods trains continued to run to Ventnor until May when the line south of Shanklin was completely closed. The high cost of maintaining the tunnel under Boniface Down was given as the reason for closure. The Ryde to Shanklin section was reprieved and eventually converted to third-rail electric using ex-London Underground stock. Part of the route, from Shanklin to Wroxall, is now a footpath and cycleway.

CLOSED
JANUARY
2
1967

Three Bridges to Tunbridge Wells

Following two failed proposals to build a railway between Three Bridges, on the London & Brighton Railway's main line, and the town of East Grinstead, the East Grinstead Railway opened with an intermediate station at Rowfant on 9 July 1855. Leased and operated from the outset by the London, Brighton & South Coast Railway (successor to the L&BR) the railway was purchased by that company in 1865. In 1870 another intermediate station was opened at Grange Road.

An extension to the East Grinstead Railway, the East Grinstead, Groombridge & Tunbridge Wells Railway, opened in 1866. At East Grinstead the opening of the Lewes & East Grinstead Railway (part of which is now the Bluebell Railway, see Haywards Heath to Horsted Keynes) in 1882 led to a major rebuilding of the station with the Three Bridges to Tunbridge Wells line platforms at a higher level than the new line. The latter was extended northwards in 1884 by the opening of the Croydon, Oxted & East Grinstead Railways – the two lines being connected via a spur built from St Margaret's Junction north of East Grinstead station.

Push-pull trains were introduced between Three Bridges and Tunbridge Wells in 1905 and these stayed in service until the introduction of diesel-electric multiple units in the early 1960s. The immediate years after the Second World War saw a rapid decline in traffic and the East Grinstead to Lewes line finally closed in 1958 following several reprieves. The introduction of the new diesel-electric multiple units between Three Bridges and Tunbridge Wells failed to halt the decline in passengers and the line was listed for closure in the 'Beeching Report' – the author of the report lived near East Grinstead so there was no favouritism! Despite fierce local opposition the line between Three Bridges, East Grinstead and Groombridge closed on 2 January 1967. The day before closure an engineers' special headed by D6529 was run between Three Bridges and Groombridge to collect 'valuable' station furniture and loose fittings.

The section from Groombridge to Tunbridge Wells was kept open for trains to and from Eridge until 1985. Today East Grinstead is the southern terminus of the electrified line from London and Oxted, while the line south to Sheffield Park is operated by the Bluebell Railway.

Opened in 1979, almost the entire length of the Three Bridges to East Grinstead railway is now a footpath and cycleway known as the Worth Way and forms part of National Cycle Network Route 21. At East Grinstead the Worth Way links to another footpath and cycleway known as the Forest Trail which runs for 9½ miles as far as Groombridge. Station buildings at Rowfant, Hartfield and Withyam survive albeit with different uses. Completely reopened as a heritage railway in 2011, the line between Tunbridge Wells West, Groombridge and Eridge (on the Uckfield line) is now operated by the Spa Valley Railway.

Class 'U' 2-6-0 No. 31803 and Class 'N' 2-6-0 No. 31411 leave Rowfant station en route from Three Bridges to Hastings via Heathfield with the LCGB's widely-travelled and much photographed 'The Wealdsman Rail Tour' on 13 June 1965. Railway photographers will go to great lengths to get that 'perfect' picture!

Appledore to New Romney

CLOSED
MARCH
6
1967

The 26¼-mile railway between Ashford and Hastings was opened by the South Eastern Railway in 1851. A scheme to link the railway with a branch line to a proposed deepwater harbour at Dungeness came to nothing and it was not until 1881 that the Lydd Railway received authorisation to build an 11-mile branch line from Appledore, on the Ashford to Hastings line, to the shingle banks of Dungeness. The following year a second branch, northwards from Lydd, on the Dungeness branch, to New Romney was also authorised – the junction for this branch was about one mile south of Lydd station. Construction work progressed fairly rapidly across the flat landscape and the Appledore to Dungeness branch with its numerous level crossings opened on 1 April 1883. The Lydd to New Romney branch opened on 19 June 1884. From the outset the two branches were worked by the South Eastern Railway and the Lydd Railway was taken over by it

in 1895.

Until the closure of Dungeness station in 1937 passengers on the line were treated to a magical mystery tour as trains to or from New Romney would also travel via Lydd to or from Dungeness, thus greatly adding to their journey time. Goods traffic consisted mainly of sheep and flint shingle, the latter of which was dispatched by rail to the distant Potteries in Staffordshire. The line also became increasingly busy with military traffic when a large army camp and military ranges were built at Lydd in the early twentieth century.

The 1930s saw a ribbon development of holiday bungalows along the coast between New Romney and Dungeness and to serve this the Southern Railway resited the New Romney branch closer to the coast. Reopened on 4 July 1937, the branch also served intermediate halts at Greatstone-on-Sea and Lydd-on-Sea while Lydd station was renamed Lydd Town. At the same time the passenger service between Lydd

and Dungeness was withdrawn.

The war years saw much military activity on the line – as with the neighbouring miniature Romney, Hythe & Dymchurch Railway, armoured trains were fitted with anti-aircraft guns to guard against marauding German aircraft. Following the war the Dungeness branch lost its goods service in 1953 and by the early 1960s most trains (in 1962 steam was replaced by diesel haulage) to or from New Romney started or ended their journeys at Ashford, 22 miles away.

Along with the Ashford to Hastings line the New Romney branch was listed for closure in the 'Beeching Report'. The former was reprieved but the latter was closed on 6 March 1967 – it had already lost its goods service two years earlier. However, this was not quite the end of the line as the section from Appledore to Dungeness nuclear power station was retained for the passage of nuclear waste trains, a service that continues today.

Type 2 diesel D5006 calls at Lydd Town station with the 11.15am Ashford to New Romney train on 26 August 1961.

Class 'U' 2-6-0 No. 31803 and Class 'N' 2-6-0 No. 31411 leave Hailsham, en route for Hastings, with the LCGB's widely travelled 'The Wealdsman Rail Tour' on 13 June 1965.

CLOSED
SEPTEMBER
9
1968

Polegate to Hailsham

What was to later become known as the Cuckoo Line, the railway between Eridge and Polegate was built by the London, Brighton & South Coast Railway in two sections. The southern section from Polegate, on the Eastbourne to London main line, to Hailsham opened on 14 May 1845. To the north of Hailsham the line to Eridge opened in September 1880 and closed on 13 June 1965 (see Eridge to Hailsham).

Despite being listed for closure in the 'Beeching Report' and the subsequent closure of the Cuckoo Line north of Hailsham, the expanding town continued to be served by passenger trains until 9 September 1968 when the line closed completely.

Today much the trackbed of the Cuckoo Line northwards as far as Heathfield and southwards as far as Polegate is a popular footpath and cycleway known as the Cuckoo Trail. Forming part of National Cycle Route 21, the Trail continues south from Polegate to terminate at Hampden Park in Eastbourne. Commissioned wooden and steel sculptures act as mileposts along the Trail. The station at Hailsham has long since disappeared but that at Polegate is still served by trains on the East Coastway Line.

CLOSED
FEBRUARY
24
1969

Lewes to Uckfield

Opened in 1858 the Lewes & Uckfield Railway branched off from the London, Brighton & South Coast Railway's line from Lewes to Keymer Junction, via Plumpton, at a junction 1½ miles northwest of Lewes. The railway was taken over by the LBSCR in 1864. The junction on the Plumpton line was taken out of use in 1868 when the line from Uckfield was rerouted via a 3½-mile diversion so that trains from the branch entered Lewes station from the opposite direction and could then continue unhindered to Brighton. In the same year the LBSCR extended the Uckfield branch to Eridge and Tunbridge Wells allowing trains to travel directly from Tunbridge Wells to Brighton via Eridge and Uckfield. With its eventual connections via East Croydon, Hurst Green and Ashurst the Wealden Line, as it became known, was also used as an alternative through route between London and Brighton.

A regular interval service was introduced in 1956 with through trains between London and Brighton operating during rush hours. While the Lewes to Crowborough section was listed for closure in the 'Beeching Report' the line northwards from Crowborough to Hurst Green appeared to be safe – it is shown on Map 9 and in the Appendices of the 'Report' as being retained. However, the closure of the southerly section appeared inevitable as a proposed relief road in Lewes would sever the line. By 1966 the northern section from Hurst Green to Crowborough had also been added to the closure list and the whole of the Wealden Line was now under threat. Closure of the line between Lewes and Uckfield came on 24 February 1969 although the line north of Uckfield was saved.

Today, while there are serious proposals afoot to reopen the Uckfield to Lewes line, the restored station at Isfield is home to the Lavender Line, a short heritage railway that runs for a mile southwards to Little Horsted.

BR Standard Class '4' 2-6-4T No. 80010 brings a train into the former LBSCR station at Uckfield in April 1955.

A single car diesel unit calls at Bourne End station in August 1966 with the 11.24am High Wycombe to Maidenhead train.

A three-car electric multiple unit (EMU) arrives at Dalston Junction with the 2.05pm Richmond to Broad Street train on 18 October 1978.

CLOSED
MAY 4 1970

Bourne End to High Wycombe

The Wycombe Railway was an independent company that opened a single-track broad gauge line from Maidenhead, on the GWR main line out of Paddington, to High Wycombe on 1 August 1854. The Wycombe Railway was later extended to Thame and Kennington Junction, south of Oxford (see Oxford to Princes Risborough). Operated from the outset by the GWR, the railway between Maidenhead and Oxford provided an alternative route for passengers instead of travelling on the GWR via Reading and Didcot. The railway was taken over by the GWR in 1867 and converted to standard gauge in 1870. A separate company, the Great Marlow Railway, opened its 2¾-mile branch line from Bourne End, on the Maidenhead to High Wycombe line, to Marlow in 1873. Six years later the company was taken over by the GWR.

The opening of the Great Western & Great Central Joint Railway between Princes Risborough and Northolt Junction in 1906 saw much traffic lost to this new direct route. While neither the Maidenhead to High Wycombe line or the Marlow branch were listed for closure in the 'Beeching Report' the straitened times of the mid-1960s soon caught up with the Bourne End to High Wycombe section and goods traffic was withdrawn in 1966. Passenger services ceased on 4 May 1970 although the Maidenhead-Bourne End-Marlow lines survived because of their important commuter traffic.

While the two intermediate stations of Wooburn Green and Loudwater have long since disappeared, the majority of the trackbed between High Wycombe and Bourne End is now a footpath and cycleway.

CLOSED
JUNE 27 1986

Dalston Junction to Broad Street

Broad Street station in London became the terminus of the North London Railway Extension from Dalston Junction in 1868. It was built on decking with seven platforms and by the early twentieth century was the third busiest station in London. Two further platforms were later added and the station was also used by the Great Northern Railway for some of its commuter services. Although the expansion of London's underground railways saw a decline in passenger numbers on the line, the North London Railway went ahead with electrification in 1916 with the service being extended to Watford in 1922.

Badly damaged by bombing during the Second World War, Broad Street never recovered and by the early 1960s the station was served by only a limited number of peak hour trains. Although not specifically listed for closure in the 'Beeching Report', the service from Watford to Broad Street was marked down as 'Stopping passenger services to be modified'. Whatever that meant, the writing was on the wall and by 1985, when services from Richmond ended, only 6,000 passengers were using the station each week. Demolition of the station began even before closure which came on 27 June 1986. Today, nothing now remains of this once-important London terminus. To the north, Kingsland Viaduct now carries the East London Line.

CLOSED
FEBRUARY
5
1973

Winchester to Alton

Railways first reached the town of Alton in Hampshire in 1852 when the London & South Western Railway opened its extension from Ash Junction, near Aldershot. Alton remained the end of the line until the Mid-Hants Railway opened its 17-mile line from Alton to Winchester Junction (two miles north of Winchester) via Alresford in 1865. Worked from the outset by the LSWR, it was taken over by that company in 1884. Between Alton and Alresford the switchback line became known as 'The Alps' due to the steep gradients encountered either side of the 652ft-high summit at Medstead & Four Marks station.

The line provided an alternative route for Waterloo to Southampton trains and was heavily used by military trains between Aldershot and Southampton during both World Wars. Locally produced watercress was also conveyed to market in London from stations along the line. Two other railways once branched off the Mid-Hants Railway at Butts Junction to the west of Alton: the Basingstoke & Alton Light Railway opened in 1901, closed to passengers in 1932 and to goods in 1936; the Meon Valley line to Knowle Junction near Fareham opened in 1903, closed to passengers in 1955 and to goods (to Farringdon) in 1968.

A diesel-electric multiple unit arrives at Alton with a train from Winchester on 24 August 1959.

Class 'S15' 4-6-0 No.30837 and Class 'U' 2-6-0 No. 31639 approach Medstead and Four Marks with the LCGB's 'S15 Commemorative Railtour' on 16 January 1966.

The diverted 'Bournemouth Belle' Pullman train heads through Ropley behind Brush Type 4 diesel D1686 on 1 May 1966.

Despite third-rail electrification reaching Alton from Waterloo in 1937 the Mid-Hants line remained steam hauled until the introduction of diesel-electric multiple units and a regular-interval service between Alton and Southampton Terminus in the late 1950s. Sundays often saw diverted Waterloo to Southampton and Bournemouth expresses struggling over 'The Alps' behind Bulleid Pacifics during engineering work on the main line.

Although it was listed for closure in the 'Beeching Report', a long running battle from objectors saw the line reprieved for nearly ten years. Lord Stonham stuck up for the line in 1963: 'The Clerk to the Winchester Rural District Council rang up yesterday, because they are concerned about losing the Alton line, to say: "We are sure it could be made to pay. Is that something we could put before the transport consultative council?" Well, they could talk about it, if the chairman of the committee allowed; but it is quite outside their province.' However, the inevitable finally happened on 5 February 1973 when it closed.

Fortunately this was not completely the end for much of the Mid-Hants line – in 1975 the newly-formed Winchester & Alton Railway Company purchased the 10¼ miles of track between Alton and Alresford. Opened in stages between 1977 and 1985, the Watercress Line as it is known, with its direct connection to the national rail network at Alton, is today one of the most popular steam-hauled heritage railways in Britain.

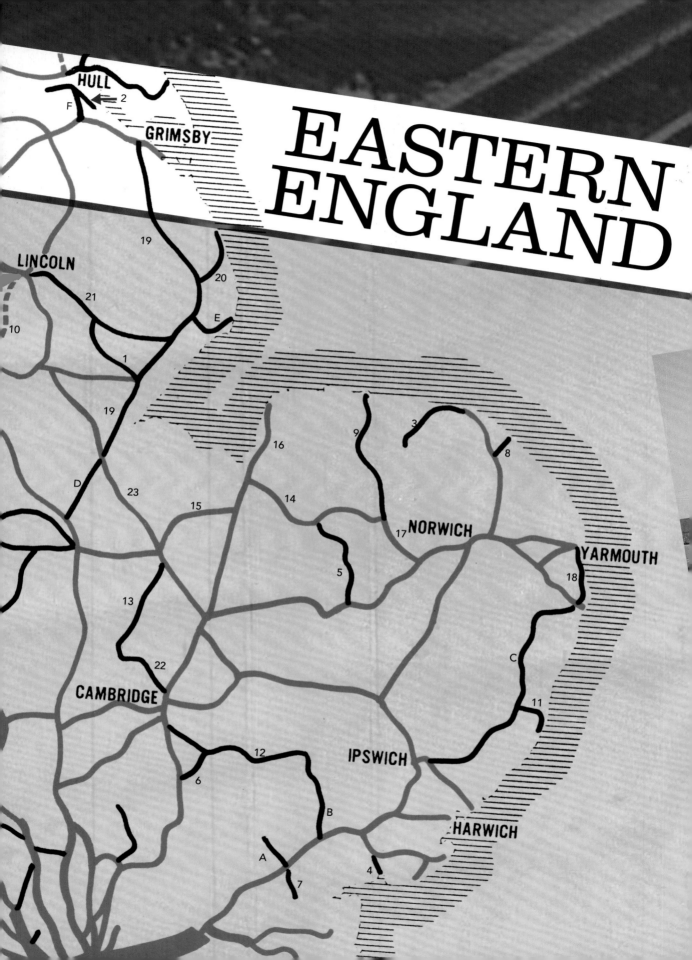

EASTERN ENGLAND

THE CASUALTIES

1. Woodhall Junction to Boston – 17 June 1963
2. Goxhill to Immingham Dock – 17 June 1963
3. Sheringham to Melton Constable – 6 April 1964
4. Wivenhoe to Brightlingsea – 15 June 1964
5. Swaffham to Roudham Junction – 15 June 1964
6. Audley End to Bartlow – 7 September 1964
7. Witham to Maldon East & Heybridge – 7 September 1964
8. North Walsham to Mundesley-on-Sea – 5 October 1964
9. Dereham to Wells-next-the-Sea – 5 October 1964
10. Lincoln to Grantham – 1 November 1965*
11. Saxmundham to Aldeburgh – 12 September 1966
12. Shelford to Sudbury via Long Melford – 6 March 1967
13. March to St Ives – 6 March 1967
14. King's Lynn to Dereham – 9 September 1968*
15. March to Magdalen Road via Wisbech – 9 September 1968*
16. King's Lynn to Hunstanton – 5 May 1969*
17. Wymondham to Dereham – 6 October 1969*
18. Lowestoft Central to Yarmouth South Town – 4 May 1970
19. Grimsby to Firsby via Louth/Boston to Spalding – 5 October 1970
20. Willoughby to Mablethorpe – 5 October 1970
21. Lincoln to Little Steeping via Woodhall Junction – 5 October 1970
22. Cambridge to St Ives – 5 October 1970
23. March to Spalding – 7 May 1973*

Note: Dates given are for withdrawal of passenger services
* = not listed for closure in the 'Beeching Report' Note:

THE SURVIVORS
A. Witham to Braintree
B. Marks Tey to Sudbury
C. Ipswich to Lowestoft
D. Peterborough to Spalding
E. Boston to Skegness
F. Habrough to Barton-on-Humber

A busy scene outside Wells-next-the-Sea station on the last day of services, 3 October 1964. The building survives today.

Fallen from grace: the former royal station at Wolferton on the King's Lynn to Hunstanton line which closed on 5 May 1969. The station has since been beautifully restored and after a period as a museum is now a private residence.

Made by Wagon und Maschinenbau of Germany, four-wheel railbus E79961 calls at the rickety platform at Bartlow with a service from Audley End on 8 June 1961. The line closed on 7 September 1964.

Woodhall Junction to Boston

Opened in 1848 as part of the Great Northern Railway's Lincolnshire Loop Line, the 31-mile railway between Lincoln and Boston was the temporary route for London to York trains until the completion of what became known as the East Coast Main Line in 1852. Closely following the Witham Navigation, its construction was speedy and cheap across the fens but, after the opening of ECML, it reverted to life as a secondary rural railway serving only scattered agricultural communities along its route. The opening of the 18-mile line from Woodhall Junction eastwards to Little Steeping via Coningsby and Midville in 1913 provided a shorter route for summer holiday trains from the East Midlands to Skegness via Lincoln.

Along with Lincolnshire's other rural railways, diesel multiple units and other cost-saving measures such as unstaffed stations and guard conductors were introduced as early as 1955. This was all to no avail, however, as the Lincoln to Boston line (along with many other railways in the county) was listed for closure in the 1963 'Beeching Report'.

The northern section from Lincoln to Woodhall Junction and from there to Little Steeping was reprieved until 1970. However, British Railways wasted no time in closing the 15¼-mile line southwards from Woodhall Junction to Boston –this loss-making line across the fens, serving the intermediate stations of Tattershall, Dogdyke and Langrick, was wound up on 17 June 1963.

Serving a small scattered community, Dogdyke station was immortalised in the Flanders and Swann song 'Slow Train', which mourned the loss of Britain's rural railways during the Beeching era.

The former Great Northern Railway station at Woodhall Junction, where the lines from Lincoln to Boston and Skegness diverge, circa 1969.

Ex-Great Central Railway Class 'A5/1' 4-6-2T No. 69820 waits to depart from Immingham Dock station with the 12.10pm train to New Holland on 28 April 1954. The loco was withdrawn in 1960 and the line closed in 1963.

Goxhill to Immingham Dock

The 7½-mile single-track line from Goxhill to Immingham Dock was opened by the Barton & Immingham Light Railway in 1911 and taken over by the Humber Commercial Railway & Dock the following year. It was served by trains to and from New Holland Pier where connections were made with the ferry across the River Humber to Hull. With intermediate stations at Killingholme Halt and East Halton Halt the railway was listed for closure in the 'Beeching Report'. Operated in later years by diesel multiple units, passenger services were withdrawn on 17 June 1963 although the section from Immingham to Killingholme remains open for oil traffic. Following closure, passenger trains for Immingham Dock were diverted via the freight-only line from Ulceby until 6 October 1969 when they, too, were withdrawn.

The bleak scene at Melton Constable station on the last day of passenger services to Sheringham, 4 April 1964.

CLOSED
APRIL
6
1964

Sheringham to Melton Constable

The seaside village of Sheringham was first reached by the Eastern & Midlands Railway which opened its steeply graded 15¼-mile branch line from its important hub junction at Melton Constable to Cromer Beach in 1887. In 1893 the E&MR was in a parlous financial position and it was taken over by the Midland Railway and the Great Northern Railway to form the Midland & Great Northern Joint Railway.

The mainly single track M&GNJR via Bourne in Lincolnshire, South Lynn and Fakenham was a popular route for holiday trains from the Midlands during the summer months but it fell on hard times after the Second World War and almost the whole system including lines to Peterborough, Norwich City and Yarmouth Beach was closed on 2 March 1959. The only exception was passenger services between Cromer Beach (reached by through diesel trains from Norwich via Wroxham and North Walsham) and Melton Constable which were retained for a further five years until closure east of Sheringham on 6 April 1964. On that date trains to and from Norwich reversed direction at Cromer Beach to continue along the coast to Sheringham.

Today, the 3-mile section between Cromer Beach and Sheringham (served by trains from Norwich on the Bittern Line) is the only part of the M&GNJR to remain open as part of the national rail network. However, in 1969 the 6¼-mile section from Sheringham to Holt was saved by the first railway preservation scheme in the UK to be floated as a public company. Fully opened in 1989, the North Norfolk Railway is today a popular attraction for holidaymakers and steam enthusiasts alike.

CLOSED
JUNE
15
1964

Wivenhoe to Brightlingsea

The five-mile single-track branch line from Wivenhoe, on the Great Eastern Railway's line from Colchester to Clacton-on-Sea and Walton-on-the-Naze, to the fishing village of Brightlingsea opened on 18 April 1866. From the outset the branch was worked by the GER and taken over by it in 1893. Oysters and fish throughout the year and daytrippers during the summer months provided most of the traffic on the branch until the 1950s. Severely damaged during the 'Great Storm' of January 1953, the line was first threatened with closure but eventually repaired and reopened 11 months later. Despite dieselisation and an intensive shuttle passenger service of 19 return trips each weekday the line suffered from road competition and was listed for closure in the 'Beeching Report' – the excuse being given was the cost of maintaining a swing bridge over Alresford Creek. The end came on 15 June 1964 and track was lifted soon after. Today, much of the trackbed from the former site of Brightlingsea station to Alresford Creek is a footpath.

A Class '105' DMU waits to depart from Brightlingsea station for Wivenhoe in May 1964. A month later the line had closed.

Swaffham to Roudham Junction

The 18¾-mile railway between Roudham Junction, on the Cambridge to Norwich main line to the east of Thetford, and Swaffham, on the King's Lynn to Dereham line, opened in two stages. First on the scene was the Thetford and Watton Railway which opened between Roudham Junction and Watton in 1869. The nine-mile northerly section was opened by the Watton & Swaffham Railway in 1875 – north of Watton an embankment had to be built to carry the line over the valley. It was initially worked by the T&WR but in 1879 both railways were leased by the Great Eastern Railway, the latter company taking over both the T&WR and the W&SR in 1897.

Passenger services along the line consisted of five return trains on weekdays while goods traffic consisted of cattle to and from local markets, poultry, butter, eggs, milk and sugar beet. Known as the Crab & Winkle Line it saw its busiest period during the Second World War when an RAF aerodrome was opened at Watton.

Diesel multiple units were introduced in the late 1950s when all intermediate stations except Watton became unmanned – the exchange station at Roudham Junction had already closed in 1932. Watton station was famous for a hedge on the platform that was carefully clipped into the shape of the station name and a locomotive.

Listed for closure in the 'Beeching Report', the end came for passenger trains on 15 June 1964 – freight continued between Swaffham and Watton until April 1965.

Audley End to Bartlow

The railway first reached Audley End in 1845 when the Eastern Counties Railway opened its main line from London to Cambridge – routing the railway via the nearby town of Saffron Walden had been blocked by the local landowner, Lord Braybrooke. The townsfolk and merchants of Saffron Walden were not best pleased, seeing the absence of a railway to their town as having a negative impact on their livelihoods. Eventually Lord Braybrooke relented and the 1¾-mile branch line from Audley End to the town opened in 1865. Meanwhile a 5½-mile northeasterly extension to Bartlow, on the Eastern Counties Railway's newly-opened Stour Valley line, had also been authorised and this opened in 1866.

The line was heavily used during both World Wars but by 1958 increasing competition from road transport led to a reduction in staff and the introduction of diesel railbuses. By 1960 the frequent weekday service consisted of 12 return shuttle journeys between Audley End and Saffron Walden with a further seven along the entire route to and from Bartlow. Listed for closure in the 'Beeching Report', passenger services ceased on 7 September 1964. Goods services survived only until the end of that year. The track was left in situ until 1968 when it was lifted. Surprisingly, the platform and wooden shelter (a wooden carriage body) at Ashdon Halt still survive. The Stour Valley line was closed between Shelford (south of Cambridge) to Sudbury at the end of 1966.

Henry Casserley's view of Stow Bedon station taken from a Swaffham to Thetford train on 9 May 1953.

German-built four-wheel diesel railbus E79961 rolls into Audley from Bartlow on a sunny day in May 1964.

German-built four-wheel diesel railbus E79963 calls at Wickham Bishops station on the Witham to Maldon East branch line on 14 March 1964.

CLOSED
SEPTEMBER
7
1964

Witham to Maldon East & Heybridge

What was effectively two separate branch lines, the double track Maldon, Witham & Braintree Railway opened in 1848. In conjunction with the building of the railway, the proposed development of Maldon Harbour for the export of grain never saw the light of day as the Eastern Counties Railway – whose main line the MW&BR had to cross at Witham – had already taken over the railway before it had even opened. While the Witham to Braintree line continues to flourish, the branch line from Witham to Maldon East & Heybridge was not so lucky and by the 1950s much of its traffic (daytrippers in the summer, and seasonal fruit and vegetable produce) had been lost to road transport. A second

line to Maldon from Woodham Ferrers had opened in 1889 – this 8¾-mile single track line saw little traffic and had closed to passengers as early as 1939, with goods lingering on until 1953.

Despite the introduction of diesel railbuses in 1958 passenger traffic continued to fall but British Railways must have clung on to some hope of revival as even in the winter of 1960/61 there were still 17 return trains each weekday. Listed for closure in the 'Beeching Report', the Witham to Maldon branch line succumbed to the inevitable on 7 September 1964. Goods traffic continued until April 1966. The wonderfully ornate station building at Maldon East has been restored and is now used as offices.

The station clock says 11.15am – the grand station building at Mundesley-on-Sea on the last day of services from North Walsham, 3 October 1964.

CLOSED
OCTOBER
5
1964

North Walsham to Mundesley-on-Sea

The 5¼-mile branch line from North Walsham to Mundesley-on-Sea was opened by the Midland & Great Northern Joint Railway in 1898. In a bid to open up the coast between Mundesley and Cromer as potential holiday destinations a unique arrangement was made in that year between the Great Eastern Railway and the M&GNJR; jointly owned by the two companies, the Norfolk & Suffolk Joint Railway was authorised to continue the Mundesley branch along the coast to Cromer. This is the only instance of a joint railway becoming a partner in another joint railway!

Opened in 1906, this 8¾-mile extension was never a great success and it closed completely on 17 April 1953. The grand station at Mundesley with its three platforms then reverted to being the terminus of the branch line from North Walsham, with diesel multiple units being introduced in 1956. This was all to no avail and while reasonably patronised during the summer months the branch was listed for closure in the 'Beeching Report'. Along with its delightful camping coaches the line was swept away on 5 October 1964. Goods traffic ceased at the end of that year and the track was ripped up. Today the station site at Mundesley has long since disappeared beneath modern housing although the intermediate station at Paston & Knapton survives as a private house.

CLOSED
OCTOBER
5
1964

Dereham to Wells-next-the-Sea

Built by the Norfolk Railway, the first railway to reach the town of Dereham was opened from Wymondham, on the Norwich to Thetford mainline, in 1847. Although an extension northwards to Wells-next-the-Sea had been authorised, construction stopped at Fakenham and the 12-mile line from Dereham opened in 1849. The remaining 9½ miles to Wells was built by the Wells & Fakenham Railway which had been part funded by the Earl of Leicester of Holkham Hall. The line opened in 1857 with a short branch to Wells Harbour being added two years later. The entire route from Wymondham to Wells became part of the Great Eastern Railway in 1862.

Popular with holidaymakers in the summer heading for the beaches at Wells and with pilgrims visiting the shrine of Our Lady of Walsingham, the line also carried vast quantities of milk to London, imported potash and exported corn via Wells Harbour and was extensively used during the Second World War when it was guarded by an armoured train. Traffic declined after the war and despite the introduction of diesel multiple units in 1955 the line became increasingly uneconomic and was listed for closure in the 'Beeching Report'. Despite this a fairly healthy service of 11 return trains each weekday, the majority starting or ending their journey at Norwich, continued up until closure on 5 October 1964.

While Dereham finally lost its passenger service on 6 October 1969 (see Wymondham to Dereham) the line to Fakenham stayed open for goods until the 1980s. The northerly section from Wells-next-the-Sea to Walsingham has since been reopened as the Wells & Walsingham Light Railway – the longest 10¼in gauge miniature railway in the world also operates the most powerful steam locomotives in that gauge in the world.

A Metropolitan Cammell lightweight DMU leaves Walsingham station with a Wells to Dereham train in June 1960.

CLOSED
NOVEMBER
1
1965

Lincoln to Grantham

Seen as a more direct route for trains between King's Cross and Lincoln via Grantham, the 18¼-mile railway between Honington and Lincoln was opened by the Great Northern Railway in 1867. Also serving intermediate stations at Caythorpe, Leadenham, Navenby, Harmston and Waddington (for the RAF air station), the line was mainly used by King's Cross to Lincoln expresses until closure. Diesel multiple units for the few stopping trains were introduced in the late 1950s but the line was closed on 1 November 1965 despite not being listed for closure in the 'Beeching Report'. After that date trains from London to Lincoln were diverted via Newark and Swinderby.

Although not listed for closure in the 'Beeching Report', the main line between Grantham and Lincoln closed on 1 November 1965. This is the sorry state of Navenby station a few years later after the track had been lifted.

CLOSED
SEPTEMBER
12
1966

Saxmundham to Aldeburgh

The 8¼-mile branch line from Saxmundham, on the East Suffolk Line between Ipswich and Lowestoft, to Aldeburgh was opened in two stages. The first four miles to Leiston was opened by the East Suffolk Railway in 1859, primarily to serve the engineering works of Richard Garrett & Sons which had been established in the town since 1778. The ESR was taken over by the Eastern Counties Railway which then extended the branch from Leiston to the small fishing village of Aldeburgh in 1860. The ECR became part of the newly formed Great Eastern Railway two years later.

With its terminus station some distance from the town centre and shingle beach, the village of Aldeburgh was slow to develop, although until the First World War, large quantities of fish were daily dispatched by train to London. Through coaches also ran from Liverpool Street until the outbreak of the Second World War. Following the war passenger usage declined dramatically and although diesel multiple units (some operating through services to and from Ipswich) were introduced in 1956 the branch would have closed by 1960 if it hadn't been for the construction of the nearby Sizewell 'A' magnox nuclear power station. By 1966 the power station had been completed and the branch, listed for closure along with the East Suffolk Line (the latter subsequently reprieved), succumbed on 12 September.

On the last day, Saturday 10 September, the flag flew at half mast at Aldeburgh, while Thorpness Halt was decorated with bunting. Packed with local residents, enthusiasts and journalists, the last train from Aldeburgh, a two-car DMU displaying the Royal Train headcode, left at 7.22pm. However, the branch from Saxmundham, to a loading point one mile east of Leiston, was kept open for the removal of spent uranium fuel rods by rail from Sizewell to Sellafield in Cumbria; this traffic continues today.

Metro-Cammell twin diesel unit E79066 waits to depart from Aldeburgh station on the final day of services to Saxmundham, 10 September 1966.

CLOSED
MARCH
6
1967

Shelford to Sudbury via Long Melford

The meandering 43¼-mile cross-country route between Shelford, south of Cambridge, and Marks Tey (on the London to Colchester main line) was opened by the Colchester, Stour Valley, Sudbury & Halstead Railway in several stages. First to open, in 1849, was the 11¾-mile section from Marks Tey northwards to the market town of Sudbury. This heavily engineered line involved the excavation of deep cuttings and the building of the massive brick viaduct at Chappel & Wakes Colne. The high construction costs incurred during the building of this first section led to a delay in the completion of the rest of the line which opened throughout in 1865. The railway was taken over by the Great Eastern Railway in 1898.

Normally carrying agricultural goods and cattle, the line saw its busiest period during the Second World War when it delivered building materials, fuel and armaments to several RAF airfields along its route. Passenger traffic consisted of through trains between Cambridge and Colchester – from 1959 these were operated by diesel multiple units when most stations became unmanned with tickets being issued by the guard conductor on the train. Listed for closure in the 'Beeching Report', the line lost its goods services in 1966. Withdrawal of passenger services between Shelford and Sudbury came on 6 March 1967 – an enthusiasts' two-car DMU special organised by the Midland & Great Northern Society ran over the line on 4 March – although the section from Sudbury to Marks Tey was reprieved and is still open today.

'B2' Class 4-6-0 No. 61616 'Falloden' pauses at Linton station between Cambridge and Bartlow with a Cambridge University Railway Club (CURC) special on 3 May 1959.

Somersham station on the GN&GE Joint line from St Ives to March was also the junction for the branch line to Warboys and Ramsey.

CLOSED
MARCH
6
1967

March to St Ives

The 19-mile line between March and St Ives was opened by the Wisbech, St Ives & Cambridge Railway in 1847. Even before it opened the railway had been taken over by the Eastern Counties Railway, one of the companies that became part of the newly-former Great Eastern Railway in 1862. Twenty years later the line from March to St Ives and westwards to Huntingdon became a joint line operated by the GER and the Great Northern Railway. A 5½-mile branch line from Somersham to Ramsey via Warboys opened in 1889 and also became part of the GN&GE Joint Line – it lost its passenger service in 1930 and the line closed completely in 1964.

With passenger numbers declining, diesel multiple units were introduced in 1959 with most trains running beyond St Ives to Cambridge. Avoiding the congestion at Ely, the majority also continued their journey to and from other destinations including Peterborough, King's Lynn (via Wisbech) and Birmingham. The line was also occasionally used as a diversionary route for trains diverted from the East Coast Main Line between Peterborough and Hitchin, running instead via Cambridge. Listed for closure in the 'Beeching Report', the March to St Ives line was closed to goods traffic in 1966 and to passengers on 6 March 1967.

CLOSED
SEPTEMBER
9
1968

King's Lynn to Dereham

The 26½-mile railway between King's Lynn and Dereham was originally seen as part of a cross-country trunk route and was designed for double track. However, despite strong objections from landowners (resulting in sky-high land purchase costs) and the owners of the Nar Navigation, the line was only built as single track and opened from King's Lynn to Narborough in 1846, to Swaffham in 1847 and to Dereham in 1848. Here it met the Norfolk Railway's branch line from Wymondham where it connected with the main line from Ely to Norwich.

Diesel multiple units were introduced in 1955 when a more frequent service from King's Lynn to Norwich was introduced. Freight consisted of agricultural goods, cattle, sugar beet and, during the Second World War, fuel and armaments for the RAF airbase at Marham. Despite not being listed for closure in the 'Beeching Report', the line became a casualty of the financial constraints imposed by a beleaguered Labour Government in 1966. In that year all goods services, except industrial sand from Middleton Towers, were withdrawn, passing loops removed and stations became unmanned. This last ditch attempt to save the line from closure failed and the end came on 9 September 1968. Today only the three-mile stub from King's Lynn to Middleton Towers remains open for sand traffic to four destinations around Britain.

The porter at Middle Drove station passes the time of day with the driver of a Wisbech to King's Lynn DMU on 21 June 1967.

CLOSED
SEPTEMBER
9
1968

March to Magdalen Road via Wisbech

By the 1820s the town of Wisbech was handling large quantities of imported Baltic timber carried by ship up the River Nene from The Wash. While the docks were enlarged and the river dredged to take larger ships, the absence of a railway in the 1840s was having a detrimental effect on the town. First to reach Wisbech was the Wisbech, St Ives & Cambridge Railway (worked by the Eastern Counties Railway) which opened via March in 1847. From the east the East Anglian Railway opened from Magdalen Road, on the Ely to King's Lynn main line, to Wisbech East in 1848. The short connection between the two rival stations at Wisbech was the source of much disagreement between the two companies which was only solved when the Eastern Counties Railway took over the running of the East Anglian Railway in 1852. Both railways later became part of the newly-formed Great Eastern Railway in 1862.

Goods traffic in the form of imported timber, timber products, beer, jam, agricultural machinery and cut flowers was the lifeblood of the line from Wisbech to March and remained substantial even after closure to passenger services. Diesel multiple units were introduced in the late 1950s and a frequent passenger service was complemented by through trains running between Peterborough, Ely, Cambridge and King's Lynn. Despite not being listed for closure in the 'Beeching Report', the straitened times of the late 1960s saw the line lose its passenger service on 9 September 1968 although goods traffic continued to operate from Wisbech to March until the end of the twentieth century. Today, the mothballed line between Wisbech and March awaits a possible reopening.

Ex-Great Eastern Railway Class 'J17' No. 65567 pauses at Swaffham station with a Rail Correspondence and Travel Society (RCTS) special from Norwich to Thetford on 21 March 1962. The loco was withdrawn five months later.

By 1965 Hunstanton station was but a shadow of its former self. Seen here on 11 August the empty platforms and sidings were still in situ waiting for excursion trains that would never come. On the right is a DMU waiting to depart for King's Lynn.

CLOSED
MAY
5
1969

King's Lynn to Hunstanton

The 15¼-mile single-track Lynn & Hunstanton Railway opened in 1862. Four years later the West Norfolk Junction Railway opened its 18¼-mile line from Heacham (the penultimate station on the Hunstanton branch) to Wells-next-the-Sea. Worked by the Great Eastern Railway, the two companies merged in 1874 to form the Hunstanton & West Norfolk Railway – the latter was then absorbed by the GER in 1890.

At the time of the railway's opening, Hunstanton was but a small village – land had either been given or sold cheaply by local landowners to the railway company in the hope of future development. Their optimism paid off and within ten years the village was expanding into a popular seaside resort – the purchase of nearby Sandringham House by the Prince of Wales in 1862 had already attracted much public interest. The nearest station to the royal residence was Wolferton on which Prince Edward lavished much expense befitting its royal patronage. At the end of the nineteenth century the track between King's Lynn and Wolferton was doubled – so popular was Sandringham with the royal family that no fewer than 645 Royal Trains visited Wolferton between 1884 and 1911. The station also witnessed the aftermath of the sad occasion of King George VI's death at Sandringham in 1952 when his body was taken by train back to London for burial at Windsor. The last Royal Train visit to the station was in 1966 – following closure of the line it became a museum for a while but has since been restored as a private house.

By the early twentieth century, Hunstanton's growing popularity as a seaside resort saw through trains running from Liverpool Street for the first time – by the onset of the Second World War there were trains running from Liverpool Street, St Pancras and King's Cross daily during the summer months. After the war through trains such as 'The Fenman' were reintroduced and the popularity of caravan holidays along this stretch of coastline further boosted patronage of the line. The severe floods at the beginning of 1953 brought disaster to the line when a train was stranded in rising waters near Heacham and was then hit by a floating wooden bungalow!

By the late 1950s changing holiday patterns and increased car ownership prompted a terminal decline in passenger numbers; diesel multiple units were introduced in 1958 and the line somehow escaped the death sentence in the 1963 'Beeching Report'.

In 1962 the Hunstanton branch was immortalised in a classic short BBC Television documentary – *John Betjeman Goes By Train* – which saw the future Poet Laureate travel along it to celebrate the centenary of its opening.

By 1967, in a bid to cut ever-deepening losses, all stations had become unstaffed with tickets being issued on the train by a guard conductor; the line from King's Lynn to Wolferton was singled; signal boxes were closed; and manually operated level crossing gates were replaced by automatic barriers. The entire branch line was now operated as a single section. Sadly this was all to no avail and, despite strong local opposition, the line finally closed on 5 May 1969.

With the station full of excursion trains, Class 'D16/3' 4-4-0 No. 62597 waits to depart from Hunstanton station with a train for Liverpool Street in August 1959. The loco was withdrawn less than six months later.

Working the daily milk train from North Elmham, Class 'J15' 0-6-0 No. 65471 is seen here north of Dereham en route to Norwich in 1960.

CLOSED

OCTOBER
6
1969

Wymondham to Dereham

The 11½-mile branch line from Wymondham, on the Norwich to Ely main line, to Dereham was opened by the Norfolk Railway in 1847. It was later extended northwards to Fakenham in 1849 and to Wells-next-the-Sea by the Wells & Fakenham Railway in 1857. While the line northwards from Dereham to Wells was listed for closure in the 'Beeching Report' (closing to passengers in 1964 – see Dereham to Wells-next-the-Sea), Dereham was also served by the line from King's Lynn and saw a through service between King's Lynn and Norwich. None of this route was listed for closure in the 'Beeching Report' but the various cost savings such as the use of diesel multiple units, unmanned stations and conductor/guards couldn't stave off the inevitable. While the King's Lynn to Dereham line closed in 1968 (see King's Lynn to Dereham), the Wymondham to Dereham line lingered on as a branch for just over another year until closure on 6 October 1969 although freight continued to use the line, as far north as Fakenham, into the 1980s. Since 1997 the railway between Wymondham to Dereham has been reopened as a heritage line – the Mid-Norfolk Railway also owns the trackbed north of Dereham to County School station.

CLOSED
MAY
4
1970

Lowestoft Central to Yarmouth South Town

The 10¼-mile line from Lowestoft Central to Yarmouth South Town was opened by the Norfolk & Suffolk Joint Railway in 1903. Together with the line from North Walsham to West Runton via Mundesley-on-Sea (opened throughout in 1906 – see North Walsham to Mundsley-on-Sea), the Norfolk & Suffolk Joint Railway was jointly owned by the Great Eastern Railway and the Midland & Great Northern Joint Railway – the latter was the only joint railway in Britain to jointly own another joint railway! Conveying catches of local fish was the lifeblood of the line for many years but by the 1950s much of this had been lost. Liverpool Street to Yarmouth trains were diverted via Norwich in 1962 although the summer Saturdays through services to and from the capital continued to use the coastal route for a few more years.

By 1966 the writing was on the wall for this under-patronised line and in an effort to reduce running costs intermediate stations became unmanned and diesel multiple units were introduced with conductor guards. Most trains then ran between Yarmouth and Ipswich, reversing direction at Lowestoft Central. With intermediate stations at Lowestoft (North), Corton, Hopton-on-Sea, Gorleston Links Halt and Gorleston-on-Sea the railway, along with the East Suffolk line to Ipswich, was listed for closure in the 'Beeching Report'. While the latter line was fortunately reprieved, the Lowestoft to Yarmouth line lost its goods service on 3 July 1967 and its passenger service on 4 May 1970.

Today, while there is now no direct rail link between Yarmouth and Lowestoft, the majority of the line's infrastructure and trackbed has disappeared beneath new roads, industrial and housing estates.

The unstaffed and neglected station at Gorleston-on-Sea shortly before closure.

CLOSED
OCTOBER
5
1970

Grimsby to Firsby via Louth/Boston to Spalding

The 47½-mile railway from Grimsby Town to Boston via Louth was built by the East Lincolnshire Railway but before completion in 1848 it had already been leased by the Great Northern Railway as part of an eventual through route to Peterborough and King's Cross. The ELR remained independent until the Big Four Grouping in 1923 when it became part of the newly-formed London & North Eastern Railway.

With through running over Manchester, Sheffield & Lincolnshire Railways' lines between Grimsby and New Holland the GNR could ostensibly offer a direct service between King's Cross and Hull, the latter reached by ferry across the River Humber. However, this slow route never fully developed, depending on local traffic to survive along with seasonal holiday traffic to Cleethorpes and, via branch lines, to the resorts of Mablethorpe and Skegness. By far the most important intermediate town on the line was Louth which was not only a major agricultural centre but home to an enormous maltings complex built near the station in 1870; destroyed by German bombing in 1940, the 90ft-high storage chambers were subsequently rebuilt in the early 1950s. Much of the freight traffic along the line was generated at Louth.

The through service of passenger trains to and from

The grand station building at Louth on 11 July 1959. Following years of dereliction the building has been tastefully converted into housing.

King's Cross continued until the early 1960s – even in 1961 there were two through buffet car services (one to Cleethorpes and one to Grimsby) to and from the capital on weekdays. In a bid to reduce ever increasing losses diesel multiple units had been introduced for local services as early as 1955 but these failed to stem a decline in passenger usage caused by slow journey times and increasing ownership of cars. The 1963 'Beeching Report' was a bombshell for the inhabitants of East Lincolnshire – all railways were to be closed leaving only Grimsby in the north and Boston in the south to serve as railheads. Closure, not only for the East Lincolnshire line but also for the branches to Mablethorpe and Skegness and lines from Lincoln to Boston and Woodhall Junction to Little Steeping, was scheduled for 1964 but a hard-fought campaign by the county and local councils brought a reprieve except for the Woodhall to Boston line which closed on 17 June 1963 (see Woodhall Junction to Boston).

Despite this hard-won battle, the East Lincolnshire line survived for only another six years and, amidst continuing protest from local councils, closed between Grimsby and Firsby and Boston to Spalding on 5 October 1970. The section south of Firsby to Boston along with the branch to Skegness was retained and is still open today. Goods traffic continued to use the line between Grimsby and Louth until 1980 when it closed completely. Today, a short section from Ludborough to North Thoreby is operated as a steam heritage railway by the Lincolnshire Wolds Railway.

CLOSED
OCTOBER 5 1970

Willoughby to Mablethorpe

When the East Lancashire Railway opened in 1848 it took an inland route to serve agricultural centres, away from small coastal villages such as Mablethorpe and Skegness. The latter was eventually reached along a 9¼-mile branch line from Firsby that opened in 1873 – this was the making of Skegness as a resort and by the twentieth century through trains from all over the Midlands and from London were carrying holidaymakers in their thousands during the summer months.

To the north, the Louth & East Coast Railway opened its 13-mile branch from Louth to Mablethorpe in 1877. Worked from the outset by the Great Northern Railway it soon led to the growing popularity of Mablethorpe as a seaside resort. A few miles down the coast there were plans to build an extensive docks system at Sutton; the seven-mile branch from Willoughby, on the East Lincolnshire main line, to Sutton was opened in 1886 by the Sutton & Willoughby Railway. Although the docks never developed, a connecting line between Sutton and Mablethorpe which opened in 1888 transformed the two branch lines into a 22¾-mile loop off the main line. The GNR took over the S&WR in 1902 and the L&ECR in 1908. Mablethorpe was never as successful as a seaside resort as Skegness but still saw extensive excursion traffic via Willoughby until the 1950s. Diesel multiple units were introduced in 1955 but the less patronised section from Louth to Mablethorpe closed on 5 December 1960. Listed for closure in the 'Beeching Report' the Mablethorpe branch closed on 5 October 1970.

Derby-built two-car diesel unit E56015 at Mablethorpe with a service for Willoughby on a sunny day in May 1967.

Time stands still at Bardney station in the late 1960s. The two-car diesel unit is heading north on a Skegness to Sheffield via Lincoln service.

Lincoln to Little Steeping via Woodhall Junction

Opened in 1848 as part of the Great Northern Railway's Lincolnshire Loop Line, the 31-mile railway between Lincoln and Boston was the temporary route for London to York trains until the completion of what became known as the East Coast Main Line in 1852. Closely following the Witham Navigation its construction was speedy and cheap across the fens but, after the opening of ECML, it reverted to life as a secondary rural route serving only scattered agricultural communities along its route.

The northern section between Lincoln and Woodhall Junction (for the Horncastle branch) took on a new lease of life in 1913 with the opening of the

A Lincoln to Skegness train departs from a sleepy Woodhall Junction on 11 September 1967.

This is what happens when you close railway lines and let buses take over – Histon station on the concrete guided busway between Cambridge and St Ives. What a daft waste of money.

CLOSED
OCTOBER
5
1970

Cambridge to St Ives

18-mile line between Woodhall Junction and Little Steeping, on the East Lincolnshire main line from Grimsby to Boston. Built primarily as a shorter route for holiday traffic from the East Midlands to Skegness, it saw little other traffic apart from seasonal seed potato trains from Tumby Woodside and, during the Second World War, traffic to and from RAF Coningsby.

As already noted, the 1963 'Beeching Report' spelt the end for Lincolnshire's rural railways. While they were all reprieved for a while the line southwards from Woodhall Junction to Boston (see Woodhall Junction to Boston) was not so lucky and was closed in indecent haste on 17 June 1963. The Lincoln to Skegness service via Woodhall Junction and Little Steeping struggled on for a few more years but the end came on 5 October 1970. By then the summer holiday traffic to Skegness – the *raison d'être* for the line – had already been reduced to a trickle and the guard conductor DMUs saw little intermediate traffic.

Today, much of the trackbed of the railway alongside the Witham Navigation between Lincoln (Waterside South) and Boston Marina is a footpath and cycleway known as the Water Rail Way (National Cycle Network Route 1). Specially commissioned modern sculptures decorate the route. Another footpath and cycleway known as the Spa Trail runs along much of the trackbed of the former branch line from Woodhall Junction to Horncastle.

The market town of St Ives in Huntingdon was once well served by railways. First on the scene were the Ely & Huntingdon Railway's line to Godmanchester and the Eastern Counties Railway's 14¾-mile branch from Cambridge, both of which opened in 1847. The planned eastward extension of the former railway to Ely did not open until as late as 1878 by which date the Great Eastern Railway was running the show. Northwards from St Ives the 19-mile line to March was opened by the ECR in 1848 and in 1882 became part of the Great Northern & Great Eastern Joint Railway (see March to St Ives).

West of St Ives the joint line to Huntingdon closed on 15 June 1959 – a year earlier diesel multiple units had been introduced between Cambridge, St Ives and March. Listed for closure in the 'Beeching Report', the line between St Ives and March closed on 6 March 1967 when the remaining service from Cambridge was reduced to its basic essentials with guard conductors issuing tickets on the trains. The end eventually came for the St Ives branch on 5 October 1970, a black day for railways in Eastern England, although freight services continued to use the line until 1992, when the track was mothballed.

In more recent years a controversial concrete guided busway has been built at great cost along the trackbed of the line from the outskirts of Cambridge to St Ives. Some say that it would have been cheaper to reopen the railway.

CENTRAL ENGLAND

THE CASUALTIES

1. Wellington to Buildwas and Much Wenlock – 23 July 1962
2. Wolverhampton (Low Level) to Stourbridge Junction – 30 July 1962
3. Bewdley to Tenbury Wells – 30 July 1962
4. Coaley Junction to Dursley – 10 September 1962
5. Cheltenham to Kingham – 15 October 1962
6. Kingham to Chipping Norton – 3 December 1962
7. Kimberley East to Pinxton South – 7 January 1963
8. Cresswell to Cheadle – 17 June 1963
9. Ashchurch to Redditch via Evesham – 17 June 1963
10. Bewdley to Shrewsbury – 9 September 1963
11. Wellington to Market Drayton and Nantwich – 9 September 1963
12. Etruria to Kidsgrove via Tunstall – 2 March 1964
12A. Stoke-on-Trent to Silverdale – 2 March 1964
13. Kemble to Cirencester – 6 April 1964
14. Kemble to Tetbury – 6 April 1964
15. Northampton to Wellingborough, Oundle and Yarwell Junction – 4 May 1964
16. Old Hill to Dudley – 15 June 1964
17. Walsall to Dudley – 6 July 1964
18. Worcester to Bromyard – 7 September 1964
19. Wolverton to Newport Pagnell – 7 September 1964
20. Verney Junction to Buckingham – 7 September 1964
21. Leicester to Burton-upon-Trent – 7 September 1964
22. Derby Friargate to Nottingham – 7 September 1964
23. Stafford to Wellington – 7 September 1964
23A. Nottingham to Worksop via Kirkby-in-Ashfield – 12 October 1964
24. Berkeley Road to Sharpness – 2 November 1964
25. Grange Court to Hereford – 2 November 1964
26. Uttoxeter to Leek – 4 January 1965
27. Castle Bromwich to Walsall via Aldridge – 18 January 1965
28. Wichnor Junction to Wolverhampton High Level via Walsall – 18 January 1965
29. Walsall to Rugeley (Trent Valley) via Cannock – 18 January 1965
29A. Leamington Spa to Coventry and Nuneaton – 18 January 1965
30. Rugby to Peterborough – 6 June 1966
31. Seaton to Stamford Town – 6 June 1966
32. Nottingham to Kettering – 6 June 1966
33. Aylesbury to Nottingham and Sheffield and Banbury to Woodford Halse – 5 September 1966
34. Gobowen to Oswestry – 7 November 1966
35. Manchester Central to Cheadle Heath – 2 January 1967
36. Miller's Dale to Buxton – 6 March 1967
37. Oxford to Bletchley and Bedford St John's to Cambridge – 1 January 1968*
38. Stratford-upon-Avon to Cheltenham – 25 March 1968*
39. Matlock to Chinley – 1 July 1968
40. Rugby Central to Nottingham Victoria – 5 May 1969
41. Bewdley to Kidderminster/Hartlebury – 5 January 1970
42. New Mills Central to Hayfield – 5 January 1970

Note: Dates given are for withdrawal of passenger services
* = not listed for closure in the 'Beeching Report'

THE SURVIVORS

A. Syston Junction to Peterborough via Oakham
B. Lincoln to Nottingham
C. Stockport to Buxton
D. Stockport to Dore via Edale (Hope Valley)
E. Wrexham to Bidston
F. Hooton to Helsby

Although not listed for closure in the 'Beeching Report', passenger trains between Oxford and Cambridge were withdrawn on 1 January 1968. This is the sorry state of Winslow station after closure following years of neglect and vandalism. Although the station building no longer exists, the platforms and overgrown track still survive today.

Numerous enthusiasts' special trains were run over threatened branch lines during the 1960s. Here, BR Standard '3MT' Class 2-6-2T No. 82003 heads a Locomotive Club of Great Britain special on the Hayfield branch, 16 April 1966.

A major victim of the 'Beeching Axe' in Central England was the Great Central route from Marylebone to Nottingham. Here, the last up train is about to depart from Nottingham Victoria behind suitably decorated Stanier 'Black 5' 4-6-0 No. 44984 on 3 September 1966.

CLOSED

JULY

23

1962

Wellington to Buildwas and Much Wenlock

A convoluted tale of many railway companies! The branch line from Ketley Junction, to the east of Wellington, to Lightmoor was opened by the Wellington & Severn Junction Railway as far as Horsehay in 1857 and extended to Lightmoor in 1858. The section between Lightmoor and Coalbrookdale had already opened in 1854 as part of a branch line from Madeley Junction. Initially worked by the Coalbrookdale Iron Company, the branch from Ketley Junction to Coalbrookdale was leased to the GWR in 1861 and taken over by that company in 1892. To the west, the Much Wenlock & Severn Junction railway was opened between Buildwas (on the Severn Valley Railway's line from Hartlebury to Shrewsbury) and Much Wenlock in 1862. This line was worked by the West Midlands Railway until taken over by the GWR in 1863. The intervening gap over the River Severn between Coalbrookdale and Buildwas was opened by the Much Wenlock, Craven Arms & Coalbrookdale Railway in 1864. From Much Wenlock the latter company extended westwards beneath Wenlock Edge to Marsh Farm Junction, north of Craven Arms on the Shrewsbury & Hereford Railway, opening in 1867.

The Wellington (Ketley Junction) to Craven Arms (Marsh Farm Junction) railway operated as a 24-mile cross-country route until 1951 when all passenger services between Much Wenlock and Craven Arms were withdrawn. Goods trains continued to use the line between Buildwas and Longville until 1963. The remaining stretch of line between Ketley Junction, Buildwas and Much Wenlock reverted to branch line status and was served by six return trains each day, the 11¼-mile journey from Wellington to Much Wenlock taking 45-50 minutes. Despite the introduction of diesel multiple units, passenger numbers continued to decline and the branch was marked on Map 9 of the 'Beeching Report' as due for closure – in fact closure came on 23 July 1962, eight months before publication of the 'Report'.

Today the section from Lightmoor to Buildwas is still used by merry-go-round coal trains serving Ironbridge Power Station via the line from Madeley Junction.

The last day of passenger services on the Wellington to Much Wenlock line – here, dwarfed by the nearby power station, a single-car diesel unit pauses at Buildwas Junction on 21 July 1962.

CLOSED JULY 30 1962
Wolverhampton (Low Level) to Stourbridge Junction

The 12-mile railway between Stourbridge Junction and Wolverhampton (Low Level) was opened by the Oxford, Worcester & Wolverhampton Railway in 1854. Nicknamed the 'Old Worse & Worse' because of its shoddy service, the company amalgamated with the Worcester & Hereford Railway in 1860 to form the West Midland Railway, which was itself then absorbed by the Great Western Railway in 1863. Although listed for closure in the 'Beeching Report', passenger services were withdrawn some eight months earlier on 30 July 1962 while goods services continued until December 1967. Serving a steel terminal at Round Oak, the line northwards from Stourbridge Junction is currently still open for freight traffic. The line north of Round Oak to Dudley and Walsall is mothballed awaiting possible reopening.

Ex-GWR streamlined diesel railcar W20W calls at Wyre Forest station with the 4.10pm Kidderminster to Tenbury Wells train on 20 June 1959.

'5700' Class 0-6-0PT No. 3778 coasts into Brettell Lane station with the 3.57pm Wolverhampton (Low Level) to Stourbridge Junction train on the last day of passenger services over this route, 28 July 1962.

CLOSED JULY 30 1962
Bewdley to Tenbury Wells

Originally part of a through route linking Woofferton, on the Shrewsbury & Hereford Railway's main line, and Bewdley, the 14-mile Tenbury & Bewdley Railway opened in 1864 and was taken over by the GWR in 1869 – the Tenbury Railway had already opened the 5¼-mile line from Woofferton to Tenbury Wells in 1861. By the 1950s the entire route was suffering from increased road competition and the section from Woofferton to Tenbury Wells closed on 31 July 1961. The rest of the line to Bewdley was reprieved for another year, with a limited weekday service, but closure to passengers came on 30 July 1962. Despite this early closure it is still shown as a black line on Map 9 of the 'Beeching Report'. On this date the section from Tenbury to Cleobury Mortimer was closed completely but east of Cleobury it was retained to serve the 12¾-mile Cleobury Mortimer & Ditton Priors Light Railway which had opened in 1908 and served a large Admiralty arms depot. Complete closure of the light railway and the section from Cleobury to Bewdley came on 16 April 1965.

Evening draws on and the mourners gather as Ivatt Class '2MT' 2-6-0 No. 46527 waits at Coaley Junction with the last train to Dursley on 8 September 1962.

The view from the train as Ivatt Class '2MT' 2-6-0 No. 46527 pulls away from Coaley Junction with the last passenger train for Dursley on 8 September 1962.

CLOSED
SEPTEMBER
10
1962

Coaley Junction to Dursley

Serving woollen and carpet mills, the 2½-mile branch line up the Cam Valley from Coaley Junction, on the Midland Railway's Gloucester to Bristol main line, to the town of Dursley was opened by the grandly named Dursley & Midland Junction Railway in 1856. The company was taken over by the Midland Railway in 1861. In 1867 the engineering company of R A Lister opened in the town and its rail-linked factory provided much of the freight traffic on the line until closure. Passenger traffic was never heavy and passenger services were withdrawn on 10 September 1962 but the branch remained open as a long siding for goods traffic serving Lister's factory until 13 July 1970. Although Coaley Junction had closed on 4 January 1965 a new station, Cam & Dursley, was opened nearby on the main line in 1994.

CLOSED
OCTOBER
15
1962

Cheltenham to Kingham

The 23½-mile single-track railway between Cheltenham and Kingham was completed as part of the Great Western Railway's Banbury & Cheltenham Direct Railway. While the 11-mile section from Kingham to Bourton-on-the-Water had been opened by the Oxford, Worcester & Wolverhampton Railway in 1862, the remainder of the line to Cheltenham was only completed by the GWR in 1881. Beyond Kingham, the Chipping Norton Railway (opened in 1855) and an extension to King's Sutton (opened in 1887) completed the B&CDR's rural route across the Cotswolds.

Although the line remained a fairly quiet backwater until its closure it did see the passage of a fascinating through service which ran from 1905 until the 1930s. Known as the 'Ports to Ports Express', the restaurant car express was operated jointly by the North Eastern Railway, the Great Central Railway and the GWR and ran between Cardiff and Newcastle via Gloucester, a south-east spur at Cheltenham, Kingham, King's Sutton, Banbury, Leicester, Sheffield and York.

Following heavy use during the Second World War, the line had reverted back to being a rural railway by the 1950s. Six trains each way on weekdays sufficed although the western section from Cheltenham to Andoversford Junction was also used by the one train each weekday on the former Midland & South Western Junction Railway's route to Southampton until its closure in 1961. Although listed for closure in the 'Beeching Report', the railway had lost its passenger service on 15 October 1962. Goods trains continued to serve Bourton-on-the-Water from Kingham until 7 September 1964.

'5101' Class 2-6-2T No. 4109 is seen here filling up with water for the last time at Chipping Norton while working the last day of passenger services from Cheltenham and Kingham on 13 October 1962.

CLOSED
DECEMBER
3
1962

Kingham to Chipping Norton

The 4½-mile Chipping Norton Railway was opened between Kingham and Chipping Norton by the Oxford, Worcester & Wolverhampton Railway in 1855. Becoming part of the Great Western Railway in 1863, the single-track Chipping Norton branch and the Bourton-on-the-Water branch became part of the GWR's Banbury & Cheltenham Direct Railway which opened throughout between Cheltenham and King's Sutton in 1887.

Despite being part of the route of the 'Ports to Ports Express' in the early twentieth century, the railway was an early victim of competition from road buses. Passenger services between Chipping Norton and King's Sutton were withdrawn in 1951 and goods services along this section in 1958. By then the remaining branch service from Kingham had dwindled to two trains each way on weekdays and it came as no surprise when the line was listed for closure in the 'Beeching Report'. Closure preceded the report's publication when passenger services were withdrawn on 3 December 1962. The last passenger train ran on the preceding Saturday hauled by BR Standard Class '2' 2-6-0 No. 78001. Goods services continued until 7 September 1964.

'5101' Class 2-6-2T No. 5184 calls at Bourton-on-the-Water station with the 10.50am train from Cheltenham St James to Kingham on 29 September 1962. On the other line No. 4101 is waiting to leave with the 11.18am ex-Kingham train. Only two weeks later this wonderful Cotswold scene passed away forever.

CLOSED
JANUARY
7
1963

Kimberley East to Pinxton South

The 8½-mile branch line from Kimberley East, west of Nottingham, to Pinxton was opened as part of the Great Northern Railway's bold extension into Derbyshire and Staffordshire in 1876 (see Derby Friargate to Nottingham). Primarily a coal-carrying line, the Pinxton South branch was also served by a sparse and infrequent passenger service to and from Nottingham Victoria until closure on 7 January 1963.

Last train from Pinxton South – bedecked with flags, 'B1' Class 4-6-0 No. 61299 leaves with the 6.55pm train to Nottingham Victoria on a cold 5 January 1963.

CLOSED
JUNE
17
1963

Cresswell to Cheadle

The opening of the four-mile branch line from Cresswell, on the North Staffordshire Railway's line from Stoke-on-Trent to Uttoxeter, to the small market town of Cheadle was dogged by delays. Although incorporated in 1878, the Cheadle Railway was abandoned in 1882. It was then reborn as the Cheadle Railway Mineral & Land Company in 1888 and opened, with the support of the NSR, to Totmanslow (later renamed Tean) in 1892. The company was then renamed the Cheadle Railway in 1896 with Cheadle being reached in 1901 – the nine-year delay was caused by the building of a tunnel through difficult rock just south of Cheadle station. Worked from the outset by the NSR it was taken over by that company in 1907.

Passing into the newly-formed LMS in 1923, the Cheadle branch continued to experience problems with the tunnel until the line was diverted around the obstacle in 1933. Passenger traffic was never heavy although the branch did serve a colliery at New Haden until 1943. By 1962 there were only two return train services on weekdays for commuters to and from Stoke. On summer Saturdays there were four trains with one surprisingly running to and from Llandudno.

Listed for closure in the 'Beeching Report', the Cheadle branch closed to passengers on 17 June 1963. The branch continued to be used for industrial sand traffic until 1986. Today, apart from a small section that has been built over at Cheadle, the heavily overgrown track is still in place.

Spot those old bangers – looking more like Steptoe & Son's junkyard, the site of the closed Tean Halt sees the passage of the 1.35pm Cheadle to Stoke-on-Trent train on 19 August 1961.

CLOSED JUNE 17 1963
Ashchurch to Redditch via Evesham

Known as the Birmingham & Gloucester Loop Line, the railway between Redditch and Ashchurch was built in stages, although since 1859 Redditch had been served by a branch line built by the Redditch Railway from Barnt Green. At the southern end the Midland Railway opened a ten-mile branch from Ashchurch to Evesham in 1864 – serving an important agricultural region, much of its goods traffic consisted of transporting soft fruit to market. The intervening 17¼-mile gap between Evesham and Redditch via Alcester was opened throughout in 1868. The loop was often used by heavy freight trains avoiding the gruelling Lickey Incline to the west and, during the Second World War, by heavy freight traffic that reached it from the Stratford-upon-Avon & Midland Junction Railway via Broom Junction.

Passenger traffic was never heavy and after the S&MJR was connected with the GWR's Birmingham to Cheltenham line at Stratford-upon-Avon in 1960 it lost its usefulness as a freight corridor. Listed for closure in the 'Beeching Report', passenger services on the Evesham to Redditch section had already been substituted by a bus service on 1 October 1962. Closure to passengers came on 17 June 1963 and to goods between Ashchurch and Evesham on 9 September and between Redditch and Evesham on 6 July 1964.

Two ex-GWR streamlined railcars meet at Bewdley in 1961 – on the left is green liveried W30 while on the right is W21. The young lad on the island platform is so excited that his feet have left the ground!

CLOSED SEPTEMBER 9 1963
Bewdley to Shrewsbury

Closely following the River Severn, the Severn Valley Railway opened its 40¾-mile line between Hartlebury, north of Droitwich, to Shrewsbury in 1862. It was initially leased by the West Midland Railway until being taken over by the GWR in 1872. A linking three-mile line was opened from Kidderminster to Bewdley in 1878.

Passenger demand was fairly low and the line saw the introduction of streamlined diesel railcars after the Second World War. Goods traffic consisted of milk and dairy products, livestock and coal from a colliery at Alveley. Journey times were slow – by the autumn of 1958 there was only one through train from Shrewsbury to Bewdley and in the opposite direction just two. At other times passengers trying to travel along the whole length of the line were forced to change trains at Bridgnorth – no doubt a deliberate ploy by BR to persuade customers to use buses instead in a run-up to closure. Their plan worked and the line was, unsurprisingly, listed for closure in the 'Beeching Report' –the end came for passenger services and through goods traffic on 9 September 1963. A sparse passenger service from Bewdley to Hartlebury and Kidderminster continued until 1970. Coal traffic continued south of Alveley until 1969 leaving only a short stub near Buildwas with merry-go-round coal trains serving Ironbridge Power Station via Madeley Junction. This traffic continues today.

This highly scenic railway came back to life in 1970 when a preservation group started running steam trains between Bridgnorth and Hampton Loade. Since then the line has reopened south to Bewdley and on to Kidderminster and today the Severn Valley Railway is one of the most popular heritage lines in Britain.

As a southbound Cross-Country DMU heads off for Cheltenham, '3600' Class 0-6-0PT No. 3745 prepares to leave Ashchurch with the 10am train to Evesham on the last day of passenger services on this line, 15 June 1963.

Wellington to Market Drayton and Nantwich

Etruria to Kidsgrove via Tunstall

While attempting to invade the North Staffordshire Railway by the back door and striking deep into the heart of Euston-controlled territory, the 27½-mile north-south route between Wellington and Nantwich (and on to Crewe) had fallen into the hands of the GWR before the end of the nineteenth century. The northern 10¾-mile section from Nantwich to Market Drayton was opened by the Nantwich & Market Drayton Railway in 1863 while the remaining 16¾ miles south of Market Drayton to Wellington was opened by the Wellington & Drayton Railway in 1867 – the latter company had already been taken over by the GWR a year earlier, while the N&MDR was taken over in 1897.

Classed as a secondary main line, the railway served a rich dairy farming region along with Market Drayton, the only intermediate town of any size. Mainly consisting of through trains between Wellington and Crewe bringing the incongruous sight of GWR locos arriving and departing from Crewe, the passenger service was sporadic and very poorly patronised. By the autumn of 1958, when the LMR took over control from the WR, there were only six return trains along the length of the line with two more between Wellington and Market Drayton. There were two return services on Sundays. Closure was already on the cards even before the 'Beeching Report' was published. The end came for passenger services on 9 September 1963 but the line remained open for through goods traffic and diverted passenger trains until the completion of the electrification of the West Coast Main Line south of Crewe in 1967.

The seven-mile Potteries Loop Line from Etruria to Kidsgrove via Hanley, Burslem and Tunstall was opened in stages by the North Staffordshire Railway between 1850 and 1875. Serving the industrial towns of the Potteries, the line was renowned for its bleak outlook, sharp curves and steep gradients. The line's heyday was in the early twentieth century when workers at the numerous brickworks, collieries and pottery works were served by around 40 trains of rattling four-wheel coaches each day.

Increased competition from buses and lorries brought a decline in its fortunes during the 1930s and by the 1950s it was living on borrowed time. The summer 1962 timetable shows only five (poorly patronised) return services each day and, inevitably, the line was listed for closure in the 'Beeching Report'. Closure to passengers came on 2 March 1964 although goods trains and diverted passenger trains continued to run until 1967 when the line was severed – the northern section from Kidsgrove to Park Farm remained open for opencast coal traffic until 1976, while the southern section from Etruria to Waterloo Road remained open for oil traffic to Hanley until 1969. A section of the trackbed at Tunstall is now a footpath and cycleway known as the Greenway.

A three-car BRCW DMU takes the Potteries Loop Line north of Etruria with the 4.42pm Wolverhampton (High Level) to Manchester via Stoke train on 28 September 1963. Heavy industry such as the steelworks in the background is now just a dim and distant memory in the Potteries.

On a cold midwinter's day Ivatt Class '2' 2-6-2T No. 41241 pulls away from Audlem station with the 10.08am train from Wellington to Crewe, 30 December 1960.

Silverdale station seen from a Market Drayton to Stoke-on-Trent train on 28 August 1954.

Made by A C Cars Ltd, four-wheel diesel railbus W79977 waits to depart from Cirencester for Kemble on 25 March 1964. Even at this late stage agricultural machinery was still being delivered to the station.

CLOSED MARCH 2 1964

Stoke-on-Trent to Silverdale

The 4¼-mile branch line from Silverdale to Stoke-on-Trent was opened as part of the North Staffordshire Railway's cross-country route to Market Drayton which was completed in 1870. Passenger services between Silverdale and Market Drayton via Keele ceased in 1956 although the section from Market Drayton to Madeley was kept open for milk traffic and as a diversionary route until 1966. Despite closure, much of the track from Pipe Gate to Madeley still survives albeit hidden beneath undergrowth.

Meanwhile Silverdale continued to be served by passenger trains to and from Stoke on weekdays although by the early 1960s these amounted to only two early morning/late afternoon commuter trains in each direction. Another two trains in each direction terminated at Newcastle-under-Lyme. One oddity of the summer 1962 timetable was a Saturdays-only return working between Silverdale and Birmingham New Street.

Listed for closure in the 'Beeching Report', the Silverdale branch lost its meagre passenger service on 2 March 1964 although coal traffic continued until 9 January 1967. Since closure the station building at Silverdale has been re-erected at the Apedale Heritage Centre while the platforms have been restored alongside a railway footpath to Newcastle-under-Lyme.

CLOSED APRIL 6 1964

Kemble to Cirencester

The branch line from Kemble to Cirencester started life as part of the Cheltenham & Great Western Union Railway which opened its line from Swindon in 1841. The C&GWUR extended its main line from Kemble to Standish, where it met the Bristol & Gloucester Railway, in 1845 leaving Cirencester at the end of a 4¼-mile branch line. The C&GWUR had already been leased by the GWR and was taken over by it in 1844. Cirencester got a second station, Watermoor, in 1883 when the Midland & South Western Junction Railway opened between Swindon Town and Cheltenham (closed 11 September 1961); to avoid confusion the GWR terminus was renamed Cirencester Town in 1924.

Along with the Tetbury branch (see Kemble to Tetbury), the Cirencester branch saw the introduction of four-wheel railbuses on 2 February 1959 – small sleeper-built halts were also opened at Park Leaze and Chesterton Lane. With an increased frequency of trains connecting with the Cheltenham to Paddington expresses at Kemble, passenger usage increased but all to no avail as the line was listed for closure in the 'Beeching Report'. Passenger services ceased on 6 April 1964 although goods traffic continued until 1965.

Passengers on the last down train on 5 April were given free beer and rolls but the burning of a life-size effigy of Mr Marples at Cirencester station was prevented by the police – it was later set alight on the pavement outside. A Gloucestershire Railway Society special train – two auto coaches hauled by 0-4-2T No. 1472 – also traversed the branch on the last day.

CLOSED
APRIL
6
1964

Kemble to Tetbury

The small market town of Tetbury was originally planned to be served by a through railway route from Stroud to Malmesbury by the Wiltshire & Gloucestershire Railway but nothing came of this and the company was wound up in 1871. Eventually a 7¼-mile branch line from Kemble, on the GWR's Swindon to Gloucester main line, to the market town of Tetbury was opened by that company in 1889. A new cattle market was also opened next to the terminus station, providing much of the branch's goods traffic until closure. It is fascinating to learn that in 1963 the contents of a complete farm were moved by a special train to Stranraer in Scotland!

Leading a fairly quiet life, the branch was one of the first to see the introduction of four-wheel diesel railbuses on 2 February 1959. In an attempt to generate more traffic three small halts (built from sleepers) were also opened at Church's Hill, Culkerton and Trouble House and a more frequent service was introduced. Despite an increase in passengers this

bucolic country railway was listed for closure in the 'Beeching Report' and the end came on 6 April 1964 when the line closed completely.

The last day of regular services on 4 April saw some fun and games along the line. A coffin addressed to Dr Beeching was conveyed on the last train (7.35pm) from Tetbury and at Kemble was loaded on to the 8.15pm to Paddington. The return journey was delayed by bonfires of hay bales placed across the track near Tetbury station, which was finally reached to the sound of detonators laid on the track. A Gloucestershire Railway Society special train – two auto coaches hauled by 0-4-2T No. 1472 – traversed the branch on 5 April 1964. Today, all that remains at Tetbury is the goods shed.

A C Cars Ltd four-wheel diesel railbus W79976 waits to depart from Tetbury with the 2.15pm train for Kemble on 7 February 1964.

CLOSED
MAY
4
1964

Northampton to Wellingborough, Oundle and Yarwell Junction

The 43¾-mile railway between Northampton and Peterborough was opened by the London & Birmingham Railway in 1845 – its starting point was at Blisworth on the L&BR's main line between Euston and Birmingham. The L&BR became part of the newly-formed London & North Western Railway a year later. The line's fairly level route through the rich farmland of the Nene Valley via Wellingborough and Oundle was cheap to construct although the numerous level crossings (built instead of road overbridges) increased operating costs and the location of many stations (built in an attractive old English style) miles from the villages they purported to serve brought little extra traffic.

While useful as a through route, the line saw only a sporadic pattern of passenger services – by the summer of 1962 there were only five through trains between Northampton Castle and Peterborough (plus one to Oundle, Monday to Friday), with one on Saturdays extending to Lowestoft and Yarmouth. With competition from more convenient bus services, high operating costs and few customers, the line between Northampton and Yarwell Junction was inevitably listed for closure in the 'Beeching Report'.

Despite strong public protests, the end came on 4 May 1964 although iron ore trains continued to use the line until 1966. It was closed completely to through goods traffic in 1972.

The last train on the Northampton to Peterborough route. Stanier 'Black 5' 4-6-0 No. 44837 departs from Wellingborough London Road station with the 8.49pm Peterborough to Northampton train on 2 May 1964.

CLOSED
JUNE
15
1964

Old Hill to Dudley

Known as the Bumble Hole Line, the 3¾-mile railway between Old Hill and Dudley was opened by the Great Western Railway in 1868. Built as a double-track railway it afforded an alternative route for trains between Wolverhampton (Low Level) and Birmingham (Snow Hill). A series of four simple halts was later opened and for many years local services were operated by steam railmotors and auto trains. Single-car diesel units were introduced in the early 1960s but by then trains had become very poorly patronised and the line was inevitably listed in the 'Beeching Report'. Closure to passengers came on 15 June 1964 and to goods on January 1968. Today, the northern section from south of Dudley to Windmill End is a footpath.

Watched by a group of enthusiasts, '5700' Class 0-6-0PT No. 4665 runs through the branch platforms at Old Hill station on 21 July 1962. The Dudley auto train is on the right.

A BRCW two-car DMU moves into Dudley station to form the 4.18pm train to Walsall on 26 August 1961.

Gloucester R C & W Co single unit diesel railcar W55003 waits to depart from neglected Bromyard station with a train for Worcester on a drizzly 28 November 1963.

CLOSED
JULY
6
1964

Walsall to Dudley

The 6¼-mile railway between Walsall and Dudley was opened by the South Staffordshire Railway in 1850. Unusually it was first leased to an individual (John Robinson McClean) until it was taken over by the London & North Western Railway in 1867. Although the line was an important freight corridor through the Black Country, the line's passenger service was fairly modest and served the intermediate stations of Wednesbury Town, Great Bridge North and Dudley Port. Passing into the London Midland Region after nationalisation, by the summer of 1962 train services consisted of a fairly frequent shuttle service of auto trains between Dudley and Dudley Port in addition to 12 weekday trains along the whole route.

Listed for closure in the 'Beeching Report', the end came for passenger services on 6 July 1964 although local goods trains continued to serve factories along the line until 1972. Through freight trains continued to use the route until 1993 and since then the line, including southwards through Dudley Tunnel to Round Oak, Kingswinford and Stourbridge Junction (route closed to passengers on 30 July 1962), has lain derelict. There are currently plans to reopen the line as part of the Midland Metro tramway and also as a freight line.

CLOSED
SEPTEMBER
7
1964

Worcester to Bromyard

Authorised in 1861, the 24½-mile Worcester, Bromyard & Leominster Railway fell on hard times before it was completed. The 12 miles from Bromyard to Leominster was not initially built and the remainder from Leominster Junction, south of Worcester, to Bromyard was only opened in 1877, worked by the GWR. A separate company, the Leominster & Bromyard Railway, revived the missing section which opened in 1897 – in the meantime both companies had been taken over by the GWR in 1888.

The poorly patronised Bromyard to Leominster section closed as early as 1952 but the rest of the line struggled on until listed for closure in the 'Beeching Report'. In the meantime passenger services had dwindled to three trains each weekday to Bromyard (plus two extra services on Tuesday and Saturday), with four (plus two on Tuesday and Saturday) in the opposite direction. With increasing competition from buses and a journey time for the 14½-mile journey a leisurely 40 minutes it is hardly surprising that the line was closed on 7 September 1964.

CLOSED
SEPTEMBER
7
1964

Wolverton to Newport Pagnell

Replacing the closed Newport Pagnell Canal, the four-mile branch line from the railway town of Wolverton, on the Euston to Birmingham main line, to Newport Pagnell was opened completely in 1867. The railway was taken over by the London & North Western Railway in 1875 and provided a convenient commuter route for workers at that company's railway works in Wolverton. Construction of an eastward extension from Newport Pagnell to Olney and Wellingborough was started but abandoned in 1871.

Listed for closure in the 'Beeching Report', the branch closed despite many local objections on 7 September 1964. Goods traffic continued until 1967 when the track was lifted. Today, part of the trackbed is a footpath and cycleway forming part of the Milton Keynes Redway. While all of the line's station buildings have long since disappeared the platforms at Bradwell and Great Linford have survived alongside the cycleway.

BR Derby-built single-unit diesel railcar M79901 gets ready to leave Buckingham station with a train for Verney Junction on 28 May 1964.

CLOSED
SEPTEMBER
7
1964

Verney Junction to Buckingham

Supported by the London & North Western Railway, the Buckinghamshire Railway opened between Bletchley, on the LNWR Euston to Birmingham main line, to Banbury (Merton Street) via Buckingham on 1 May 1850. The following year the Buckinghamshire Railway extended its line from Verney Junction, 4½ miles south of Buckingham, to Oxford (Rewley Road) and the LNWR now had a direct through route from Euston to Oxford.

In 1872 the Northampton & Banbury Junction Railway (later part of the Stratford-upon-Avon & Midland Junction Railway) opened a line from Blisworth to Cockley Brake Junction, on what was now the branch line from Verney Junction to Banbury. This little-used route was closed completely in 1951.

The Banbury branch settled down to a quiet life and, in 1956, was one of the first lines in Britain to see the introduction of Derby lightweight single-car diesels units. It was all too late and, despite the success of these modern trains, the section from Buckingham to Banbury was closed to passengers in 1961. The shortened branch from Verney Junction (served by trains running between Oxford and Cambridge) to Buckingham lingered on until it was listed for closure in the 'Beeching Report'. Passenger trains on the seven-minute journey were withdrawn on 7 September 1964 and goods services followed in 1966. The track had been lifted by the end of 1967.

Today, only the platforms and station building at Verney Junction survive on the mothballed Bicester to Bletchley line, waiting patiently for the promised reopening which will once again see trains running between Oxford, Aylesbury and Bedford.

Watched by a group of mourners at Wolverton, the crew of Ivatt Class '2' 2-6-2T No. 41222 hold up a wreath for the last train on the Newport Pagnell branch, 5 September 1964.

Great interest is shown by local train spotters on the arrival at Bardon Hill of unrebuilt Bulleid 'West Country' Pacific No. 34006 'Bude' on 11 May 1963. It was heading a special that ran between Leicester and Burton-upon-Trent organised jointly by the RCTS and the LCGB.

CLOSED
SEPTEMBER
7
1964

Leicester to Burton-upon-Trent

The 30¾-mile railway between Leicester and Burton-upon-Trent had its origins in one of the earliest railways to be built in Britain. Opened throughout in 1833, the Leicester & Swannington Railway was built to carry coal and minerals to Leicester for onward shipment along the River Soar. The main engineering features were the 1,786-yard Glenfield Tunnel and inclines at Bagworth and Swannington. The railway was bought by the Midland Railway in 1846 which then completed the route and opened diversions around the inclines and the narrow Glenfield Tunnel.

While serving numerous collieries and quarries along its length the railway also provided a fairly regular passenger service which, by the early 1960s, amounted to ten return trains each weekday. On summer Saturdays the line was also served by a service to and from Blackpool North. Listed for closure in the 'Beeching Report', the railway lost its passenger service on 7 September 1964 although both coal and stone traffic continued for many more years. Today, apart from the Knighton North spur at Leicester, the entire line remains in situ and sees the passage of stone trains from Bardon Hill Quarry. A proposal to reopen it to passenger trains stalled following the privatisation of BR in 1995.

CLOSED
SEPTEMBER
7
1964

Derby Friargate to Nottingham

Opened in 1878, the 18½-mile railway between Nottingham and Derby Friargate formed part of the Great Northern Railway's incursion deep into Derbyshire and Staffordshire. The GNR reached Nottingham from Grantham in 1855 by working, and then leasing, the Ambergate, Nottingham, Boston & Eastern Junction Railway. At Nottingham the GNR opened its own terminus at London Road in 1857 and in 1900 jointly opened Victoria station with the newly-established Great Central Railway. The railway between Nottingham and Grantham remains open for business today.

Eastwards from Nottingham the GNR opened its Derbyshire & Staffordshire Extension through Ilkeston and Derby Friargate to Egginton in 1878. This was followed in 1881 with the takeover of the Stafford & Uttoxeter Railway so that, with running powers over the North Staffordshire Railway between Egginton and Uttoxeter, the GNR was knocking on the door of both the London & North Western and Great Western railways.

Passenger services westward from Derby Friargate were withdrawn as early as 1939 although goods trains continued to use the route until 1968. However, this was not the end for the line through Mickleover and Etwall as it was used as a test track by BR's Research Division at Derby.

Listed for closure in the 'Beeching Report' the remaining passenger service between Derby Friargate and Nottingham Victoria was withdrawn on 7 September 1964. Goods trains continued until 4 September 1967. Today, all that remains of the GNR's incursion into Midland Railway territory is the enormous bonded warehouse and cast-iron bridge at Derby's Friargate.

'L1' Class 2-6-4T No. 67746 arrives at Kimberley station with the 1.20pm Derby Friargate to Nottingham Victoria train on 19 October 1961.

Fowler Class '4' 2-6-4T No. 42389 heads the 5.40pm Stafford to Wellington train about half a mile west of Newport station on 5 August 1961.

CLOSED SEPTEMBER 7 1964
Stafford to Wellington

The 18¾-mile cross-country route between Stafford and Wellington was built by an amalgamation of several canal and railway companies which, in 1846, formed the Shropshire Union Railways & Canal Company (SUR&CC). It also became a partner in the Wellington to Shrewsbury section of the Shrewsbury & Birmingham Railway. From its opening in 1849 the railway was leased by the London & North Western Railway who primarily saw it as a through route to Shrewsbury and beyond. As a company, the SUR&CC remained independent until it was swallowed up by the newly formed LMS in 1923.

While the vast majority of passenger services along the line started or ended their journeys at Shrewsbury, the average journey time between Wellington and Stafford was a leisurely 1hr 10min. In the winter of 1962 there were eight return trains stopping at all five intermediate stations each weekday plus a late evening/early morning non-stop service and two trains on Sundays. Apart from a colliery and Ministry of Defence (MoD) ordnance depot (opened in the 1930s) at Donnington, intermediate traffic was very light but the route was important for through freight trains even after closure to passengers on 7 September 1964. The line was completely closed east of Donnington in 1966. Granville Colliery at Donnington continued to be rail-served until 1979 and the stub is still open to the new but little-used Telford International Railfreight Park that was built on the site of the MoD depot.

CLOSED OCTOBER 12 1964
Nottingham to Worksop via Kirkby-in-Ashfield

The Midland Railway's 32-mile route through the Nottinghamshire coalfields started life in 1848 when the section from Nottingham to Kirkby-in-Ashfield opened for business. The MR also purchased the horsedrawn Mansfield & Pinxton Tramway which ran north of Kirkby and rebuilt it to extend the Nottingham line up to Mansfield. Linking numerous collieries en route, the line was further extended up the Leen Valley to Worksop in 1875. Coal was the lifeblood of this route and consequently the passenger services suffered – even in 1962 it still took around 1½ hours for the 32-mile journey. One interesting working was the summer Saturdays-only train for holidaymakers between Radford and Blackpool North (21 July – 11 Aug) while there was a 7.35am departure from Mansfield to London St Pancras on summer Saturdays (14 July – 11 Aug) but no return working.

Listed for closure in the 'Beeching Report' the line lost its passenger service on 12 October 1964. The closure left Mansfield as one of the largest towns in Britain without a railway station. However, much of the line remained open for coal traffic and as a diversionary route and in 1993 part of it (from Nottingham to Newstead) was reopened for passenger traffic. Known as the Robin Hood Line, passenger services were extended in stages until Worksop was again reached in 1998.

There are still plenty of parcels and sundry traffic at Bulwell Market station on the last day of services on the Nottingham Midland to Worksop route, 10 October 1964. On the platform a few onlookers take in their last sight of the 8.45am Nottingham Midland to Worksop train about to depart behind Fairburn Class '4' 2-6-4T No. 42218.

CLOSED NOVEMBER 2 1964 — Berkeley Road to Sharpness

Built to serve docks at Sharpness, the 4¼-mile branch line from Berkeley Road, on the Gloucester to Bristol main line, was opened in 1876 by the Midland Railway. Meanwhile, on the west bank of the River Severn, the Severn Bridge Railway, backed by the Severn & Wye Railway and the MR, had been authorised in 1872 to build a four-mile line from Lydney across the River Severn via a 1,387yd bridge to link up with the branch from Berkeley Road.

With 22 cast-iron spans, work began on the bridge in 1875 but the company ran into financial trouble and had to be rescued by the GWR and the MR. The new company, known as the Severn & Wye & Severn Bridge Joint Railway, opened for traffic across the bridge in 1879. However, it's usefulness was shortlived as the GWR's Severn Tunnel to the south opened in 1886 while the ailing S&WR was merged with the S&W&SBJR in 1894 to form the Severn & Wye Joint Railway. A south facing 1¼-mile loop was opened by the GWR at Berkeley Road in 1908 to enable goods trains from Sharpness to reach Bristol and as a diversionary route.

Passenger services between Berkeley Road and Lydney were brought to an abrupt end in 1960 when two petroleum barges collided with the bridge on 25 October. It was never repaired and later dismantled – the remaining train service between Berkeley Road and Sharpness was operated by an auto train until closure on 2 November 1964. Still used by nuclear flask trains from the decommissioned Berkeley and Oldbury nuclear power stations, the branch remains open for occasional freight traffic to and from Sharpness Docks.

CLOSED NOVEMBER 2 1964 — Grange Court to Hereford

The 22½-mile Hereford, Ross & Gloucester Railway from Grange Court, on the Gloucester to South Wales main line, to Hereford via Ross-on-Wye was financially backed by the GWR-leased Gloucester & Dean Forest Railway. Built to the broad gauge, the single-track line opened throughout in 1855 and was taken over by the GWR in 1862. Its many engineering features included four bridges over the River Wye and four tunnels. Mixed-gauge track was laid in 1866 with the broad gauge element being lifted as early as 1869 as a precursor to the removal of the gauge throughout the entire GWR system.

By the late 1950s passenger services, for many years in the capable hands of Gloucester-based GWR Class '4300' 2-6-0s, consisted of eight trains each way on weekdays with the majority calling at the 11 intermediate stations of which Ross-on-Wye was by far the most important. The average journey time for the 30-mile trip from Gloucester to Hereford was around 1 hour 15 minutes. Although there were no timetabled trains on Sundays the line was often used on the Sabbath as a diversionary route for North-West expresses when the Severn Tunnel was closed for maintenance.

Listed for closure in the 'Beeching Report', this delightful country railway lost its passenger service on 2 November 1964, the same day as the withdrawal of the much-loved (and profitable) Gloucester Central to Chalford auto trains. The line between Grange Court and Ross remained open for goods traffic until 1 November 1965. Along the entire route only Ballingham station survives today, as a private residence.

'1400' Class 0-4-2T No. 1453 awaits departure from Sharpness with the last train for Berkeley Road on 31 October 1964.

'5101' Class 2-6-2T No. 4107 waits to depart from Ross-on-Wye station with the 12.15pm Gloucester Central to Hereford train on the last day of services on this line, 31 October 1964.

Fowler Class '4' 2-6-4T No. 42323 arrives at Alton Towers station with the 11.25am (SO) Leek to Uttoxeter train on 19 August 1961.

Watched by a gaggle of Boy Scouts, Stanier 'Black 5' 4-6-0 No. 45333 restarts from Streetly station with a return empty excursion working on 4 August 1957 in connection with the Boy Scouts' Jubilee Jamboree held at nearby Sutton Park.

CLOSED
JANUARY
4
1965

Uttoxeter to Leek

The 19-mile branch line from Uttoxeter to Leek was once part of a scenic double-track through route along the Churnet Valley which was opened from North Rode (south of Macclesfield) to Uttoxeter by the North Staffordshire Railway in 1849. Heavily promoted by the NSR for its scenic beauty, the Churnet Valley line was also used by through freight traffic and special trains run for the agricultural and livestock market at Leek and the racecourse at Uttoxeter.

Increased competition from road transport saw a decline in traffic along the Churnet Valley line after the Second World War and through passenger trains between Macclesfield and Uttoxeter were withdrawn in 1960. Goods trains were withdrawn north of Leek on 15 June 1964, leaving just a skeleton service of workmen's trains still running between Uttoxeter and Leek – in 1962 these consisted of one early morning and one afternoon train southbound, and three northbound. Already listed for closure in the 'Beeching Report', the end came for passenger services on 4 January 1965. The line from Uttoxeter to Oakamoor was closed completely and goods trains ceased running to Leek (from Stoke-on-Trent via Leekbrook Junction) on 3 July 1970. The remainder of the Churnet Valley line southwards from Leekbrook Junction to Oakamoor remained open for industrial sand traffic until 1988.

Since then the Churnet Valley Railway has reopened the line between Leekbrook Junction and Oakamoor as a heritage railway. While there are plans to extend the line southwards to Alton Towers station, the trackbed between Oakamoor and Denstone, near Rocester, is currently a footpath and cycleway.

CLOSED
JANUARY
18
1965

Castle Bromwich to Walsall via Aldridge

The 13¾-mile railway between Castle Bromwich and Walsall was opened by the Wolverhampton, Walsall & Midland Junction Railway in 1879 although the company had already been taken over by the Midland Railway in 1874. West of Sutton Coldfield, the railway controversially ran for two miles through Sutton Park – its 2,400 acres containing lakes, ancient woodland, heathland, wetlands and marshes made it the largest urban park in Europe.

Passenger services along the line were served by trains running between Birmingham New Street and Wolverhampton High Level, with some having to reverse directions at Walsall. The passenger service between Wolverhampton and Walsall via Wednesfield was withdrawn as early as 1931. Serving several collieries, a branch from Aldridge to Brownhills was opened in 1882; a passenger service along the branch ceased in 1930 and much of the line had closed by 1960. Part of this colliery railway has since been reopened as a heritage line known as the Chasewater Railway.

By 1962, passenger services along the line between New Street and Walsall amounted to only five trains each way on weekdays although a fairly intensive shuttle service was operated on summer Sundays between Walsall and Sutton Park. Listed for closure in the 'Beeching Report', the line (by now operated by DMUs) closed to passengers on 18 January 1965 although its entire length is still open for freight trains.

BR Sulzer Type 4 diesel D42 heads the 8.40am Sheffield Midland to Bristol Temple Meads through Alrewas station on Sunday 13 October 1963. The train was diverted off the Tamworth route due to engineering works.

CLOSED
JANUARY
18
1965

Wichnor Junction to Wolverhampton High Level via Walsall

Serving the important Cannock coalfield, the 17½-mile railway between Wichnor Junction, south of Burton-on-Trent, and Walsall (and thence to Dudley) was opened by the South Staffordshire Railway in 1849. Unusually, the railway was leased by its chief engineer, John McClean, until 1861 when the London & North Western Railway took over the lease before absorbing the company in 1867.

In addition to the heavy coal traffic the line was served by passenger services operating between Burton-on-Trent and Wolverhampton High Level. By the summer of 1962 these amounted to ten trains each way on weekdays with the 29-mile journey taking just over an hour. Listed for closure in the 'Beeching Report', the line lost its passenger service on 18 January 1965. Today, only the Wichnor Junction to Lichfield High Level section remains open as a through freight and diversionary route to and from the West Coast Main Line. The short section south from Lichfield Trent Valley to Lichfield City is still open for trains to New Street via Four Oaks – just to the south of City station the former line to Walsall is now a disused siding which once served an oil distribution depot at Anglesey until 17 May 2001.

CLOSED
JANUARY
18
1965

Walsall to Rugeley (Trent Valley) via Cannock

John McClean, lessee of the South Staffordshire Railway, was keen to exploit the enormous coal reserves lying beneath Cannock Chase. Opened in 1858, his seven-mile branch ran north from Walsall to Cannock serving intermediate stations at Bloxwich and Wyreley & Church Bridge. McClean's lease of the SSR was taken over by the London & North Western Railway in 1861. Meanwhile, to the north, and also with an eye on reaching the coalfield, the Cannock Mineral Railway had already opened from Rugeley, on the LNWR's main line between Stafford and Lichfield, to Cannock in 1859 – it was worked from the outset by the LNWR and taken over by that company in 1869.

Serving not only many collieries, the two railways also served as a through route for passenger trains between Birmingham New Street and Rugeley until closure. Listed for closure in the 'Beeching Report', the line lost its passenger service on 18 January 1965 – a black day for railways in this area. Along with the closure of lines to Wichnor Junction (for Burton) and Castle Bromwich, the town of Walsall was left at the end of a short branch line, its days as an important railway centre seemingly over. However, freight traffic continued to use the line from Walsall to Rugeley (and its coal-fired power station) and in later years also served an open-cast mine at Mid Cannock while the line from New Street to Walsall via Bescot was also electrified.

Fortunately the freight-only line survived and in 1989 it was reopened for passengers from Walsall to Hednesford, and extended to Rugeley Trent Valley in 1998. Now marketed as the Chase Line, future plans include upgrading and electrifying the route and the opening of a container terminal at Cannock.

Two two-car Metro-Cammell DMUs head the 2.50pm Rugeley (Trent Valley) to Walsall and Birmingham service south of Cannock on 7 March 1964.

Rugby to Peterborough

The 51-mile cross-country railway between Rugby and Peterborough was opened in several stages. First on the scene was the London & Birmingham Railway's Rugby & Stamford branch line which ran via Market Harborough, Seaton and Luffenham Junction and opened throughout in 1851 (see Seaton to Stamford Town). From Luffenham Junction trains for Peterborough were forced to use the Midland Railway's route via Stamford. This unsatisfactory arrangement lasted until 1879 when the London & North Western Railway opened a direct route from Seaton to Peterborough along the Nene Valley through Wansford.

As a cross-country route the railway from Rugby to Peterborough also saw through trains between Birmingham and East Anglia, becoming the major route for this holiday traffic after the Midland & Great Northern Joint Railway closed in 1959. Listed for closure in the 'Beeching Report', the route closed on 6 June 1966. Since then the 7½-mile section from Yarwell Junction to Peterborough has been opened as a heritage railway by the Nene Valley Railway.

BR Standard Class '2' 2-6-2T No. 84013 stands in the bay platform at Seaton station with a push-pull train for Stamford on 17 June 1965.

BR Sulzer Type 2 diesel D5085 calls at Welford & Kilworth station with the last up train, the 8.12pm Peterborough East to Rugby Midland, on 4 June 1966.

Seaton to Stamford Town

The six-mile line from Seaton to Luffenham was opened as part of the London & Birmingham Railway's line from Rugby to Stamford in 1851. Despite being double-track, the railway was relegated to branch line status in 1879 when the London & North Western Railway opened the direct route from Seaton to Peterborough via Wansford (see Rugby to Peterborough). Apart from the occasional goods train, the line saw around six return passenger trains each day operating from Seaton through to Stamford Town – in its latter years the service was operated by Ivatt Class '2' 2-6-2Ts fitted for push-pull operation and was the last such steam-hauled train to operate in Britain. Listed along with the dieselised Rugby to Peterborough route for closure in the 'Beeching Report', the Seaton to Stamford service ceased on 6 June 1966 and the line as far as Luffenham Junction closed completely.

CLOSED

JUNE
6
1966

Nottingham to Kettering via Melton Mowbray

The 51-mile railway between Nottingham and Kettering via Melton Mowbray and Corby started life as three separate railways but was opened as a through route by the Midland Railway (MR) in 1880. The northern section from Nottingham to Melton Junction (west of Melton Mowbray) involved the construction of four tunnels (1,330-yard Stanton Tunnel, 1,305-yard Grimston Tunnel, 543-yard Saxelby Tunnel and 419-yard Asfordby Tunnel). The southern section from Wymondham Junction, east of Saxby, to Glendon Junction, north of Kettering, involved the construction of two long tunnels (1,842-yard Glaston Tunnel and 1,920-yard Corby Tunnel) and the magnificent 82-arch, 1,275-yard Welland Viaduct – the longest masonry viaduct across a river valley in Britain.

Not only was it the shortest route for MR trains between London (St Pancras) and Nottingham, it was also a useful diversionary route for express trains such as the 'Thames-Clyde Express' and 'The Waverley'. Heavy freight traffic was also important, especially to and from the enormous steel works which had grown up around Corby in the 1930s.

Despite all this, the entire route, along with the Syston Junction to Peterborough line, was listed for closure in the 'Beeching Report'. While the latter was reprieved, the former lost its passenger service on 6 June 1966. Despite closure to passengers the majority of the route fortunately survived.

The 13-mile northerly section from Melton Mowbray to Tollerton is now known as the Old Dalby Test Track and is equipped to test new designs of trains operating with either 25kV AC overhead wires or with London Underground-style conductor rails.

Since closure the double-track railway bridge over the River Trent at Nottingham has been converted to carry a single-track road. Progress, indeed. The southern section from Manton Junction to Glendon South Junction is used as a diversionary route for trains between London and Leicester and freight traffic to and from Corby. The Kettering to Corby passenger service was reinstated in 1987 but was withdrawn in 1990. The line reopened to regular passenger services in 2009 and is currently served by trains between London (St Pancras), Corby, Oakham, Melton Mowbray and East Midlands Parkway.

Years before the line became a test track for new locomotives and electric trains, Fowler '4F' 0-6-0 No. 44076 trundles through Old Dalby station at the head of a freight train, c.1962.

CLOSED SEPTEMBER 5 1966 Aylesbury to Nottingham and Sheffield and Banbury to Woodford Halse

Seen as part of a major trunk route linking the North of England and the East Midlands with London and the Continent, the Great Central Railway's 88¾-mile London Extension from Nottingham (Victoria) to Aylesbury opened in 1899. To the north of Nottingham the GCR had already opened a loop line from Sheffield via Chesterfield while to the south of Quainton Road in Buckinghamshire the new railway was jointly owned with the existing Metropolitan Railway to Marylebone. Built to the Continental loading gauge and with no level crossings, the new double-track railway was designed for fast freight and passenger traffic although the extension south from London through a planned Channel Tunnel to northern France never materialised.

An 8¼-mile line linking the London Extension at Culworth Junction (south of Woodford Halse) with the Great Western Railway at Banbury was opened in 1900. This was by far the busiest section of the Great Central with vast amounts of freight including coal and iron ore and through cross-country passenger trains passing over it day and night until the early 1960s.

Competing with the parallel Midland Railway route out of St Pancras and the Great Northern route out of King's Cross, the Great Central never lived up to its promoters' expectations as an important high-speed passenger railway. Freight traffic was far more lucrative although a few named trains, such as the 'Master Cutler' and the 'South Yorkshireman' ran between Marylebone and Sheffield until 1960 when the whole route was transferred from the Eastern Region of British Railways to the London Midland Region. From that date passenger services were restricted to around four stopping trains between Marylebone and Nottingham along with

one overnight train to Manchester – the through coach carried on this train to and from Liverpool (Central) was withdrawn on 5 March 1962. The two inter-regional trains using the route ran between Bournemouth and York and overnight between York and Swindon.

With economies and rationalisation looming throughout the British Railways network, the writing was on the wall for the Great Central, its duplication of other routes being its final downfall. Listed for closure in the 'Beeching Report' (BR had estimated this would save £900,000 per year), the line lost its through freight trains in 1965 and the Marylebone to Nottingham steam-hauled passenger service on 5 September 1966. The last scheduled steam services – the 5.15pm Nottingham (Victoria) to Marylebone and the 10.45pm return – ran on Saturday 3 September and were hauled by Stanier Class '5' 4-6-0 No. 44984. The Great Central had indeed 'Gone Completely' although the 43¼-mile section from Rugby Central to Nottingham Victoria continued to be served by a DMU shuttle service until 5 May 1969 (see Rugby Central to Nottingham Victoria).

Today the line north of Aylesbury remains open for trains as far as the Calvert waste terminal. Passenger services may return one day as part of the reopening of the currently mothballed Bicester to Bletchley route.

Complete with wreath on the smokebox door, Stanier 'Black 5' 4-6-0 No. 44984 storms out of Woodford Halse with the last ever up train to Marylebone, the 5.15pm from Nottingham Victoria.

A two-car later-type Derby Lightweight DMU leaves tiny Park Hall Halt with the 6.05pm train from Gobowen to Oswestry on 30 August 1964.

CLOSED

NOVEMBER
7
1966

Gobowen to Oswestry

The 2½-mile single-track branch line from Gobowen, on the Shrewsbury to Wrexham main line, to Oswestry was opened by the Shrewsbury & Chester Railway in 1848 – the company was amalgamated with the GWR six years later. From 1864 Oswestry was also served by the Cambrian Railway's line from Whitchurch to Welshpool, the town also becoming the headquarters and main workshops of that railway. Following the CR's absorption by the GWR in 1922 all trains from Gobowen were then diverted to the former company's station in 1924.

Both listed for closure in the 'Beeching Report', the CR line closed on 18 January 1965 (see Whitchurch to Welshpool), while the branch from Gobowen survived until 7 November 1966. Despite closure to passenger services the branch, along with the former CR line south of Oswestry to Llynclys Junction and Llanddu Quarry near Blodwell (on the closed Llangyog branch line along the Tanat Valley), remained open for stone traffic until 1989 when it was mothballed. The intact line was purchased by Shropshire County Council from Network Rail in 2008 and an umbrella organisation known as the Cambrian Heritage Railway plans to reopen the entire route as a heritage railway in the near future. In the meantime trains run from Llynclys South to Pen-y-Garreg Lane and also for a short distance from Oswestry station.

'Jubilee' Class 4-6-0 No. 45703 'Thunderer' calls at Cheadle Heath station with a southbound excursion from Manchester Central on 17 August 1963.

CLOSED

JANUARY
2
1967

Manchester Central to Cheadle Heath

The railway from Manchester Central to Cheadle Heath was opened as the Manchester South District Line by the Midland Railway in 1880. Extended through Disley Tunnel to New Mills in 1902, the line was also used as a through route for expresses between Manchester Central, Liverpool Central and London St Pancras including the diesel Blue Pullman service which ran from 1960 to 15 April 1966. Diesel multiple units replaced steam on the Cheadle Heath commuter service in 1960. Listed for closure in the 'Beeching Report', the line not only lost its local passenger service between Manchester Central and Cheadle Heath on 2 January 1967 but also the remaining through trains which, after Central station closed on 5 May 1969, were diverted along the former LNWR route through Stockport and into Manchester Piccadilly via a new chord to the west of Hazel Grove.

The trackbed of the line from Manchester to Didsbury is scheduled to reopen as part of the Manchester Metrolink Big Bang Extension in 2013.

CLOSED
MARCH 6 1967
Miller's Dale to Buxton

The 5½-mile line from Miller's Dale, on the Derby to Manchester main line, to Buxton was opened by the Manchester, Buxton, Matlock & Midlands Junction Railway in 1863. It had been a long time coming as the first section of this railway, from Ambergate to Rowsley, had opened 14 years earlier. Seen by the Midland Railway as a through route to Manchester, the line was extended northwards from Miller's Dale, through the long Dove Holes Tunnel to Chinley and New Mills in 1867 – Miller's Dale to Buxton effectively becoming a branch off the new main line. Having already opened its own line to Buxton from Stockport in 1863, the London & North Western Railway gave up its joint lease of the MBM&MJR which itself was taken over by the MR in 1871.

Despite it having branch line status, the MR route to Buxton was served by through trains to and from London St Pancras up until the 1960s. However the majority of passenger trains (around 20 return services each weekday) connected with main line services at Miller's Dale. Strangely, in the 'Beeching Report', the main line between Ambergate and Stockport is shown on Map 9 as being kept open for through passenger services (although losing its stopping trains) while the Miller's Dale to Buxton branch doesn't even appear! However, all intermediate stations on the main line and the Buxton branch lost their passenger services on 6 March 1967. Despite closure to passengers, the former MR route from Chinley to Miller's Dale Junction and Buxton is still very much alive for stone, lime and cement traffic – its signal boxes and semaphore signalling belonging to a bygone age.

An Oxford-bound DMU calls at a busier than usual Bicester London Road station on the last day of passenger services between Oxford and Cambridge, 30 December 1967.

CLOSED
JANUARY 1 1968
Oxford to Bletchley and Bedford St John's to Cambridge

What became the London & North Western Railway's 77-mile cross-country route between Oxford and Cambridge was built in several stages: the Bedford Railway opened the 16-mile line from Bedford to Bletchley in 1846; the Buckinghamshire Railway opened the line from Bletchley to Banbury via Verney Junction in 1850 (the 9½ miles from Bletchley to Verney Junction eventually forming part of the main cross-country route) and the 21¾ miles from Oxford to Verney Junction in 1851; the 3½-mile Sandy & Potton Railway opened in 1857 but was built without an Act of Parliament because it was on private land owned by the son of the then prime minister, William Peel; and the final link in the chain was opened by the Bedford & Cambridge Railway in 1862. All of these company's had become part of the LNWR by 1879. Until 1951 trains from Cambridge terminated at the LNWR's Rewley Road terminus in Oxford.

Although the route was not listed for closure in the 'Beeching Report', the end came, despite much opposition from rail users, universities and local councils, on 1 January 1968 – well, not quite the end as the Bedford St John's to Bletchley section retained a local passenger service and Bletchley to Oxford was kept open for freight movements including access to the large MoD Depot at Bicester. The Oxford to Bicester section was reopened to passenger services in 1987 and this, plus the currently mothballed section from Bicester to Claydon Junction and south to Aylesbury, will hopefully reopen in the near future as a new direct rail service between London Marylebone and Oxford.

The scene of dereliction at Buxton's Midland station on 20 April 1968; just over a year since closure and the tracks have been lifted. The station clock is stuck at 8.46 while on the other face it reads 5.56!

Stratford-upon-Avon to Cheltenham

Seeking to compete with the Midland Railway's main line from Birmingham to Bristol via the Lickey Incline, the Great Western Railway belatedly opened its own through route via Stratford-upon-Avon and Cheltenham in 1908. Until the mid-1960s the route was heavily used by a variety of through passenger services from the Midlands including express diesel railcars to South Wales, the 'Cornishman' express from Wolverhampton (Low Level) to Penzance, summer Saturday holiday trains from the Midlands to various destinations in the southwest and iron ore trains from Northamptonshire to South Wales. Although the auto train service between Cheltenham and Honeybourne was withdrawn on 7 March 1960 the route was not listed for closure in the 'Beeching Report'. Despite this all through passenger services were withdrawn in September 1965 leaving only a poorly patronised twice-daily diesel 'bubble car' service along the route from Gloucester to Leamington until this, too, was withdrawn on 25 March 1968 – it did not stop at Cheltenham as both Malvern Road and St James stations had been closed on 3 January 1966. The route continued to be used for special trains to Cheltenham Racecourse station, through freight trains and as a diversionary route when the former Midland Railway route via the Lickey incline was closed for engineering work.

The end came suddenly on 25 August 1976 when a coal train was derailed at Winchcombe – the damaged track was considered uneconomic to repair and the line apparently closed for good. Since 1984 the Gloucestershire-Warwickshire Railway have reopened the line as a heritage railway southwards from Toddington to Cheltenham Racecourse and are currently extending northwards to Broadway.

How the mighty are fallen: Gloucester R C & W Co single-car diesel unit W55007 heads east of Winchcombe Tunnel with the 3.45pm Leamington Spa to Gloucester service on 26 June 1965.

Matlock to Chinley

Although the former Midland Railway route between Derby and Manchester lost its stopping trains on 6 March 1967 the line was not listed for closure in the Beeching Report'. The first section of this scenic route through the Peak District had been opened by the Manchester, Buxton, Matlock & Midlands Junction Railway (MBM&MJR) from Ambergate to Rowsley in 1849. The high cost of building numerous tunnels and bridges through these limestone hills soon put a halt to further construction and Rowsley remained at the end of a branch line for the next 14 years. Leased jointly by the LNWR and the MR, the MBM&MJR eventually completed its heavily engineered line to Buxton in 1863 and from Miller's Dale to Chinley in 1867. The LNWR let go of its lease in 1871 and the MBM&MJR was then taken over by the MR.

Now owning a through route from London St Pancras to Manchester, the MR heavily promoted the line for its scenic beauty and ran through trains between London, Buxton and Manchester. The diesel 'Blue Pullman' was introduced in 1960 but withdrawn in 1967 on the completion of electrification of the West Coast Main Line. In the same year many intermediate stations were closed and on 1 July 1968 the section from Matlock to Chinley was closed to through passenger trains. While Matlock to Miller's Dale Junction closed completely, the northerly section through Dove Holes Tunnel remains open for stone, limestone and cement traffic. Today, Matlock is served by trains from Derby. The scenic section of the line from Rowsley to Miller's Dale is a footpath and cycleway known as the Monsal Trail while the line from Matlock to Rowsley South has been reopened as a heritage railway by Peak Rail.

Stanier 'Black 5' 4-6-0s Nos 45110 and 44949 emerge from Dove Holes Tunnel with the 'North West Tour' organized by the Manchester Rail Travel Society and the Severn Valley Railway Society on 20 April 1968. The tour was so popular it ran again on 27 April. Just over two months later this line closed as a through route for trains between Manchester and Derby.

Following its closure as a through route in 1966, all that remained of the mighty Great Central Railway was a humble DMU service, seen here heading southwards near Quorn on 11 May 1968, which continued to operate between Nottingham and Rugby until closure on 5 May 1969.

A Derby-built three-car suburban DMU arrives at Kidderminster station with the 1.55pm Birmingham (Snow Hill) to Stourport-on-Severn train on 30 March 1958.

CLOSED
MAY
5
1969

Rugby Central to Nottingham Victoria

Following the closure of the former Great Central Railway as a through route between Marylebone and Sheffield on 5 September 1966, the 43¼-mile section from Rugby Central to Nottingham Victoria was reprieved and continued to be served by a DMU service until closure on 5 May 1969. Today, the line from Loughborough to East Leake is still open for gypsum traffic – this latter section as far north as Ruddington is also operated as a heritage railway by the Great Central Railway (Nottingham). Finally, one of Britain's most popular heritage railways, the eight-mile Great Central Railway, now operates between Loughborough Central and Leicester North; reopened in stages since 1973 it is the only heritage railway in Britain featuring double track (from Loughborough to Rothley).

CLOSED
JANUARY
5
1970

Bewdley to Kidderminster/ Hartlebury

The 5½-mile line from Bewdley to Hartlebury via Stourport-on-Severn was opened as part of the Severn Valley Railway from Shrewsbury in 1862 and taken over by the GWR in 1872. Meanwhile, a 3½-mile linking line was opened from Bewdley to Kidderminster in 1878. Following closure of the line north of Bewdley in 1963, the two short lines serving Bewdley from Kidderminster and Hartlebury continued to be operated by a single diesel car service. While the Hartlebury line was listed for closure in the 'Beeching Report', the line from Kidderminster was not – despite this both routes were closed to passengers on 5 January 1970. Stourport to Hartlebury was retained for freight until 1980.

The Kidderminster line fared better and was eventually bought by the Severn Valley Railway as part of its 16-mile heritage railway from Bridgnorth.

CLOSED
JANUARY
5
1970

New Mills Central to Hayfield/Marple Rose Hill to Macclesfield

The three-mile branch line up the Sett Valley from New Mills to Hayfield was opened by the Manchester, Sheffield & Lincolnshire Railway (MS&LR) in 1868. At the beginning of the 20th century it was temporarily extended a further two miles up the valley to aid in the construction of Kinder Reservoir which was completed in 1911. Listed for closure in the 'Beeching Report', the Hayfield branch closed on 5 January 1970. The trackbed has since been reopened as a footpath and cycleway known as the Sett Valley Trail.

The 10-mile line from Marple Rose Hill to Macclesfield was opened by the Macclesfield, Bollington & Marple Railway in 1869. It was jointly owned by the North Staffordshire Railway and the MS&LR and featured a 23-arch viaduct at Bollington. Listed for closure in the 'Beeching Report', the line also closed on 5 January 1970. It has since been reopened as a footpath and cycleway known as the Middlewood Trail.

THE CASUALTIES

1. Barry to Pontypridd – 10 September 1962
2. Whitland to Cardigan – 10 September 1962
3. Wrexham to Ellesmere – 10 September 1962
4. Neath to Brecon – 15 October 1962
5. Neath to Cymmer Afan – 3 December 1962
6. Moat Lane Junction to Three Cocks Junction via Rhayader – 31 December 1962
7. Hereford to Brecon via Three Cocks Junction – 31 December 1962
8. Newport to Brecon – 31 December 1962
9. Llandilo to Carmarthen – 9 September 1963
10. Tondu and Pyle to Porthcawl – 9 September 1963
11. Pontypool Road to Neath – 15 June 1964
12. Bridgend to Barry – 15 June 1964
13. Swansea Victoria to Pontardulais – 15 June 1964
14. Nelson & Llancaiach to Dowlais (Cae Harris) – 15 June 1964
15. Caerphilly to Senghenydd – 15 June 1964
16. Johnston to Neyland – 15 June 1964*
17. Porth to Maerdy – 15 June 1964
18. Abercynon to Aberdare (Low Level) – 30 October 1964
19. Gaerwen to Amlwch – 7 December 1964
20. Caernarfon to Afonwen – 7 December 1964
21. Carmarthen to Aberystwyth – 14 December 1964 (Aberystwyth to Lampeter)/22 February 1965 (Carmarthen to Lampeter)
22. Whitchurch to Welshpool – 18 January 1965
23. Llanymynech to Llanfyllin – 18 January 1965
24. Ruabon to Barmouth Junction and Bala Junction to Bala – 18 January 1965 (part closed by floods on 11/12 December 1964)
25. Penarth to Cadoxton via Lavernock – 6 May 1968 (not shown on Beeching Map 9)*
26. Bangor to Caernarfon – 5 January 1970
27. Bridgend to Treherbert – 22 June 1970

Dates given are for withdrawal of passenger services
* = not listed for closure in the 'Beeching Report'

THE SURVIVORS

A. Llandudno Junction to Blaenau Ffestiniog
B. Craven Arms to Llanelli
C. Cardiff to Coryton

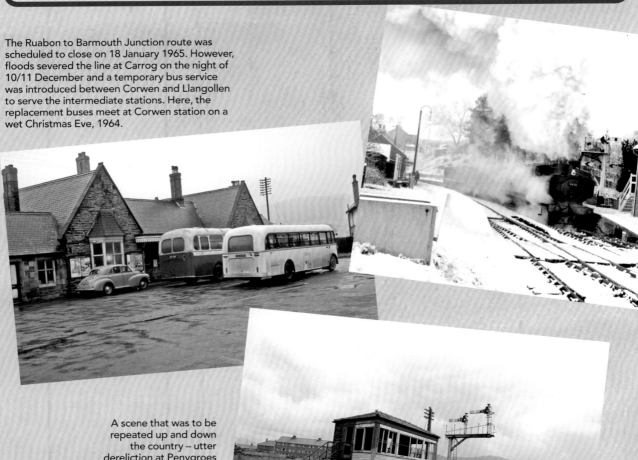

The Ruabon to Barmouth Junction route was scheduled to close on 18 January 1965. However, floods severed the line at Carrog on the night of 10/11 December and a temporary bus service was introduced between Corwen and Llangollen to serve the intermediate stations. Here, the replacement buses meet at Corwen station on a wet Christmas Eve, 1964.

A scene that was to be repeated up and down the country – utter dereliction at Penygroes on the Caernarfon to Afon Wen line which had closed on 7 December 1964. By 1970 all that was left are some forlorn signals and this vandalised signal box.

WALES

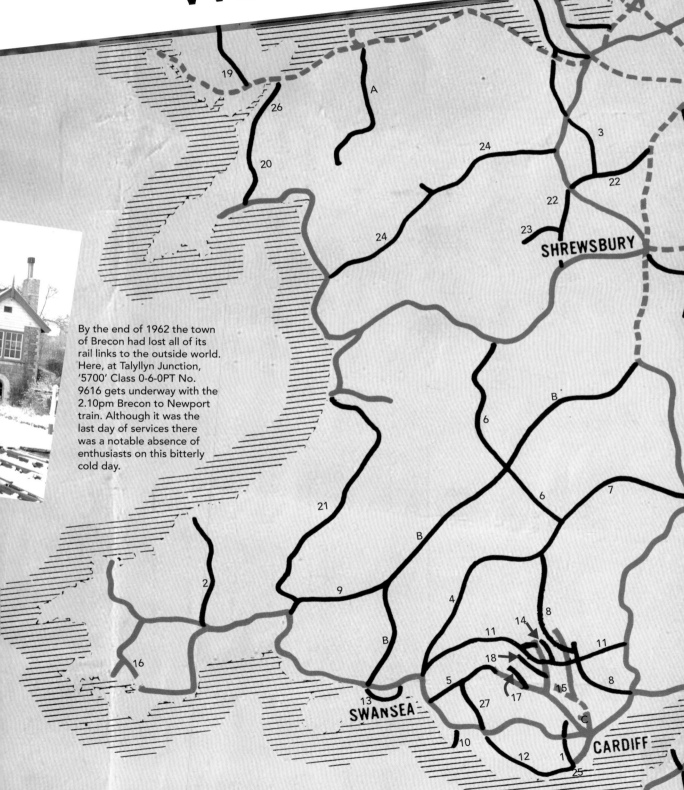

By the end of 1962 the town of Brecon had lost all of its rail links to the outside world. Here, at Talyllyn Junction, '5700' Class 0-6-0PT No. 9616 gets underway with the 2.10pm Brecon to Newport train. Although it was the last day of services there was a notable absence of enthusiasts on this bitterly cold day.

19
26
A
20
24
3
24
22
22
23
SHREWSBURY
B
6
7
6
21
B
2
B
9
4
8
B
11
14
16
18
11
5
27
17
15
8
13
10
C
SWANSEA
12
1
CARDIFF
25

CLOSED
10
1962

Barry to Pontypridd

Although arriving on the scene rather late in the day, the Barry Dock & Railway Company (renamed the Barry Railway in 1891) was an enormous financial success. The line was built to link the collieries of the South Wales Valleys with a new deepwater dock at Barry. Bypassing Cardiff Docks, the Barry Railway ended up carrying 30 per cent of South Wales's coal for export by 1913 with Barry becoming the largest coal exporting port in the world. The 68-mile railway was built between Cadoxton Junction (east of Barry) and Trehafod Junction (for the Rhondda Valley) via Wenvoe and Pontypridd with a freight-only branch diverging at St Fagan's to Barry Junction (for the Merthyr and Rhymney Valleys). Engineered by Sir John Wolfe Barry and Henry Marc Brunel, the railway featured two long tunnels and four enormous steel and masonry viaducts. All four viaducts – Llanbradach, Penyrheol, Penrhos and Walnut Tree were on the St Fagans to Barry Junction line and have all since been demolished.

The railway from Trehafod and the new dock at Barry opened with a fanfare in 1889 and both were an immediate success. A further dock was opened at Barry in 1898 and railway extensions were opened at the beginning of the twentieth century to siphon even more coal away from other railways – huge profits were made by Davies and the railway's shareholders until the early 1920s. The Barry Railway became one of the constituent companies of the enlarged Great Western Railway in 1923 but coal traffic fell into decline soon after the 1926 General Strike, never to recover – as a result the freight-only line from Penrhos Junction to Barry Junction and the section from Tonteg Junction to Pontypridd Craig both closed in 1930.

Naturally, passenger traffic was of secondary importance to the Barry Railway and the through service between Barry and Pontypridd was fairly meagre right up until closure. Despite this the line came into its own on summer Sundays and bank holidays with packed trains taking daytrippers from the Valleys to Barry Island. Closure came on 10 September 1962 when the remaining passenger service from Barry to Wenvoe, Treforest Low Level and Pontypridd was withdrawn, goods trains ceased on 6 April 1964 and within a few years all traces of this once hugely successful railway had been erased.

Rush hour at Efail Isaf station as a Barry to Pontypridd auto train gets ready to leave after unloading its precious human cargo on 15 July 1959.

With only three days to go before closure of this delightful rural railway, '4500' Class 2-6-2T No. 4557 takes on water at Glogue station, mid-way between Whitland and Cardigan, 7 September 1962.

Neyland shed's ex-GWR '4500' Class 2-6-2T No. 4557 waits patiently at Cardigan station while luggage is unloaded from a train from Whitland on 9 June 1960. Closed on 10 September 1962, this 27-mile branch line meandered through bucolic Cardiganshire countryside serving small farming communities.

CLOSED
SEPTEMBER
10
1962

Whitland to Cardigan

The 27½-mile meandering single-track rural branch line from Whitland to Cardigan was opened by the Whitland & Cardigan Railway as an extension of the previously authorised (but not built) Whitland & Taff Vale Railway in 1886. Worked from the onset by the Great Western Railway, the picturesque branch line was absorbed by that company in 1890.

Serving only small intermediate villages, the steeply-graded branch led a fairly quiet life carrying agricultural produce, livestock and milk for distant markets via the important junction at Whitland. Passenger traffic was never heavy and consisted of four trains from Whitland to Cardigan and three returns on weekdays only – the journey time was a very gentle 1hr 45min. Closure had been on the cards for some years and the end came for passenger services on 10 September 1962 (although the branch was still shown in black on the 'Beeching Report' Map No. 9) and for goods traffic on 27 May 1963.

With just over a week before closure of this line, '1400' Class 0-4-2T No. 1432 heads an auto train away from Bangor-on-Dee station between Wrexham and Ellesmere on 1 September 1962.

CLOSED SEPTEMBER 10 1962 — Wrexham to Ellesmere

Although the 12¾-mile railway from Wrexham to Ellesmere was authorised in 1885, the Wrexham & Ellesmere Railway eventually opened in 1895. Its station in Wrexham, Central, was shared with the Wrexham, Mold & Connah's Quay Railway which was taken over by the Great Central Railway in 1905; from 1923 part of the LNER. The W&ER remained independent until 1923 when it became part of the enlarged Great Western Railway. A north-west loop was also installed at Ellesmere to allow through running of trains from the Great Central Railway to Oswestry and the Cambrian line. In addition to the three intermediate stations already open at Marchwiel, Bangor-on-Dee and Overton-on-Dee, six halts were opened between 1914 and 1938. The line was closed to passenger services during the Second World War due to heavy munitions traffic from the ordnance factory at Marchwiel.

Passenger services were reinstated in 1946 and consisted of eight return trains on weekdays – these were usually operated by GWR auto trains. Passenger traffic was never heavy and the through freight and passenger traffic to and from the former LNER system dried up. Closure came on 10 September 1962.

CLOSED OCTOBER 15 1962 — Neath to Brecon

The 33¼-mile railway from Neath to Brecon started life as the Dulais Valley Mineral Railway which opened up the Neath Valley to collieries around Onllwyn in 1864. Changing its name to the Neath & Brecon Railway, a further 23 miles of track across bleak country to Brecon was opened in 1867. Here it met the Hereford, Hay & Brecon Railway which was taken over by the Midland Railway in 1876, thus providing a through route for MR trains to Swansea via the N&BR and the Swansea Vale Railway via Colbren Junction, Ynys-y-Geinon Junction and Pontardawe.

Serving numerous collieries along the valley, the southern part of the line up to Onllwyn was by far the busiest section of the N&BR – beyond, both goods and passenger traffic was light. The N&BR was absorbed by the GWR in 1922 although MR, and later LMS, trains from Birmingham via Hereford continued to use the line between Brecon and Colbren Junction until the 1930s. Closure had been mooted for the loss-making railways to Brecon for some years and the passenger service from Neath ceased on 15 October 1962. As around 1,000 people turned up to travel on the last train from Brecon a relief also had to be run – the final train left at 7.46pm behind 0-6-0PTs Nos 3621 and 3693 with five coaches. Goods services also ceased north of Craig-y-Nos where a quarry continued to be rail served until 1977.

Today, the southern section of the N&BR down the Neath Valley remains open for coal traffic from the Onllwyn coal washing plant. This was the first of the Brecon closures – these four routes (from Neath, Hereford, Moat Lane and Newport) were claimed by BR to lose £287,000 a year with another £380,000 due for renewals and maintenance over the next five years.

With plenty of activity from railway enthusiasts, '5700' Class 0-6-0PTs Nos 9796 and 3706 wait to depart from Neath Riverside station with the 11.25am train to Brecon on the last day of services on this line, 13 October 1962.

Ex-GWR '5700' Class 0-6-0PT No. 9766 heads north out of Pontrhydyfen station with the 1.55pm Aberavon to Cymmer Afan train on 27 September 1960.

CLOSED
DECEMBER
3
1962

Neath to Cymmer Afan

The 27¾-mile railway between Swansea and Treherbert was opened throughout by the Rhondda & Swansea Bay Railway as late as 1895. Heavily engineered, it followed the Afan Valley up from Port Talbot before burrowing through the 3,443-yard-long Rhondda Tunnel (the longest in Wales) to emerge at the head of the Rhondda Valley at Treherbert, where it connected with the Taff Vale Railway. Designed to carry coal direct from the Rhondda down to Swansea Docks, the railway successfully bypassed the Marquess of Bute's monopoly at Cardiff Docks. The Great Western Railway took over working the line in 1906, absorbing it in 1922. However, the hoped-for volumes of coal traffic never lived up to expectations due to the steep gradients encountered on the line, especially inside the Rhondda Tunnel.

Passenger trains originally ran into Swansea Riverside station but by 1936 they ended their journey at the GWR's High Street terminus. By 1958 there were only two through return trains each weekday between Swansea and Treherbert although there was a more frequent service along the line from Neath via Aberavon Town. A Saturday-only late night train also burrowed through the Rhondda Tunnel to terminate at Blaenrhondda, no doubt for the benefit of drinkers being turned out of Treherbert's pubs!

Lord Stonham in 1963: 'There are literally scores of what I regard as daft proposals in this Plan. In the Rhondda, there is a two-mile railway tunnel under the mountains. It is proposed to continue the railway for freight but not for passengers. To get to the other side of the mountain by road entails travelling 40 miles and the roads round are not suitable for buses.'

Although listed for closure in the 1963 'Beeching Report', this had already been on the cards for some years. The loss-making railway finally met its end on 3 December 1962 when the line closed between Briton Ferry and Cymmer Afan. The service of workmen's trains between Cymmer Afan and collieries at Duffryn Rhondda continued to operate until 7 November 1967, while the line from Cymmer Afan to Treherbert via the Rhondda Tunnel remained open for passenger trains from Bridgend and Maesteg until 22 June 1970 (see Bridgend to Treherbert). Today, the trackbed of the railway up the picturesque Afan Valley is a popular footpath and cycleway.

Moat Lane Junction to Three Cocks Junction via Rhayader

The Mid-Wales Railway (M-WR) from Llanidloes to Talyllyn Junction opened for traffic in 1864. North of Llanidloes, the Llanidloes & Newtown Railway had already opened in 1859, eventually forming a junction at Moat Lane with the Newtown & Machynlleth Railway (later to form part of the Cambrian Railways route from Whitchurch to Aberystwyth). At the southern end, the M-WR met the Hereford, Hay & Brecon Railway at Three Cocks Junction which also opened in 1864 and which was taken over by the Midland Railway in 1876. The 7¾ miles from Three Cocks Junction to Talyllyn Junction was built along the course of a horse-drawn tramway which had opened in 1816. At Talyllyn Junction the M-WR met the Brecon & Merthyr Tydfil Junction Railway which had partially opened as far as Talybont in 1863 (and on to Merthyr in 1868). From 1888 the M-WR was worked by the Cambrian Railways which eventually took over the company in 1904.

Mid-Wales desecration – Rhayader station on the Mid-Wales line on 2 April 1964. R.I.P.

With the entire 48¼-mile route from Moat Lane to Talyllyn Junction now in the hands of the Cambrian Railways, through trains started running between Moat Lane and Brecon, passing through sparsely populated countryside. The line was heavily used by coal trains (nicknamed 'Jellicoe Specials') from South Wales destined for the far north of Scotland where the Royal Navy's Grand Fleet lay at its base at Scapa Flow during the First World War.

For some years the Cambrian Railways also ran a through passenger service over the route between Aberystwyth and Merthyr – with only two stops, at Llanidloes and Builth Road (Low Level), the journey took 5hrs 15min. In a bid to increase passenger traffic, the Great Western Railway also opened six

wayside halts along the line during the inter-war years. Despite this measure, passenger traffic was never heavy along this picturesque route and by British Railways' days in 1958 there were just two through return trains along the entire route. Other services provided (not all connecting) ran from Moat Lane to Builth Road, Builth Road to Three Cocks and Three Cocks to Brecon.

By this time closure had already been mooted for the four loss-making steam-hauled railway routes to Brecon – the Neath line (see Neath to Brecon) had already succumbed on 15 October 1962 and all of the other routes, from Moat Lane, Hereford and Newport, lost their passenger services on the last day of that year. The last train, an enthusiasts' special hauled

The last day of service on the Mid-Wales line was 29 December 1962. Here, at Three Cocks Junction, Ivatt Class '2MT' 2-6-0s Nos 46518 and 46505 wait to depart tender to tender with the 11.15am to Builth Road (Low Level).

by an Ivatt Class '2' 2-6-0, ran in a blizzard with the exhausted passengers arriving back at their homes in the early hours of the following morning.

Needless to say the die had already been cast even though all of these railways still appeared on Map 9 of the 'Beeching Report' published on 27 March 1963. At the northern end of the Mid-Wales Line, the section from Moat Lane to Llanidloes remained open until 1967 for cement traffic for the construction of the Clywedog Dam.

Green-liveried Ivatt Class '2MT' 2-6-0 No. 46521 arrives at Talyllyn Junction with a train from Moat Lane Junction heading for Brecon on 10 September 1962.

Hereford to Brecon via Three Cocks Junction

Opened throughout in 1864, the Hereford, Hay & Brecon Railway was partly built along the course of a 24-mile horse-drawn 3ft 6in gauge tramway (the Hay Railway) which had opened between Brecon and Eardisley in 1816. Following an illegal merger with the Brecon & Merthy Tydfil Junction Railway (see Newport to Brecon) in 1865, the HH&BR was worked by the Mid-Wales Railway until the Midland Railway took over operations in 1869 – the latter company eventually leased the line in 1874 and absorbed it in 1876.

Under MR ownership this country railway was also used for through traffic between the Midlands and South Wales – in 1922 the 79¼ miles from Hereford to Swansea took just under four hours for the two return train services timetabled on weekdays. Following nationalisation in 1948 all of the railways serving Brecon came under new Western Region management – the through trains to Swansea were withdrawn leaving a sparse three to four trains a day (plus one with a change at Three Cocks) with a journey time of around 1hr 45 mins for the 38½-mile journey. With declining passenger and goods traffic the inevitable closure came on 31 December 1962.

Ivatt Class '2MT' 2-6-0 No. 46511 has just arrived at Three Cocks Junction with a Hereford to Brecon train on 11 December 1962.

West end of Brecon station looking east. Ivatt Class '2MT' 2-6-0 No. 46512 is on the right having terminated here with the 9.02am train from Hereford on the penultimate day of service, 28 December 1962.

CLOSED
DECEMBER
31
1962

Newport to Brecon

With under four months to go before closure of this route '2251' Class 0-6-0 No. 3201 calls at Talybont-on-Usk with a Brecon to Newport train on 10 September 1962.

The Brecon & Merthy Tydfil Junction Railway was opened between Brecon and Talybont in 1863. From Brecon to Talyllyn Junction (for the Mid-Wales Railway) the railway followed the course of the horse-drawn tramway – the Hay Railway – opened in 1816. The railway was extended southwards through Torpantau Tunnel – at 1,312 feet above sea level, the highest in Britain – to Merthyr in 1868 and to Dowlais (the latter jointly with the London & North Western Railway) in 1869. Also wishing to reach Newport, the B&MTJR bought the Rumney Tramroad in 1868; this had originally opened as a horse-drawn tramway from Rhymney Ironworks to Bassaleg Junction (west of Newport) in 1825. The company remained independent until becoming part of the Great Western Railway in 1922. While the southern half of the railway remained fairly busy, especially with coal traffic, the section north of Merthyr was quieter; trains, often double-headed, had to cope with gradients as steep as 1-in-37 up to Torpantau Tunnel.

As with all the railways to Brecon, the line from Newport was already living on borrowed time by the late 1950s. In 1958 there were three return through services (plus an extra on Saturdays) along the 47-mile route – journey time was 2½ hours. Along with the other loss-making railways to Brecon the line from Newport lost its passenger service on 31 December 1962. Coal traffic continued to use the section down

the Rhymney Valley from Bedwas until 1985 but all that remains today is the 4¾ mile section from Bassaleg Junction to a limestone quarry at Machen. North of Merthyr the narrow gauge steam-hauled Brecon Mountain Railway today follows part of the trackbed of the B&MTJR between Pant and Dolygaer. Beyond here rusting narrow gauge track snakes its way up the valley to a forgotten terminus at Torpantau – will it ever reopen?

'4500' Class 2-6-2T No. 4555 and '5700' Class 0-6-0PT No. 3690 pause at Talybont-on-Usk en route from Merthyr to Brecon with the Stephenson Locomotive Society (Midland Area) 'Last Train to Brecon' on 2 May 1964.

'7400' Class 0-6-0PT No. 7439 pauses at Llandilo Bridge station on the Llandilo to Carmarthen line on 6 September 1963, just three days before closure.

With the River Tywi and the ruins of Drysllwyn Castle in the background, '7400' Class 0-6-0PT No. 7439 heads for Llandilo with a train from Carmarthen in July 1963.

CLOSED
SEPTEMBER
9
1963

Llandilo to Carmarthen

The 13½-mile single-track railway from Llandilo to Abergwili Junction, north of Carmarthen on the Aberystwyth line, was opened by the Llanelly Railway in 1865. The company changed its name to the Swansea & Carmarthen Railway in 1871 and was worked from that date by the London & North Western Railway – running powers over mixed-gauge track were also obtained for the last 1¾ miles of the broad gauge Carmarthen & Cardigan Railway from Abergwili Junction to Carmarthen. Two years later the railway was effectively taken over by the LNWR and changed its name yet again; the Central Wales & Carmarthen Junction Railway as it was now called was finally absorbed by the LNWR in 1891. With most of the Central Wales Line from Craven Arms to Swansea also now in its possession the LNWR could operate through trains from the North of England and the Midlands to the seaside resorts of Pembrokeshire and Pembroke Dock via Llandilo and Carmarthen.

Connecting with trains on the Central Wales Line, the passenger service between Llandilo and Carmarthen usually consisted of three eastbound and four westbound on weekdays with a journey time for the 15¼ miles of around 40 minutes. Passenger and goods traffic declined steadily after the Second World War and the line was listed for closure in the 'Beeching Report' – apparently this would save the taxpayer £21,800 per year. Closure came on 9 September 1963, the same day as one other post-Beeching casualty in Wales.

CLOSED
SEPTEMBER
9
1963

Tondu and Pyle to Porthcawl

The 3¾-mile branch line from Pyle to the seaside resort of Porthcawl began life in 1829 as a part of a 4ft 7in gauge horse-drawn tramway from collieries north of Tondu and beyond Maesteg to a company-owned harbour at Porthcawl. The tramway was taken over by the Llynvi Valley Railway in 1847 which converted the line to broad gauge, introduced steam locomotives in 1861 and passenger trains in 1864. In 1865 the neighbouring standard gauge Ogmore Valley Railway started running goods trains over the LVR from Tondu down to Pothcawl Pier on mixed gauge track. The two companies combined forces in 1866 to become the Llynvi & Ogmore Railway, enlarged the harbour and dock at Porthcawl and then removed the broad gauge rails in 1872. The final twist in this story came when the Great Western

Railway took over the working of L&OR in 1873 and absorbed it in 1883. By that date trade through the harbour was in serious decline and the GWR subsequently closed it in 1898.

Porthcawl took on a new lease of life at the beginning of the twentieth century when the harbour was rebuilt as an esplanade and a new station opened on the site of the dock in 1916. The town soon became a popular holiday destination for workers from around the South Wales Valleys – by the late 1930s around 70,000 passengers each week were being carried on the branch during the summer months. Through trains from Swansea, Cardiff and Newport were also able to bypass Pyle with the construction of new junctions. Optimism still reigned after the Second World War when there were plans to build a new six platform station at Porthcawl to

cope with the demand; this never materialised as visitor numbers soon started to decline and by the 1950s had dropped to 10,000 a week during the summer. The May 1959 timetable says it all: there were only five return train services on the branch on Sundays of which two originated or ended their journey at either Cardiff or Newport and there were no timetabled services between Tondu and Pyle on any day. Inevitably the branch (and the line north to Tondu) was listed for closure in the 'Beeching Report' – the end came at the end of the summer timetable of 1963 when the final passenger train ran, although goods trains continued until 1 February 1965.

Excursion time at Porthcawl on 12 August 1962. On the left is '5101'Class 2-6-2T No. 4160 with the 7.05pm to Treherbert, while on the right is '4300' Class 2-6-0 No. 6373 with the 6.55pm to Newport. A DMU with a local service to Pyle waits in the middle road.

Pontypool Road to Neath

This is the story of two separate railways that eventually formed an important through route cutting across the South Wales Valleys from Neath to Pontypool Road. The first of these railways was the broad gauge Vale of Neath Railway which opened the 26¾ miles from Neath to Aberdare (High Level) in 1851. A branch was opened from Gelly Tarw Junction, north of Hirwaun, to Merthyr Tydfil via the 2,497-yard-long Merthyr Tunnel (the third longest in Wales) in 1853.

From the north, the standard gauge Newport, Abergavenny & Hereford Railway opened to Pontypool along the courses of existing tramways in 1854 – its double-track Taff Vale Extension from Pontypool Road to Quaker's Yard took longer to build. This involved the construction of two massive viaducts – at Crumlin, across the Ebbw Valley, and at Hengoed, across the Rhymney Valley – with the line opening in 1858. At that time Crumlin Viaduct, 1,658 feet long and 208 feet high at its highest point above the valley, was the third highest man-made structure in the world.

In 1860 the NA&HER became one of three constituent companies of the newly formed but short-lived West Midland Railway – the latter was absorbed by the Great Western Railway in 1863 which then completed the missing five miles from Quaker's Yard through Quaker's Yard Tunnel to Middle Duffryn where it met the VoNR a year later. In the meantime the latter company had been converted to mixed gauge to allow through trains to run between Pontypool Road and Neath. The VoNR would be absorbed by the GWR in 1866.

Primarily a coal-carrying line linking many of the Valleys, the Neath to Pontypool Road line came into its own during the First World War when it was used to transport vast amounts of Welsh coal on the first part of the long journey to Thurso in the far north of Scotland – from here it was then shipped to the Grand Fleet at anchor in Scapa Flow in the Orkneys. Naturally passenger services were of secondary importance with many trains terminating their journey at Aberdare High Level – by 1958 there were five through trains between Pontypool Road and Neath on weekdays with four in the opposite direction (plus an extra late night service on Saturdays).

Listed for closure in the 'Beeching Report', the railway struggled on for over a year until passenger services were withdrawn on 15 June 1964. The last train was hauled by 0-6-0PT No. 4639 carrying a commemorative headboard and the Welsh dragon emblem – its four coaches were so packed that there was standing room only. The train was cheered on its way by residents all along the line and its crossing of Crumlin Viaduct was accompanied by the blast of closely spaced detonators.

Parts of the VoNR route are still open for coal traffic – the two sections are from Neath up the valley to Cwmgwrach and from Aberdare up to the Tower Washery. The VoNR's station at Aberdare (previously High Level) was reopened in 1988 to be served by passenger trains from Cardiff via the Taff Vale Railway's line up the Aberdare Valley from Abercynon as far as Cwmbach and then via a new connection to the newly-reopened station. Crumlin Viaduct was demolished in 1967, but the curving Hengoed Viaduct still stands and is now crossed by a footpath and cycleway known as the Celtic Trail.

With only five days to go before closure of this long route '5101' Class 2-6-2T No. 4121 calls at Crumlin High Level station with a Neath to Pontypool Road train, 10 June 1964.

'5600' Class 0-6-2T No. 6614 pauses at Rhoose station on 27 June 1964 with the West Glamorgan and Monmouthshire Railway Societies' special 'The Leek'. A Class 37 diesel approaches on the other line.

CLOSED JUNE 15 1964 Bridgend to Barry

Sponsored by the Barry Railway, the 19-mile standard gauge Vale of Glamorgan Railway was opened from Bridgend to Barry in 1897. The railway was worked from the outset by the BR but remained an independent concern until being amalgamated with the Great Western Railway in 1921. Local passenger traffic on the line was never heavy (amounting to around five trains in each direction on weekdays) although it was used as diversionary route when the main line between Cardiff and Bridgend was closed for maintenance. Goods traffic included limestone and cement from Aberthaw and Rhoose and, from 1966 (after closure to passengers), coal trains to the Aberthaw Power Station and, during the Second World War, to the RAF base at St Athan. Listed for closure in the 'Beeching Report', passenger services were withdrawn from the line on 'Black Monday', 15 June 1964.

Despite the cessation of passenger services the line survived, not only as a diversionary route but also for freight traffic. Today this includes merry-go-round coal trains to Aberthaw Power Station and engine parts to the rail-connected Ford factory near Bridgend (since 1980). By the 1990s the expansion of Cardiff International Airport at Rhoose saw plans to reopen the line to passengers again and after a period of nearly 41 years regular passenger trains began running again on 10 June 2005.

CLOSED JUNE 15 1964 Swansea Victoria to Pontardulais

Opened in 1867 by the Llanelly Railway (later to become the Swansea & Carmarthen Railway), the 12¼-mile line across the Gower Peninsula from Pontardulais to Swansea Victoria formed the southern part of what was to become the London & North Western Railway's Central Wales Line from Craven Arms. The entire 95¼-mile route through sparsely populated country and serving small intermediate spa towns and villages was completed in 1868. Apart from the section between Llandilo and Pontardulais, which was operated jointly with the GWR, the long single-track route had been taken over by the LNWR by 1891. With their entry into Great Western Railway territory the LNWR were able to operate through coaches to Swansea Victoria station from as far afield as London Euston, Manchester and the Midlands and, with the GWR rail link from Llanelli, the railway north of Pontardulais also saw heavy freight traffic including northbound anthracite and livestock.

Although the entire Central Wales Line was listed for closure in the 'Beeching Report', (apparently with a saving of £200,000 per year) only the section southwards from Pontardulais to Swansea Victoria succumbed – from 15 June 1964 Central Wales Line trains were diverted from Pontardulais to Llanelli and the line to Swansea Victoria closed. Steam-hauled to the end, the last service was the overnight Swansea to York mail train which left the dishevelled Victoria terminus behind Stanier Class '5' 4-6-0 No. 45406 (complete with wreath and headboard) at 6.30pm on 13 June.

Shrewsbury's green-liveried BR Standard Class '5MT' 4-6-0 No. 73036 gets ready to leave Swansea Victoria with a train for Shrewsbury on 2 June 1962.

A landscape of lower quadrant signals – '5600' Class 0-6-0PT No. 5655 enters Nelson & Llancaiach station with a train from Dowlais on 22 March 1964.

Some joker has painted out the first and last letters of Penyrheol's station sign. Time stands still here for a few locals as they wait for a Caerphilly to Senghenydd train on 10 July 1958.

CLOSED JUNE 15 1964
Nelson & Llancaiach to Dowlais (Cae Harris)

The 9½-mile railway from Nelson & Llancaiach to Dowlais was opened by the Taff Bargoed Joint Railway (operated jointly by the Great Western Railway and the Rhymney Railway) in 1876 – its *raison d'être* to haul iron ore from Cardiff Docks to the iron works at Dowlais. With gradients as steep as 1-in-40 it took three locomotives to haul trains of loaded iron ore wagons up the double-track line. Passenger services were of secondary importance and were laid on mainly for the benefit of workmen – in 1958 there were just four trains to Dowlais and five back down to Nelson, and all of these were extended to and from either Hengoed (High Level) or Ystrad Mynach. The picture on Saturdays was much improved with two additional trains being laid on for late night drinkers. Sunday was a day of rest! Although the railway closed to passengers on 15 June 1964 it still remains open as a single-track line from Ystrad Mynach to the open-cast coal depot at Cwm Bargoed.

CLOSED JUNE 15 1964
Caerphilly to Senghenydd

The steeply graded 3¾-mile branch line up the Aber Valley from Aber Junction, north of Caerphilly, to Senghenydd was opened by the Rhymney Railway in 1894. As well as serving several collieries the railway saw a fairly frequent service of passenger trains all calling at the intermediate stations of Aber Junction, Penyrheol and Abertridwr. Extra trains were laid on during summer weekends and bank holidays to take miners and their families on day trips to Barry Island. Closed to passengers on 15 June 1964, the branch remained open as far as Windsor Colliery until 1977. The last train, a three-car DMU carried a large party of pupils from Groeswen Secondary School and members of the local council.

CLOSED

Johnston to Neyland

Engineered by Isambard Kingdom Brunel, the 3¾-mile single-track branch line from Johnston to Neyland was opened by the South Wales Railway as an extension of its broad railway from Carmarthen to Haverfordwest in 1856. Neyland station was originally named Milford Haven until 1859 when the line from Johnston to Milford Haven opened. Steam packet boats operated from a floating pier adjacent to Neyland station to Cork in southern Ireland. The opening of the direct line to Fishguard by the GWR in 1906 saw Neyland's importance decline although the line was still kept busy with daily fish trains and a direct service to and from Paddington. Even in the late 1950s there were three through trains from Paddington to Neyland with the Milford Haven portion being detached at Johnston. Also opened in 1856, Neyland's engine shed and its turntable remained in use until 9 September 1963. Despite not being listed for closure in the 'Beeching Report', the Neyland branch lost its goods service in late 1963 and was closed to passengers on 15 June 1964 – the Milford Haven line remains open today.

'4300' Class 2-6-0 No. 7318 gets ready for its next turn of duty at Neyland shed (87H) on 14 August 1962.

CLOSED
JUNE
15
1964

Porth to Maerdy

Built in part along existing colliery railways, the 6½-mile branch line up the Rhondda Fach from Porth to Maerdy was opened by the Taff Vale Railway in 1856. Serving collieries along the valley, the railway reached 900 feet above sea level at its terminus which was approached on gradients as steep as 1-in-41. Connecting with Cardiff to Terherbert trains at Porth, passenger services were only introduced on the branch as far as Ferndale in 1876 and to Maerdy in 1889.

By the late 1950s the line was still being served by 11 return services each day with an additional five on Saturdays – as with many other Valleys branch lines, the latter included the all-important late night train for pub-goers which arrived at Maerdy at 12.23am on a Sunday morning. Listed for closure in the 'Beeching Report', the Maerdy branch lost its passenger service on 15 June 1964 – the same day as six other line closures in South Wales. Coal trains continued to use the branch until the closure of Maerdy Colliery in 1986.

At the head of the Rhondda Fach, '4575' Class 2-6-2T No. 5574 waits to depart from Maerdy with the 12.25pm train for Porth on 6 November 1957. The loco was withdrawn from Tondu shed at the end of 1958.

CLOSED
OCTOBER
30
1964

Abercynon to Aberdare (Low Level)

Served by a canal since 1812, the Aberdare Valley and its numerous coal mines and ironworks had become a world-renowned industrial centre by the 1850s. Promoted by ironworks' owners keen to see improved transport communications, the 7¼-mile railway from Abercynon, on the Taff Vale Railway's Pontypridd to Merthyr Tydfil line (opened in 1841), to Aberdare was opened by the Aberdare Railway in 1856. Leased and worked by the TVR the AR was absorbed by that company in 1902, itself becoming part of the Great Western Railway in 1923.

The decline in the steel-making and coal mining industries from the 1930s saw a dramatic reduction in goods traffic along the branch, although passenger services held up well until the early 1960s when there were over 20 return trains each weekday with many originating or ending their journeys at Barry Island, Cardiff or Pontypridd. Listed for closure in the 'Beeching Report', the passenger service ceased on 30 October 1964 although the line (singled in 1968) was kept open for coal traffic from several collieries – the last one to remain open, Tower Colliery (closed 2008) near Hirwaun, was reached via a new connection over the River Cynon near Cwmbach to the Vale of Neath line and then through the site of Aberdare (High Level) station. Freight trains still run along this route to serve Tower Washery.

Passenger services were restored to the line in 1988 when it was reopened for trains to and from Barry Island, Cardiff and Pontypridd.

A scene full of local colour at Mountain Ash in the Aberdare Valley – '8700' Class 0-6-0PT No. 3753 shunts loaded coal wagons by the Cresselly Arms pub in May 1962. The road sign warning of a rail crossing with no gates is correct as there was a National Coal Board ungated line in front of the BR level crossing gates.

A dog takes a keen interest in BR Standard Class '2' 2-6-2T No. 84003 as it calls at Rhosgoch station with the 2.05pm train from Amlwch to Bangor in August 1964.

CLOSED
DECEMBER
7
1964

Gaerwen to Amlwch

The 17¾-mile single-track branch line from Gaerwen, on the Chester to Holyhead main line, to the important mineral mining coastal town of Amlwch, was opened in fits and starts by the Anglesey Central Railway. The first 4½ miles to Llangefni opened to passenger traffic in 1865 by which time the company had tried, but failed, to lease or sell it to the London & North Western Railway. The rest of the railway opened in 1867 but it was another nine years before the LNWR took over.

For the first few years the line was kept busy carrying mineral traffic from the copper mine at nearby Parys Mountain but this closed in 1871. Goods traffic thereafter consisted of livestock to and from Llangefni market, agricultural produce and artificial fertiliser. To cope with this traffic an extra passing loop was installed at Llangwyllog in 1916. Passengers were also well catered for with some trains continuing their journey to and from Bangor. There were around 20 LNWR railmotor services each day by the First World War – these were also used for the Holland Arms to Red Wharf Bay branch line which closed to passengers in 1930 and completely in 1950.

However, by the late 1950s, the service had shrunk to only seven return trains on weekdays with a journey time of 36 minutes between the junction at Gaerwen and Amlwch. In the meantime, prototype Derby lightweight DMUs had already been introduced to the line as early as 1953 but steam traction returned once more in 1963 and trains remained steam-hauled until closure. A short extension was opened at Amlwch in 1953 to serve the new bromine extraction plant at the Octel factory.

Listed for closure in the 'Beeching Report', the line closed to passengers and goods on 7 December 1964. Despite this, the line still saw trains carrying ethylene dibromide from Amlwch until 1993 when the Octel plant closed. Today the overgrown, mothballed line has been overtaken by nature although there are various proposals to reopen it as a heritage railway or as a cycle track. To further the former aim, the newly-formed Anglesey Central Railway has opened a heritage centre at Llanerchymedd station.

Caernarfon to Afonwen

Although Caernarfon had been reached from the north by the Bangor & Carnarvon Railway in 1852, the historic harbour town had been served by the horse-drawn narrow gauge slate-carrying Nantlle Tramway since 1828. Built southwards from Caernarfon over the tramway as far as Penygroes, the 18¾-mile standard gauge Carnarvonshire Railway was opened thus far in 1866. The southward extension to Afonwen, on the Cambrian Railways' coastal line from Barmouth to Pwllheli, was completed the following year. Enter the mighty London & North Western Railway, which, having already taken over the Chester & Holyhead Railway and the B&CR, took over the CR in 1870. Connecting with this railway at Dinas Junction, the North Wales Narrow Gauge Railway opened to slate mines at Bryngwyn in 1877, and this was extended to Beddgelert and Porthmadog by the Welsh Highland Railway in 1923.

With the LNWR in charge, the single-track railway from Caernarfon to Afonwen soon saw through coaches to the seaside resort of Pwllheli via the Cambrian Railways line, from as far afield as Liverpool, Manchester, Birmingham and Euston. This pattern continued until the Second World War. Goods traffic consisted of livestock, stone and slate – the latter being delivered to the line via the NWNGR and the Nantlle and Llanberis branches. The opening of Butlin's Holiday Camp at Penychain after the war saw a through train from Euston reinstated during the summer months – known as 'The Welshman', this express also carried through coaches for Porthmadog and took over seven hours to complete its journey from the capital. A through service from Liverpool Lime Street to Penychain also ran on summer Saturdays. Derby lightweight DMUs were introduced for local services in the mid-1950s but the steady drip-drip away from railways and on to roads soon saw passenger numbers in serious decline.

Listed for closure in the 'Beeching Report', the Caernarfon to Afonwen line closed to all traffic on 7 December 1964. Since then, 12 miles of the trackbed from Caernarfon to Bryncir has been converted into a footpath and cycleway known as Lon Eifion. Running alongside this cycleway from Caernarfon to Dinas Junction, the first stage of the reborn narrow gauge Welsh Highland Railway opened in 2000 – since 2011 it has reopened throughout to Porthmadog.

The sad remains at Llangybi station on the Caernarfon to Afonwen line in 1970. The railway had closed on 7 December 1964.

A busy scene at Strata Florida station on 9 June 1960 with '4300' Class 2-6-0 No. 6310 working the 11.55am Aberystwyth to Carmarthen train, crossing the corresponding northbound service. A '2251' Class 0-6-0 shunts in the goods yard.

CLOSED FEBRUARY
22
1965

Carmarthen to Aberystwyth

The 56¼-mile single-track railway from Carmarthen to Aberystwyth started life at its southern end when the impoverished broad gauge Carmarthen & Cardigan Railway opened to Conwil in 1860. This 6½-mile line was worked by the South Wales Railway with Great Western Railway locomotives. Unable to pay its way, the C&CR closed at the end of that year but reopened in August 1861. The railway was extended to Pencader and Llandyssul in 1864 but within a few months an Official Receiver had been called in. However, the line kept operating until it was taken over by the GWR in 1881 – the latter company eventually extended the line to Newcastle Emlyn in 1895 but there it stopped, its hoped-for goal of Cardigan never being achieved.

From the north, the Manchester & Milford Railway had aspirations to link the important port of Milford Haven with Manchester. Their plan was to build an independent line from Llanidloes (on the Mid-Wales Railway) and through the mountains to link with the C&CR at Pencader and thence use running powers

to Milford Haven via Carmarthen. Despite making a start on the new line at Llanidloes this was soon abandoned. Instead, the M&MR chose a cheaper option by opening a new railway between Pencader and Aberystwyth – this opened in stages: to Lampeter and Strata Florida in 1866 and throughout in 1867. Never financially successful the railway was leased to the GWR in 1906 before being absorbed by that company in 1911.

With the opening of the M&MR line between Pencader and Aberystwyth, the original C&CR's line to Llandyssul (and from 1895 to Newcastle Emlyn) effectively became a branch line. The other branch line to open was from Aberayron Junction, north of Lampeter, to Aberayron (for New Quay) – built as a Light Railway it was opened by the GWR in 1911.

Both passenger and goods traffic was never heavy and the railway failed miserably as a through route between the North of England and Milford Haven. Trains were slow and by the late 1950s the end was nigh for passenger services – the three weekday trains then operating each way took up to 2½ hours to

complete the 56¼-mile journey. The Aberayron branch closed to passengers on 10 February 1951 and the Newcastle Emlyn branch closed to passengers on 15 September 1952.

Listed for closure in the 'Beeching Report', the end came prematurely for the section from Aberystwyth to Lampeter when floods effectively severed the northern part of the line on 14 December 1964. From that date passenger services from Carmarthen terminated at Lampeter until they too ceased on 22 February 1965. However this was not quite the end for this delightful country railway as goods and milk traffic continued to run from a large creamery at Felin Frach (on the Aberayron branch) and from Newcastle Emlyn and Lampeter until road transport won the day on 1 October 1973.

Fortunately, there is still life on parts of the line today: the standard gauge Gwili Railway operates steam trains for 2½ miles from Bronwydd Arms to Danycoed; and the 2ft gauge Teifi Valley Railway operates steam trains for two miles along the former Newcastle Emlyn branch between Henllan and Llandyfriog.

Whitchurch to Welshpool

The 15¾-mile railway between Oswestry and Welshpool was opened by the Oswestry & Newtown Railway in 1860. The railway was joined from the east at Buttington, 2¾ miles north of Welshpool, by the Shrewsbury & Welshpool Railway in 1861. This latter line was later jointly worked by the London & North Western Railway and the Great Western Railway and subsequently became the most important route for trains from the GWR system to the Cambrian Railways.

An 8½-mile branch line from Llanymynech to Llanfyllin was opened in 1863. From the east, the 18¼-mile railway from Whitchurch, on the LNWR's line between Crewe and Shrewsbury, to Oswestry was built across peat bogs in two stages by the Oswestry, Ellesmere & Whitchurch Railway. The first 11 miles from Whitchurch to Ellesmere was opened in 1863 with the remainder to Oswestry in 1864. Just days before the line was completed the OE&WR amalgamated with the O&NR, the Llanidloes & Newtown Railway and the Newtown & Machynlleth Railway to form the Cambrian Railways. Soon becoming a boom town, Oswestry became the new company's headquarters where it also had its main workshops. The CR was absorbed by the GWR on 1 January 1922. A 16-mile branch line from Llynclys Junction, south of Oswestry, to Llangynog was opened by the Tanat Valley Light Railway in 1904. It was taken over by the CR in 1921 and had been completely closed west of Blodwel by 1964.

Despite being used by through passenger trains (for example, London Euston to Aberystwyth via Crewe) and goods traffic (especially during both World Wars), the Whitchurch to Welshpool line was never as important as the Shrewbury to Welshpool route. Relegated to secondary status and with traffic in decline it was listed for closure in the 'Beeching Report'. All passenger services between Whitchurch and Buttington were withdrawn on 18 January 1965, leaving Oswestry at the end of the 2½-mile branch line from Gobowen (see Gobowen to Oswestry) until 1966 when the railway works also closed.

The line south of Oswestry to Llynclys Junction and Llanddu Quarry near Blodwell (on the closed Tanat Valley branch line) remained open for stone traffic until 1989 when it was mothballed. The intact line was purchased by Shropshire County Council from Network Rail in 2008 and an umbrella organisation known as the Cambrian Heritage Railway plan to reopen the entire route as a heritage railway in the near future. In the meantime trains run from Llynclys South to Pen-y-Garreg Lane and also for a short distance from Oswestry station.

Close to the summit of the Whitchurch to Welshpool line is Frankton station. Here, Ivatt Class '2MT' 2-6-0 No. 46514 enters with a full head of steam on 27 November 1964.

A busy scene at Llanfyllin station in the summer of 1960. Ivatt Class '2MT' 2-6-0 No. 46522 shunts in the goods yard while sister engine No. 46509 gets the road ahead for its train to Llanymynech.

CLOSED
JANUARY
18
1965

Llanymynech to Llanfyllin

Following the valley of the River Cain, the 8½-mile branch line from Llanymynech, on the Oswestry to Welshpool line, to the small market town of Llanfyllin was opened by the Oswestry & Newtown Railway in 1863. Trains were required to reverse into and out of the branch line at Llanymynech in order to cross the Montgomeryshire Canal. The branch was also joined by the Potteries, Shrewsbury & North Wales Railway (though it never served the Potteries or North Wales!) which opened from Shrewsbury to

Llanymynech in 1866; closing in 1880, it was reopened as the Shropshire & Montgomeryshire Railway in 1911.

The Llanfyllin branch was heavily used during the construction of the nearby Lake Vyrnwy dam between 1881 and 1888 but for most of its life led a fairly quiet existence. By the late 1950s the passenger service consisted of four return trains each weekday with an extra working on Saturday nights. Along with the former Cambrian Railways' main line from Whitchurch to Welshpool (see Whitchurch to Welshpool), the branch was listed for closure in the 'Beeching Report'. Goods services were withdrawn in 1964 and passenger services on 18 January 1965.

Ruabon to Barmouth Junction and Bala Junction to Bala

Although the mainly single-track 53-mile railway between Ruabon, on the Great Western Railway's main line between Chester and Shrewsbury, and Barmouth Junction was built by five different railway companies, on its completion it formed an important cross-country route for the GWR. From east to west, the first railway to be built was the Vale of Llangollen Railway which opened along the Dee Valley from Ruabon to the small town of Llangollen in 1862. It was worked from the outset by the GWR and absorbed by that company in 1896.

The second railway to be built along the Dee Valley was the Llangollen & Corwen Railway which opened in 1865. The third railway was the Corwen & Bala Railway which opened throughout in 1868. Both railways were also worked from the outset by the GWR and absorbed in 1896. Next to be built and worked by the GWR was the Bala & Dolgelly Railway which opened in 1868 – it was absorbed by the GWR in 1877. From that date the town of Bala was served by a shuttle service to and from the isolated Bala Junction station. At the western end, the Cambrian Railways had already opened a branch line from Barmouth Junction alongside the Mawddach Estuary to Penmaenpool in 1865. The intervening 2¼-mile gap between Dolgellau and Penmaenpool was opened by the B&DR in 1870. Worked throughout by the GWR, the entire route was now open for through traffic from the GWR system to North Wales.

Although only serving small towns, villages and farming communities along its route, the Ruabon to Barmouth line was kept busy during the summer months with holiday traffic from Birmingham destined for the seaside resort of Barmouth. Feeder traffic from the GWR branch from Blaenau Ffestiniog to Bala and the LNWR line from Rhyl and Denbigh also kept the line alive until their closures in 1960 and 1953 respectively.

The end is nigh! On a very frosty morning Ivatt Class '2MT' 2-6-0 No. 46446 approaches Garneddwen Halt with a Barmouth to Corwen train, 19 December 1964.

Ivatt Class '2' 2-6-2T No. 41241 (now preserved) approaches Drws-y-Nant station with a Barmouth to Corwen train on 19 December 1964.

With increasing competition from road transport and little intermediate traffic, the line's future was in doubt by the early 1960s. To the south it was duplicated by the Cambrian main line from Shrewsbury to Machynlleth on to which all through freight trains were soon diverted. Listed for closure in the 'Beeching Report', the end came earlier than the planned 18 January 1965 when floods cut the line at Carrog on the night of 11/12 December 1964. From that date the short Bala Junction to Bala line also closed and only the eastern (Ruabon to Llangollen) and western (Corwen to Barmouth Junction) sections (linked by a temporary bus service) continued to operate a passenger service until complete closure on the planned date.

It was reported in early 1967 that Merioneth County Council recommended that the track bed should be retained intact for possible future use by hovertrains or monorails! Goods traffic continued between Ruabon and Llangollen until 1 April 1968. Since closure several sections of this railway have seen a renaissance: The Llangollen Railway operates a standard gauge heritage line between Llangollen and Corwen; the 2ft 6in gauge Bala Lake Railway runs alongside Lake Bala from near Bala to Llanuwchllyn; and the eight-mile section from Barmouth Junction (now renamed Morffa Mawddach) to the outskirts of Dolgellau is now a footpath and cycleway known as the Mawddach Trail.

A rarely photographed line that does not even appear on the 'Beeching Report' Map 9. Here, in his inimitable style, Henry Casserley has photographed the station at Lavernock while on a Penarth-bound train on 6 April 1947.

CLOSED
MAY
6
1968

Penarth to Cadoxton via Lavernock

The first steeply graded section of the coastal railway from Cogan Junction to Cadoxton was opened as far as Penarth by the Penarth Extension Railway in 1878. It was worked and leased by the Taff Vale Railway until becoming part of the Great Western Railway in 1923. Opened throughout in 1890, the line was extended by the TVR-owned Cardiff, Penarth & Barry Junction Railway southwards from Penarth and around the coastline through Lavernock and Sully before joining the Barry Railway at Biglis Junction. Normally carrying local traffic from cement and brick works, the scenic route came to life during the summer months when thousands of daytrippers from Cardiff and the Valleys descended on the beaches and bays at Lavernock and Swanbridge. In its heyday during the first half of the twentieth century the railway saw trains running every half an hour from early morning until late at night. Lavernock was so popular as a holiday destination that the GWR hired out a camping coach at the station.

Diesel multiple units were introduced in 1958 but, strangely, the railway is not even shown on Map 9 of the 'Beeching Report' – its existence somehow escaping the attentions of the Doctor's cartographic team. However, it did not escape closure which came on 6 May 1968. The line continued to be used for cement trains to Cosmeston until 1970 when it was cut back to Penarth; the latter station is still served by trains from Cardiff and beyond. The trackbed between Lavernock and Penarth is now a footpath and cycleway.

Bangor to Caernarfon

The seven-mile railway from Menai Bridge to Caernarfon was opened by the Bangor & Carnarvon Railway in 1852. The line was initially leased by the Chester & Holyhead Railway and then taken over by that company in 1854. The C&HR was itself taken over by the London & North Western Railway in 1859. The line was extended southwards from Caernarfon to Afonwen by the Carnarvonshire Railway in 1867 (see Caernarfon to Afonwen) which was also taken over by the LNWR in 1870.

The opening of the railway to Afonwen soon brought increased through traffic and the Menai Bridge to Caernarfon section was relaid with double track in 1872. The LNWR soon made good use of this approach into North Wales with through coaches from Euston, Liverpool and Manchester to Porthmadog and Pwllheli. The opening of Butlin's Holiday Camp at Penychain after the Second World War brought increased traffic with through trains from Liverpool and Euston running during the summer months until the early 1960s, including 'The Welshman' which carried through coaches from London to Porthmadog, Pwllheli and Holyhead.

This all came to a halt when the line south of Caernarfon was closed in 1964 leaving the town at the end of a branch line from Menai Bridge. Also listed for closure in the 'Beeching Report', the line was singled in 1966 – its survival for a few more years no doubt helped by the investiture of the Prince of Wales at Caernarfon Castle on 1 July 1969. Following that event closure was swift: goods services ended on 4 August 1969 and passenger services on 5 January 1970. But this was not quite the end as on 23 May the Britannia Tubular Bridge across the Menai Strait was seriously damaged in a fire, and train services to Holyhead were suspended. While the bridge was being repaired container freight traffic to and from Holyhead was carried along the branch line to Caernarfon, where it was shipped across to Anglesey. The line finally closed on 30 January 1972 when the bridge reopened to rail traffic.

A double-headed RCTS special to Porthmadog halts at Caernarfon station on 22 July 1962. Train engines Stanier Class '3' 2-6-2Ts Nos 40116 and 40178 fill up their tanks while, in the background, is evidence of the cattle traffic that was once all carried by rail.

End of the line! The 5.08pm train from Bridgend has terminated at Cymmer Afan station on the last day of services up the Llynfi Valley, 20 June 1970.

CLOSED
JUNE
22
1970

Bridgend to Treherbert

Incorporated in 1846, the broad gauge Llynfi Valley Railway was opened along the course of two existing horse-drawn tramroads from Bridgend and up the Llynfi Valley to ironworks and zinc smelters at Maesteg in 1861. The railway amalgamated with the standard gauge Ogmore Valley Railway to become the Llynfi & Ogmore Railway in 1866. This railway was initially of mixed gauge but the broad gauge element was abandoned in 1872. It was extended through the 1,591-yard Cymmer Tunnel to the Afan Valley in 1877 and was absorbed by the Great Western Railway in 1883. An extension from Cymmer Afan to Abergwynfi was opened in 1886.

Serving numerous collieries along its length, the line from Bridgend to Abergwynfi also saw a regular passenger service of around nine trains each weekday until 1960 – the journey time for the 14-mile journey was around 50 minutes. On 13 June of that year the line from Cymmer to Abergwynfi closed with trains

from Bridgend diverted to Blaengwynfi and through the Rhondda Tunnel to Treherbert – the alternative mountain road was considered too dangerous for a replacement bus service. While the Rhondda & Swansea Bay Railway's line from Neath to Cymmer Afan closed on 3 December 1962 (see Neath to Cymmer Afan), the service from Bridgend to Maesteg, Cymmer Afan and Treherbert continued to operate until 26 February 1968 when the long and dank Rhondda Tunnel was closed due to its poor state of repair. From that date trains terminated at Cymmer Afan until they were withdrawn on 22 June 1970.

Despite the loss of passenger services, the line up the Llynfi Valley remained open for coal traffic from Maesteg Washery and, following a long campaign, it was reopened for passengers between Bridgend and Maesteg in 1992. Unfortunately an extension through the sealed-up Cymmer Tunnel is no longer possible due to housing developments at Nantyffyllon and Caerau.

NORTHERN ENGLAND

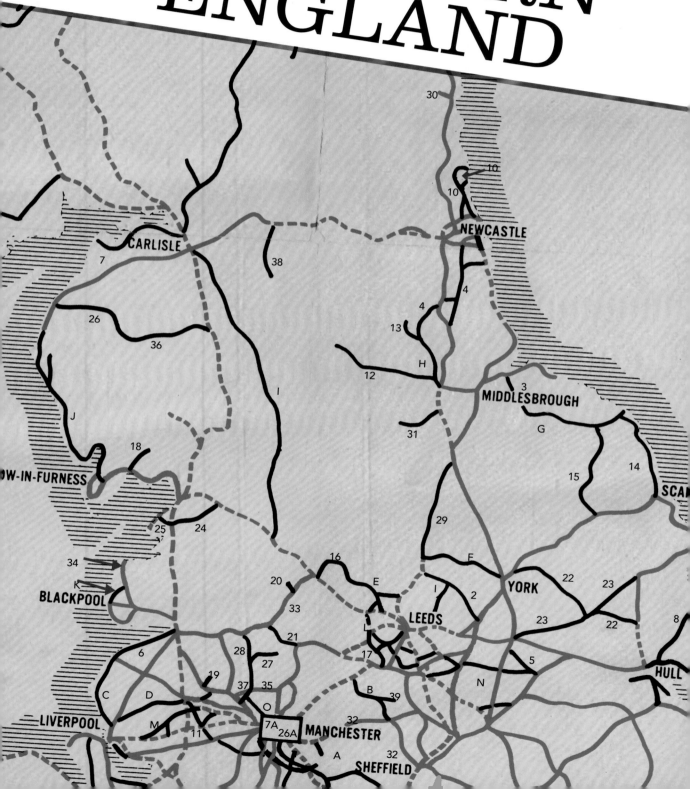

THE CASUALTIES

1. Cross Gates to Wetherby – 6 January 1964
2. Church Fenton to Harrogate – 6 January 1964
3. Nunthorpe to Guisborough – 2 March 1964
4. Bishop Auckland to Durham and Sunderland – 4 May 1964
5. Selby to Goole – 15 June 1964
6. Preston to Southport – 6 September 1964
7. Carlisle to Silloth – 7 September 1964
7A. Oldham to Middleton – 7 September 1964
8. Hull to Hornsea – 19 October 1964
9. Hull to Withernsea – 19 October 1964
10. Monkseaton to Newbiggin-on-the-Sea and Newsham to Blyth – 2 November 1964
11. Wigan Central to Glazebrook Junction – 2 November 1964
12. Darlington to Barnard Castle and Middleton-in Teesdale – 30 November 1964
13. Bishop Auckland to Crook – 8 March 1965
14. Scarborough to Whitby – 8 March 1965
15. Grosmont to Malton – 8 March 1965
16. Skipton to Ilkley – 22 March 1965
17. Low Moor to Mirfield via Cleckheaton – 14 June 1965
18. Ulverston to Lakeside – 5 September 1965
19. Blackrod/Lostock Junction to Horwich – 27 September 1965
20. Earby to Barnoldswick – 27 September 1965
21. Rose Grove to Todmorden – November 1965
22. York (Bootham Junction) to Beverley via Market Weighton – 29 November 1965
23. Selby to Driffield via Market Weighton – 14 June 1965
24. Lancaster (Green Ayre) to Wennington – 3 January 1966
25. Lancaster (Green Ayre) to Morecambe – 3 January 1966
26. Keswick to Workington – 18 April 1966

26A. Royton Junction to Royton – 18 April 1966
27. Clifton Junction to Bury (Bolton Street) and Rawtenstall to Bacup – 5 December 1966
28. Stubbins Junction to Accrington – 5 December 1966
29. Northallerton to Harrogate – 6 March 1967
30. Alnmouth to Alnwick – 30 January 1968*
31. Eryholme to Richmond – 3 March 1969
32. Sheffield to Manchester via Woodhead – 5 January 1970*
33. Colne to Skipton – 2 February 1970*
34. Poulton-le-Fylde to Fleetwood – 1 June 1970*
35. Bolton (Trinity Street) to Bury (Knowsley Street) and Heywood North Junction – 5 October 1970*
36. Penrith to Keswick – 6 March 1972
37. Bury (Bolton Street) to Rawtenstall – 3 June 1972
38. Haltwhistle to Alston – 3 May 1976
39. Shepley Junction to Clayton West – 24 January 1983
Note: dates given are for withdrawal of passenger services
* = not listed for closure in the 'Beeching Report'

THE SURVIVORS

A. Dinting to Glossop
B. Huddersfield to Penistone
C. Liverpool to Southport
D. Walton Junction to Wigan (Wallgate)
E. Apperley Junction to Ilkley
F. Harrogate to York
G. Middlesbrough to Whitby
H. Darlington to Bishop Auckland
I. Settle Junction to Carlisle
J. Barrow-in-Furness to Whitehaven
K. Poulton to Blackpool (North)
L. Shipley to Bradford (Forster Square)
M. Huyton to Wigan via St Helen's
N. Goole to Knottingley, Castleford and Wakefield
O. Manchester to Bury

It wasn't just steam that got the order of the boot... Looking like an exhibit in a Victorian museum, electric multiple unit No. 29021 waits to leave the old Morecambe Midland station with a train for Lancaster Castle on 9 October 1965. This groundbreaking line closed less than three months later.

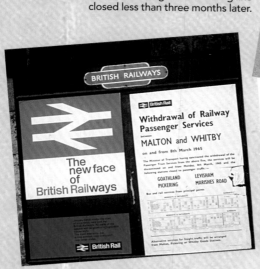

The new face of British Rail! A new logo, a new name and massive cutbacks in the rail network. We were not fooled! The closure of the Malton to Whitby line is thus announced.

Beeching dereliction in Teesdale. The sad remains of Middleton-in-Teesdale station in 1967. R.I.P.

CLOSED
JANUARY
6
1964

Cross Gates to Wetherby

The 10¼-mile line from Cross Gates, east of Leeds, to Wetherby was opened by the North Eastern Railway in 1876. Serving five intermediate stations, the steeply-graded railway was also used by through freight trains until the East Coast Main Line was quadrupled between Thirsk and York in 1959. By the early 1960s the passenger service along the line was operated by diesel multiple units with virtually all trains travelling between Harrogate and Leeds – the one exception was an early morning through train from Church Fenton (see Church Fenton to Harrogate) to Leeds via Wetherby. Costly to operate with 16 signal boxes, staffed stations and heavy trains needing rear end assistance up to the summit of the line north of Scholes, the line was inevitably listed for closure in the 'Beeching Report'. Passenger services were withdrawn on 6 January 1964 although goods trains continued until 4 April 1966.

Today, parts of the trackbed of the line between Wetherby and Cross Gates are a footpath and cycleway.

Class 'J39/2' 0-6-0 No. 64821 and a 'B16' 4-6-0 pound up the gradient through Thorner station with a southbound freight on the heavily-graded Wetherby to Leeds line on a rainy day, circa 1959.

CLOSED
JANUARY
6
1964

Church Fenton to Harrogate

The 18-mile railway between Church Fenton, on the Leeds to York main line, to Harrogate via Wetherby was opened by the York & North Midland Railway in 1848. In 1854 the railway became part of the newly-formed North Eastern Railway. A new junction was installed at Wetherby in 1901 to allow trains from Harrogate to travel via the Coss Gates line to Leeds. During the Second World War a circular railway was opened from Thorp Arch, east of Wetherby Racecourse station, to serve a Royal Ordnance munitions factory – four small wooden halts were built along this line which opened in 1942.

By the early 1960s passenger traffic had dwindled to such an extent that there was only one early morning train between Church Fenton and Wetherby on weekdays. The Wetherby to Harrogate section via Spofforth also had a pretty dire service so it was hardly surprising when the entire route was listed for closure in the 'Beeching Report'. The end came for the negligible passenger services on 6 January 1964 although goods traffic continued until 30 November 1966.

Today, the trackbed between Spofforth and Wetherby is a footpath and cycleway known as the Spofforth Railway Path. The path continues east of Wetherby as far as the restored Tudor-style station at Thorp Arch and there are currently plans to extend it across the River Wharfe to Tadcaster.

A scene from a bygone age – 'B1' 4-6-0 No. 61224 has just arrived at Wetherby East with the local pick-up goods train from Church Fenton on 25 September 1963. Note the Lambretta scooter outside the goods office.

Watched by a small group of photographers, a DMU waits to leave the overall-roof station at Guisborough with a train for Middlebrough on the last day of services, 29 February 1964.

CLOSED
MARCH
2
1964

Nunthorpe to Guisborough

The ten-mile railway from Middlesbrough to Guisborough was opened by the Middlesbrough & Guisborough Railway in 1854. At Nunthorpe it connected with the North Yorkshire & Cleveland Railway's line from Battersby and Grosmont in the Esk Valley which opened in 1865. The Guisborough line was worked from the outset by the Stockton & Darlington Railway with which it was amalgamated in 1858.

Guisborough, with its glass-roofed trainshed, also became the western terminus of the Cleveland Railway which opened throughout from Loftus in 1867. Built primarily to carry iron ore from Skinningrove to Teesside, the railway met the coastal route from Whitby at Loftus. Passenger trains between Scarborough, Whitby and Middlesbrough were rerouted via Guisborough instead of Saltburn in 1933. This service involved trains of up to seven coaches being propelled in and out of Guisborough terminus and lasted until the line to Loftus and Whitby closed on 2 May 1960 – after this date trains between Scarborough, Whitby and Middlesbrough were again rerouted, this time via the Esk Valley Line, Battersby Junction (reverse) and Nunthorpe.

Coinciding with the introduction of diesel multiple units, the closure of the Loftus line saw Guisborough revert back to branch line status served by seven trains to and from Middlesbrough each weekday (six on Saturdays). The branch, along with the Esk Valley Line to Whitby, was listed for closure in the 'Beeching Report' (though strangely, Beeching's cartographic team omitted it from Map 9). While the latter was fortunately saved – it is still open for business today – the five miles from Nunthorpe Junction to Guisborough was not so lucky and closed to passengers on 2 March 1964. Packed with dozens of enthusiasts, the last DMU service from Guisborough was formed of a four-car Metro-Cammell buffet set and a two-car set. Goods traffic continued until 31 August 1964.

Today, the trackbed from Hutton Gate to Guisborough is a footpath and cycleway known as the Guisborough Walkway.

Preserved Class 'K4' 2-6-0 No. 61994 'The Great Marquess' heads across Newton Cap Viaduct with an RCTS special on 10 April 1965. The viaduct once carried the Bishop Auckland to Durham railway over the Wear Valley but in 1995 it was converted to carry the A689 road.

CLOSED

MAY
4
1964

Bishop Auckland to Durham and Sunderland

The 11-mile railway between Durham and Bishop Auckland was opened to passengers by the North Eastern Railway in 1857. There were initially three intermediate stations at Hunwick, Willington and Brancepeth but a station serving Brandon Colliery opened in 1861. The railway served a number of other coal mines, some of which had their own colliery lines, and was also occasionally used as a diversionary route when the East Coast Main Line was closed between Durham and Darlington. Diesel multiple units were introduced in the late 1950s and by 1961 there were just five return journeys each weekday – two of these started or ended their journey at Sunderland. Extra steam-hauled trains were run on Saturdays during the summer months including through trains between Blackpool and South Shields and Blackpool and Newcastle (both via the line over the Stainmore Summit from Tebay to Barnard Castle which closed in January 1962).

Listed for closure in the 'Beeching Report', the Bishop Auckland to Durham line, along with the service to Sunderland via Penshaw, lost its passenger service on 4 May 1964. Local goods services were withdrawn on 10 August but the line remained open for through freight trains until 1968. Today, the trackbed between Brandon and the outskirts of Bishop Auckland is a footpath and cycleway.

Henry Casserley leaned out of the rear coach of a Selby to Goole train to take this photograph of Barlow's wooden platform and signal box on 31 August 1956.

CLOSED
JUNE
15
1964

Selby to Goole

The 12-mile railway between Selby and Goole was opened by the North Eastern Railway in 1910. It was initially built with double-track but the hoped-for through goods traffic failed to materialise and the line was singled in 1923. During the early years passenger trains were operated by steam railcars although by the early 1960s steam had given way to diesel multiple units. By 1961 there were four return passenger trains on weekdays with an additional working on Saturday early afternoons. Listed for closure in the 'Beeching Report', the railway lost its passenger service on 15 June 1964 with goods traffic ceasing on 7 December. Much of the route has long since disappeared beneath the A645 road.

CLOSED
SEPTEMBER
6
1964

Preston to Southport

The 16-mile double-track railway along the south shore of the Ribble Estuary between Preston and Southport was opened by the West Lancashire Railway in 1882. An independent concern, it had its own termini at Preston (Fishergate Hill) and at Southport (Central) until taken over by the Lancashire & Yorkshire Railway in 1897. Trains were then routed into Southport Chapel Street and at Preston into the joint LNWR/L&YR station. The section from Southport to Crossens was electrified with a third-rail system in 1904 and to Meols Cop in 1909 – the electric trains started or ended their journeys at Liverpool.

Closure of the line had been considered as early as 1959 and a number of intermediate stations were closed on 30 April 1962. Steam-hauled to the end, the Preston to Southport line saw a frequent service of trains – in the summer of 1962 there were no fewer than 22 each way including a through train to and from Blackpool. These were augmented on summer Saturdays with through trains from Colne and Blackburn and excursion trains from further afield. Listed for closure in the 'Beeching Report', passenger services along the line between Meols Cop and Preston ceased on 6 September 1964. Most of the track had been lifted by 1965 although goods trains continued to serve Hesketh Park until 1967.

Stanier Class '4' 2-6-4T No. 42461 arrives at Hundred End station with a Southport to Preston train in 1960.

With less than six months to go before closure of the line, a Derby Lightweight DMU waits to depart from Silloth station with a train for Carlisle on 20 April 1964.

CLOSED
SEPTEMBER
7
1964

Carlisle to Silloth

The 22½-mile railway from Carlisle to Silloth was built in two stages. First was the Port Carlisle Dock & Railway which opened over the course of the Carlisle Canal in 1854. The impoverished company had to hire locomotives and rolling stock from the Newcastle & Carlisle Railway for a year until its own locomotive was delivered. An extension from Drumburgh to Silloth, where a new wet dock had been built, was opened by the Carlisle & Silloth Bay Railway & Dock Company in 1856 – also impoverished, this company had to borrow the sole engine owned by the PCD&R but a year later passenger trains reverted to horse-haulage. The two railways were only saved from oblivion when the North British Railway took on a lease in 1862, eventually absorbing them in 1880.

Silloth soon became a popular seaside destination for Carlisle's factory workers but by the 1950s the town had lost its appeal and had became very rundown. In an effort to reduce operating costs, BR introduced new Derby lightweight DMUs in 1954 – the branch was the first in Britain to see these modern trains. Listed for closure in the 'Beeching Report', the end came for the Silloth branch on 7 September 1964. But it was far from a quiet ending. Scenes of public disorder were witnessed at Silloth station as the last train got ready to leave behind Ivatt Class '4' 2-6-0 No. 43139 the night before – a cheering and jeering crowd estimated to number about 9,000 halted proceedings and eight policeman and an Alsatian dog tried to restore some semblance of peace. The train eventually left 30 minutes late to the sound of detonators exploding and the transistorised strains of the Beatles' *Do You Love Me?*.

CLOSED OCTOBER **19** 1964

Hull to Withernsea

The 17½-mile branch line across rich agricultural land from Hull to Withernsea was opened by the independent Hull & Holderness Railway in 1854. Withernsea was then just a small village but with the coming of the railway it expanded into a seaside resort. Trains initially terminated at the York & North Midland Railway's Victoria Dock station until 1864 when they continued around the city to Paragon station. In the meantime the North Eastern Railway took over working the line in 1860 and absorbed it in 1862. Mainly double-track apart from two single-track sections, the Withernsea branch came to life on summer weekends when hordes of Hull factory workers took a train ride to the coast.

Diesel multiple units were introduced in 1957, and all intermediate stations became unstaffed in 1960 with tickets being issued by the guard conductor on the train. Despite these economies, the service of 15 trains each way (plus three more on Saturdays) was a loss-making affair and the line was listed for closure in the 'Beeching Report'. The last passenger train ran on 19 October 1964 although goods trains to Withernsea continued until 3 May 1965, after which the line was cut back to Hedon until 1968. It was then cut back to Marfleet until 1972 when the remaining rump was closed for good.

Today, several sections of the trackbed are used as a footpath and cycleway while all of the stations, except Withernsea, have survived albeit with different uses.

CLOSED OCTOBER **19** 1964

Hull to Hornsea

Built across flat agricultural land, the 13-mile Hull & Hornsea Railway was opened in 1864 between the small coastal resort of Hornsea and Wilmington, on the eastern outskirts of Hull, where it met the existing branch line from Withernsea (see Hull to Withernsea). Double track throughout, the line was worked from the outset by the North Eastern Railway and, within a few months of opening, trains were extended from Wilmington to Hull Paragon station. The railway was absorbed by the NER in 1866. It was particularly popular on summer weekends when extra trains were laid on to carry daytrippers from Hull.

As on the Withernsea branch, diesel multiple units were introduced in 1957, and all intermediate stations became unstaffed in 1960 with tickets being issued by the guard conductor on the train. Despite these economies, the service of 13 trains each way (plus three more on Saturdays) was a loss-making affair and the line was listed for closure in the 'Beeching Report'. The last passenger train ran on 19 October 1964 although goods trains continued to run to Hornsea Bridge until 3 May 1965.

Today, many of the intermediate stations (including the 'market day' station at Wassand) survive as private residences while the fine Grade II terminus building at Hornsea has been restored. Almost the entire line is now a footpath and cycleway known as the Hornsea Rail Trail.

A DMU waits to depart from Withernsea station with a service to Hull, circa1962.

Happy days at Hornsea station in the early 1960s with a DMU recently arrived from Hull.

Still life at Blyth station on 1 May 1964.
Passengers seem to be in short supply!

CLOSED
NOVEMBER
2
1964

Monkseaton to Newbiggin-on-the-Sea and Newsham to Blyth

The 13¾-mile railway between Monkseaton and Newbiggin-on-the-Sea and the 1½-mile branch line to Blyth were both casualties of the 'Beeching Axe' when they lost their passenger services on 2 November 1964. Also closed on that day were passenger services between Newcastle and Newbiggin via Backworth, Seghill, Seaton Delaval and Hartley.

The railways forming these axed routes have a fascinating history going back to the horse-drawn wagonways of the early nineteenth century. These early lines were local affairs built by colliery owners to transport coal from mines to ports on the coast. An early steam-hauled railway to be built was the Seghill Railway which ran from Seghill Colliery to Blyth in 1840 (from 1841 it also carried passengers) – this was later extended south to reach the River Tyne. A branch from Newsham to Bedlington was opened by the Bedlington Coal Company (BCC) in 1850. In 1852, the SR and the BCC's line, along with other wagonways, became two of the constituent companies of the newly formed Blyth & Tyne Railway. The Bedlington line was extended to Morpeth in 1858 and the following year a branch was opened to North Seaton. Further expansion came in 1872 with the extension of the North Seaton branch through Ashington to the

coast at Newbiggin. Serving numerous collieries, the B&TR was a highly profitable coal-carrying railway until it was taken over by the North Eastern Railway in 1874. The latter company introduced electric trains to the southern loop of the line between Newcastle (New Bridge Street), Backworth, Monkseaton and Tynemouth in 1904. At the same time the passenger service along the coast line north of Monkseaton to Hartley (closed in 1864) was reinstated.

The Bedlington to Morpeth section was closed to passengers in 1950 and the remaining non-electrified section of the old B&TR soldiered on with new diesel multiple units. The Blyth branch was also kept very busy with coal traffic – even as late as 1961 the port shipped out nearly seven million tons of coal carried to Staithes by rail. Despite closure to passengers on 2 November 1964, much of the former B&TR's route remains open for freight traffic (albeit much reduced) today. The NER's electrified lines from Newcastle were decommissioned in 1967 with services being taken over by DMUs – the North Tyneside Loop forming part of the new Tyne & Wear Metro opened from 1980. There are currently proposals to reintroduce passenger services along the freight-only route from Newcastle to Ashington via Newsham and Bedlington.

CLOSED

Wigan Central to Glazebrook Junction

As a constituent company of the Cheshire Lines Committee (CLC), the Manchester, Sheffield & Lincolnshire Railway (Great Central Railway from 1897) wished to tap into the lucrative Lancashire coalfields. To further this ambition it opened the 12¼-mile line from Glazebrook Junction, on the CLC main line between Manchester and Liverpool, to Wigan in 1879. Passenger services were introduced in 1884 and a new terminus at Wigan Central was opened in 1892. Initially, passenger trains ran between Wigan Central and Manchester Central although Warrington and St Helens were later served by through trains when a new north-west spur was opened at Glazebrook Junction in 1900.

By the 1950s, with the decline in the coal industry coupled with the more direct Wigan Wallgate to Manchester Victoria service, the line from Wigan Central had fallen into terminal decline. Many of the trains began or ended their journeys at Irlam and by 1962 there were only six through trains to Manchester on weekdays plus two extra on Saturdays for Manchester United fans. The introduction of DMUs failed to halt the decline and passenger services were withdrawn on 2 November 1964. Freight traffic continued until 1968 when the line closed for good.

The former Great Central Railway's terminus at Wigan on 23 August 1952.

CLOSED

Darlington to Barnard Castle and Middleton-in-Teesdale

Railways first reached Barnard Castle in 1856 when the Stockton & Darlington Railway opened its 16¾-mile line from Darlington. This was joined in 1861 when the South Durham & Lancashire Railway opened from Bishop Auckland to Tebay via Barnard Castle and Stainmore Summit.

An 8¾-mile branch line from Barnard Castle to Middleton-in-Teesdale was opened by the Tees Valley Railway in 1868. Featuring several viaducts, the branch was built primarily to serve several quarries in the valley but also played an important role carrying construction material during the building of two large reservoirs in the early twentieth century.

Although once important as a through freight route, the railway from Bishop Auckland and Barnard Castle to Tebay and Penrith had declined in importance by the 1950s. Served by only two through passenger trains on weekdays, the line came to life on summer Saturdays when double-headed steam trains pounded up Stainmore Summit and across Belah Viaduct carrying holidaymakers from the northeast to Blackpool. Despite the introduction of DMUs for the regular weekday services in 1957, this highly scenic line was closed at the beginning of 1962.

With dwindling stone traffic and also served by DMUs from Darlington, the Middleton-in-Teesdale branch soldiered on for a few more years. Listed for closure in the 'Beeching Report', the end came for passenger services from Darlington on 30 November 1964. Goods traffic continued until April 1965. Today, much of the Middleton branch is a footpath and cycleway known as the Tees Valley Railway Path.

Double-headed by Class 'V1' 2-6-2T No. 67646 and Stanier Class '4' 2-6-4T No. 42639, the RCTS's 'North Yorkshireman' Rail Tour crosses Mickleton Viaduct over the River Lune on the approach to Middleton-in-Teesdale on 18 April 1964.

CLOSED
MARCH
8
1965

Bishop Auckland to Crook

Bishop Auckland was once an important railway centre with railways radiating out to Weardale, Parkhead, Consett, Durham, Hartlepool, Stockton-on-Tees, Darlington and Barnard Castle. By 1965 all that remained of this once important network was the freight-only line up Weardale to Eastgate and the 18-mile branch line from Darlington to Crook – the line to Durham and Sunderland (see Bishop Auckland to Durham and Sunderland) having closed on 4 May 1964.

The coal-mining town of Crook was first reached by the Bishop

Auckland & Weardale Railway – an extension of the Stockton & Darlington Railway from Soho – in 1843. The railway was extended by the steeply graded Weardale Extension Railway in 1845, meeting the Wear & Derwent Railway at Waskerley. A 10¾-mile branch line to Frosterley was opened by the Wear Valley Railway in 1847 by which time this company had taken over the BA&WR, the WER and the W&DR. This network was then leased to the S&DR before being absorbed by it in 1858. The final twist in this complicated tale was when the S&DR was itself absorbed by the North Eastern Railway in 1863.

Passenger services on the line

north of Crook became early victims of closure, with Tow Law to Blackhill (for trains to Newcastle) ceasing in 1939 and Crook to Tow Law in 1956. Diesel multiple units were then introduced for the remaining service between Darlington and Crook via Bishop Auckland. The large complex of coke ovens, brick works, chemical plant and colliery at Crook continued to be served by rail until their closure in the early 1960s. The Darlington to Crook service was threatened with closure in the 'Beeching Report' but, at the eleventh hour, the 12½ miles as far as Bishop Auckland was reprieved with closure beyond to Crook taking place on 8 March 1965.

Coal and iron ore were once the lifeblood of railways in County Durham. Here, viewed from a DMU bound for Bishop Auckland, Class 'J39/1' 0-6-0 No. 64862 is seen in between freight duties at Crook on 9 March 1961.

CLOSED

MARCH 8 1965

Scarborough to Whitby

Closely following the dramatic Yorkshire coastline, the 21¾-mile steeply-graded single-track line between Scarborough and Whitby (West Cliff) was opened by the Scarborough & Whitby Railway in 1885. Featuring gradients as steep as 1-in-39 and the 915ft Larpool Viaduct near Whitby, construction was delayed by financial problems and took 13 years to complete. The railway was worked from the outset by the North Eastern Railway and was absorbed by that company in 1898.

At the northern end of the line, Whitby had already been reached by the Whitby & Pickering railway as early as 1836 while, to the south, Scarborough had been reached by the York & North Midland Railway in 1845. Whitby (West Cliff), linked to Whitby Town station via a steeply-graded spur, had also been reached from the north by the Whitby, Redcar & Middlesbrough Railway which was completed by the NER in 1883. Apart from continuing freight traffic to Skinningrove steelworks and Boulby potash mine, the line north of Whitby West Cliff closed on 5 May 1960.

The Scarborough to Whitby line was a popular route for excursion trains during the summer months and camping coaches were also a regular sight at many of the intermediate stations from the 1930s until closure. Steam haulage was replaced by diesel multiple units in 1958 and the line was listed for closure in the 'Beeching Report' but, despite vociferous objections from the local community and councils, the line was closed on 8 March 1965. Today, most of the trackbed of the railway is now a footpath and cycleway known as the Scarborough to Whitby Railway Path. At its northern end the path crosses the impressive Larpool Viaduct north of Whitby.

The Stephenson Locomotive Society's 'Whitby Moors Rail Tour' storms out of Staintondale behind preserved Class 'K4' 2-6-0 No. 61994 'The Great Marquess' and Class 'K1' 2-6-0 No. 62005 on 6 March 1965. This was the last day of services on the Scarborough to Whitby line.

CLOSED

MARCH 8 1965

Grosmont to Malton

The 35¼-mile line between Malton and Whitby was opened by the Whitby & Pickering Railway in 1836. One of the earliest railways in Britain, it was initially horse-drawn and included the rope-worked 1-in-15 Beck Hole Incline. The W&PR was taken over by the York & North Midland Railway in 1845. The Malton to Whitby line was then rebuilt for steam haulage but the Beck Hole Incline still impeded progress until after the North Eastern Railway had taken over in 1854. Bypassing the incline, a new deviation with a gradient of 1-in-49 was opened between Goathland and Grosmont in 1865.

By the twentieth century the line's scenic qualities through Newtondale Gorge and across the moors were being heavily promoted by the NER and its successor, the London & North Eastern Railway. During the summer months through trains from York and Leeds were running over the line to Whitby. These continued to run after the Second World War although by the late 1950s new diesel multiple units had taken over some of these duties. Even as late as the summer of 1961 there were four through trains from York (one included a through carriage from King's Cross) and one from Leeds on Saturdays. The three Sunday services included through trains from Selby and Leeds.

Listed for closure in the 'Beeching Report', the 29 miles between Malton and Grosmont (for the Esk Valley Line) closed on 8 March 1965 – on that day Whitby also lost its train service from Scarborough. Goods trains continued to run from Malton to Pickering until the following year. Since 1973, the railway between Pickering and Grosmont has been reopened as a heritage railway (the second longest standard gauge line in Britain) by the North Yorkshire Moors Railway.

What an excellent piece of signalling! BR Standard Class '3' 2-6-2T No. 82039 leaves Levisham station with the 4pm Malton to Whitby train on 13 October 1961.

Organised by the RCTS, 'The Dalesman' Rail Tour pauses at Embsay Junction outside Skipton having travelled along Wharfdale through Ilkley and Bolton Abbey on 4 May 1963. This was the first tour by preserved 'K4' 2-6-0 No. 3442 'The Great Marquess' but, some say, it did not exactly go very smoothly!

CLOSED
MARCH
22
1965

Skipton to Ilkley

The first railway to reach Ilkley was the North Eastern Railway and Midland Railway's joint line from Otley (the then terminus of the NER's branch line from Arthington Junction, on the Leeds to Harrogate line) in 1865. From the west, the MR's 11½-mile line from Skipton to Ilkley opened in 1888 – part of this line ran through the Duke of Devonshire's estate at Bolton Hall and required considerable landscaping to hide it from view! A popular destination for excursion trains, Bolton Abbey station was also frequented by royalty when visiting the Duke in his country mansion. So popular was it with daytrippers that even as late as the summer of 1961 it was still served by seven trains from Leeds and further afield on Sundays.

While diesel multiple units were introduced in 1959, all railways serving Ilkley were subsequently listed for closure in the 'Beeching Report'. The services from Leeds via Apperley Junction and from Shipley via Esholt Junction were reprieved and have since been electrified. The line from Skipton (and through Otley) was not so lucky and closed on 22 March 1965. Goods services ceased four months later.

Since 1979 the Yorkshire Dales Railway has reopened 3½ miles between Embsay and Bolton Abbey as a heritage railway. Now known as the Embsay & Bolton Abbey Steam Railway, it has ambitious plans to extend a further 2½ miles eastwards to a new station at Addingham and to reconnect the line to the national rail network at Embsay Junction.

A local service from Mirfield to Bradford Exchange enters Cleckheaton station on 20 August 1959, unusually hauled by BR Standard Class '5MT' 4-6-0 No. 73169 of Leeds Holbeck shed.

CLOSED
JUNE
14
1965

Low Moor to Mirfield via Cleckheaton

Serving the important woollen industry, the 7¾-mile railway along the Spen Valley from Low Moor, south of Bradford, to Mirfield was opened by the Lancashire & Yorkshire Railway in 1848. A branch from Heckmondwike to Thornhill (Dewsbury) was opened in 1869 (and closed in 1962). In its latter years the line was part of the North Eastern Region of BR and was served by diesel multiple units running between Penistone, Huddersfield and Bradford (Exchange). Listed for closure in the 'Beeching Report', the line lost its passenger services on 14 June 1965 although goods trains from Heckmondwike to Low Moor continued until 1981 apart from a temporary disruption for the building of the M62 motorway between 1970 and 1974.

Today, the entire route of the railway – now bisected by the M62 motorway – is a footpath and cycleway known as the Spen Valley Greenway.

CLOSED
SEPTEMBER
5
1965

Ulverston to Lakeside

The 9½-mile branch line from Ulverston, on the main line between Carnforth and Barrow-in-Furness, to Lakeside, at the southern tip of Lake Windermere, was opened in 1869 by the Furness Railway. It was connected to the main line by a triangular junction at Plumpton to the east of Ulverston. At Lakeside, trains connected directly with steamers that plied up and down Lake Windermere – the FR bought this company in 1875. The stations at each end of the line were magnificent affairs – a grand Italianate building had been opened at Ulverston in 1872 while the pier station at Lakeside was fitted out in an opulent style complete with a Palm Court restaurant and orchestra.

The branch remained popular with tourists until the Second World War but a rapid decline in passenger numbers had set in by the 1950s. Despite this, the branch was still served by through trains and carriages to and from Morecambe, Blackpool, Preston and Barrow during the summer months until the early 1960s. Listed for closure in the 'Beeching Report', the line closed to passengers on 5 September 1965. Goods traffic continued to serve ironworks at Haverthwaite until 24 April 1967 when the line closed completely. The 3½ miles from Haverthwaite to Lakeside was reopened as a heritage railway by the Lakeside & Haverthwaite Railway in 1979.

A far cry from heading the 'Condor'! Banished to Barrow, the unique Metro-Vick Co-Bo Type 2 diesels eked out their last years on menial duties in the Furness region. Here, D5708 prepares to leave Lakeside station with a train for Barrow on 22 August 1964.

CLOSED
SEPTEMBER
27
1965

Blackrod/Lostock Junction to Horwich

The 1¼-mile double-track branch line from Blackrod Junction and Horwich Fork Junction (both on the main line between Bolton and Chorley) to Horwich was opened by the Lancashire & Yorkshire Railway in 1868. It was at Horwich that the L&YR established its locomotive works in 1887 – by 1904 the town's population had risen from 4,000 to 16,000, of which around 10,000 were employed in the works.

With its north- and south-facing junctions the branch was served by trains from Chorley via Blackrod and from Bolton and Manchester Victoria via Lostock Junction and Horwich Fork Junction. Both services were run for the benefit of employees at Horwich Works and ran in the early morning and late afternoon.

Listed for closure in the 'Beeching Report', the branch line lost its passenger service on 27 September 1965. The final two-coach service was worked on Saturday 25 September by 2-6-4T No. 42626 carrying a wreath and commemorative headboard. Goods trains ceased in 1966 although the line stayed open to Horwich Works until its own closure in 1983.

Complete with wreath, Bolton's well-groomed Stanier Class '4' 2-6-4T No. 42626 heads the last train from Horwich – the 12.05 (SO) to Bolton – at Lostock Junction on 25 September 1965.

'The Last Train from Barlick' is about to leave Barnoldswick station behind BR Standard Class '2' 2-6-2T No. 84015 on a very dull-looking 25 September 1965.

CLOSED SEPTEMBER 27 1965

Earby to Barnoldswick

The 1¾-mile branch line from Earby (on the Blackburn to Skipton line, see Colne to Skipton) to Barnoldswick was opened by the Barnoldswick Railway in 1871. It was worked by the Midland Railway from the outset and absorbed by that company in 1899. Passenger traffic was never heavy and by 1962 consisted of just two trains to Earby and Skipton on weekdays and only one (plus one extra on Saturdays) in the other direction. Listed for closure in the 'Beeching Report', the minimal passenger service (mainly used by school children) ceased on 27 September 1965. The last train on Saturday 25 September was hauled by BR Standard Class '2' 2-6-2T No. 84015. Coal traffic continued to use the branch until 30 July 1966.

CLOSED NOVEMBER X 1965

Rose Grove to Todmorden

The 10¼-mile railway between Todmorden and Rose Grove was opened as far as Burnley by the Lancashire & Yorkshire Railway in 1849 and later extended to Rose Grove where it met the East Lancashire Railway. Built through difficult terrain over Copy Pit Summit (749 feet above sea level), the line also featured three tunnels, at Kitson Wood, Holme and Towneley. The long climb up to Copy Pit involved the banking of heavy coal trains until the very end of steam in 1968 when Rose Grove engine shed became one of the last steam sheds to close on British Railways. While the intermediate stations of Cornholme, Portsmouth, Towneley and Burnley (Manchester Road) had all closed by 1961 the line still saw passenger services between Todmorden and Preston via Accrington and Blackburn until it was listed for closure in the 'Beeching Report'. Closure to passenger traffic came in November 1965 although the line remained open for freight traffic. In later years an empty DMU ran on a Saturday to ensure all was well with the signalling on the Calder Valley line which was then controlled from Preston.

Passenger services were reinstated in 1986 with the help of a subsidy from the Halifax Building Society. The route is currently used by trains running between Blackpool (North) and York, and the planned reinstatement of the south-west spur at Todmorden will once more allow trains to run between Manchester and Burnley.

An enthusiasts' special, double-headed by BR Standard Class '5MT' 4-6-0s Nos 73050 (now preserved) and 73069, crosses Cornholm Viaduct on the climb from Milner Royd Junction at Todmorden to the summit of the line at Copy Pit. The date was 27 April 1968, just over three months before the eradication of standard gauge steam on BR.

Yet another victim of BR's ill-conceived railway closures – the sad remains of Pocklington station in 1974. Closed on 29 November 1965, the York to Beverley line via Market Weighton was being modernised but this all came to an abrupt halt in 1962.

The Stephenson Locomotive Society's 'Whitby Moors Rail Tour' storms past Market Weighton East signal box behind preserved Class 'K4' 2-6-0 No. 61994 'The Great Marquess' and Class 'K1' 2-6-0 No. 62005 on 6 March 1965, heading for Scarborough and Whitby via Driffield and Bridlington.

CLOSED
NOVEMBER
29
1965

York (Bootham Junction) to Beverley via Market Weighton

The 32-mile cross-country double-track railway from Bootham Junction, on the Scarborough line north of York, to Market Weighton was built in two stages. York to Market Weighton was opened by George Hudson's York & North Midland Railway in 1847 – before his downfall Hudson had his own private station at Londesborough. The single-track section from Market Weighton to Beverley was opened by the Y&NMR's successor, the North Eastern Railway in 1865. Intermediate passenger traffic along the whole route was never heavy while goods traffic consisted of agricultural produce and livestock.

While the Driffield to Selby line was slowly dying, the York to Hull route with its nine return trains each weekday saw some progress towards modernisation with the introduction of diesel multiple units in 1959. A programme of rationalisation was started in 1961 but centralised traffic control with fewer signal boxes, singling of the line and installing automatic lifting barrier level crossings all came to an abrupt halt early in 1962. The route was listed for closure in the 'Beeching Report' with the argument given that most passengers who used the line were travelling between York and Hull and this could still be achieved via the more southerly route through Selby. The line closed completely on 29 November 1965.

Today, most of the station buildings still survive and 11 miles of the trackbed between Market Weighton and Beverley has been reopened as a footpath and cycleway known, appropriately, as Hudson's Way.

CLOSED
JUNE
14
1965

Selby to Driffield via Market Weighton

The 31¼-mile single-track railway from Driffield to Selby was built in two stages. Selby to Market Weighton was opened by the York & North Midland Railway in 1848. Market Weighton to Driffield was opened by the Scarborough, Bridlington & West Riding Junction Railway in 1885. The majority of trains along this route started or ended their journeys at Bridlington with some continuing beyond Selby to Leeds. Steam railmotors were also used for some years in the 1930s by the London & North Eastern Railway. Intermediate traffic was never heavy but the route was heavily used by through excursion trains from Yorkshire to Bridlington.

Apart from Market Weighton, all intermediate stations were closed on 20 September 1954 and the entire route was listed for complete closure in the 'Beeching Report'. However, the die had been cast several years before as the summer 1961 timetable shows only two trains each day (one in the morning and one in the evening) between Bridlington and Selby (one continued to Leeds) with extra excursion trains running between West Yorkshire and Bridlington and Filey on Saturdays. The inevitable closure came on 15 June 1964.

Today, while most of the station buildings still survive, the 13-mile section from Bubwith, east of Selby, to Market Weighton is a footpath and cycleway known as the Bubwith Rail Trail. Beyond here the station at Enthorpe has remained remarkably intact since closure while Driffield station is still served by trains operating between Hull and Bridlington.

Lancaster (Green Ayre) to Wennington

The 10½-mile railway between Lancaster (Green Ayre) and Wennington was opened by the North Western Railway in 1849, and extended eastwards to Bentham and Clapham in 1850. At Clapham the line joined the NWR's ill-fated 'main line' from Skipton to Ingleton. Westwards from Lancaster, the company had already absorbed the Morecambe Harbour & Railway (see Lancaster [Green Ayr] to Morecambe) in 1846 and was itself leased by the Midland Railway in 1859. It was taken over by the MR in 1871. Wennington was linked with Carnforth and the Furness Railway system when the Furness & Midland Joint Railway opened in 1867. Although there was little traffic from the three intermediate stations at Halton, Caton and Hornby, the railway between Lancaster and Wennington was kept busy with through passenger and goods trains to and from Heysham Harbour and Morecambe from more far-flung parts of the MR system; until the early 1960s there was a regular service of trains to and from Leeds (City) and Bradford (Forster) Square.

Listed for closure in the 'Beeching Report', the railway between Lancaster and Wennington lost its passenger service on 3 January 1966 and from that date trains between Morecambe and Leeds/Bradford were routed over the former F&MJR line and via Carnforth. Goods trains continued until 8 January 1968 when the line closed completely. Today, four miles of the trackbed between Lancaster and Caton is a footpath and cycleway.

Lancaster (Green Ayre) to Morecambe

Linking Morecambe and Lancaster, the 3½-mile Morecambe Harbour & Railway opened in 1848 by which time it had been amalgamated with the North West Railway – the latter was leased by the Midland Railway in 1859 and taken over by it in 1871. A branch line from Morecambe to the new harbour at Heysham had been opened by the MR in 1904. Not only forming part of the route for through trains between Leeds/Bradford and Morecambe, the Lancaster (Green Ayre) to Morecambe and Heysham line was electrified by the MR in 1908. Unusually for the time, the line used overhead equipment with the original trains remaining in service until 1951. This pioneering line was then converted from 25-cycle, 6,600 volts AC to 50-cycle, 6,600 volts AC and reopened in 1953. Following further modifications in 1955/56, the railway became a test bed for the standard 25kV, 50Hz system soon to be introduced by BR.

Listed for closure in the 'Beeching Report', the line between Lancaster (Green Ayre) and Morecambe was closed on 3 January 1966 – carrying a commemorative headboard and wreath, the last train to run was the 11.10pm from Morecambe Promenade to Lancaster. Meanwhile, Morecambe (still served by trains from Carnforth) to Heysham trains continued to run until 4 October 1975 when that line also closed to passengers – it reopened to connect with ferries to the Isle of Man in 1987. Today, Morecambe Promenade station stands in all its restored glory while the trackbed between Morecambe and Lancaster is now a footpath and cycleway.

Fitted with a Stanier flat-sided tender, unrebuilt 'Patriot' Class 4-6-0 No. 45505 'The Royal Ordnance Corps' leaves Wennington on the Lancaster (Green Ayre) line with a Leeds to Morecambe stopping train in April 1962.

A Lancaster to Morecambe electric multiple unit crosses the River Lune just outside Lancaster (Green Ayre) station on 9 October 1965. The bridge now has a road running across it. Progress indeed!

The RCTS 'Solway Ranger Rail Tour' passes pretty Bassenthwaite Lake station en route from Workington to Penrith on 13 June 1964. The train is double-headed by Ivatt Class '2MT' 2-6-0s Nos 46426 and 46458. Note the camping coaches on the right.

CLOSED
APRIL
18
1966

Keswick to Workington

The 21½-mile line between Keswick and Workington started life as two separate railways. First to open was the Cockermouth & Workington Railway which opened in 1847 while, from the east, the Cockermouth, Keswick & Penrith Railway opened in 1865. The former company was absorbed by the London & North Western Railway in 1866 – the LNWR also worked the CK&PR from its opening. The only railway to cross the Lake District from east to west, this steeply graded route was also heavily used by mineral trains from northeast England to steel works at Workington until the 1920s. Served by through carriages from Euston, Manchester and Newcastle, tourist traffic to Keswick during the summer months

was particularly heavy and remained so until the 1950s. By then, with increased competition from road transport, both passenger and goods traffic were in decline and the entire 39¾-mile route from Penrith to Workington was listed for closure in the 'Beeching Report'. While the eastern section from Penrith to Keswick was reprieved until 1972 (see Penrith to Keswick), the western section from Keswick to Workington closed completely on 18 April 1966. Following closure, most of the trackbed of the railway westwards from Keswick and alongside Bassenthwaite Lake to Cockermouth disappeared beneath the new A66 trunk road.

Clifton Junction to Bury (Bolton Street) and Rawtenstall to Bacup

The Manchester, Bury & Rossendale Railway was incorporated in 1844 to build a railway from Clifton Junction, on the Bolton line north of Manchester, to Bury and Rawtenstall. By the time it opened in 1846 the company had changed its name to the East Lancashire Railway. Serving the important cotton spinning and weaving mills of the Rossendale valley, the ELR extended the line to Newchurch in 1848. A further extension to the town of Bacup (12¼ miles from Bury and 800 feet above sea level) was opened in 1852. Serving woollen mills and collieries, this final section of the line involved gradients as steep as 1-in-65 and the construction of two tunnels. The railway was absorbed by the Lancashire & Yorkshire Railway in 1859.

Bacup station was also served by another steeply-graded line which was opened over a 967-foot summit by the L&YR from Rochdale in 1881. This lost its passenger service in 1947 although stone traffic continued for some years after. Although an increased frequency of new diesel multiple units was introduced to the Bury to Bacup service as early as 1956, the route, along with the line to Accrington (see Stubbins

A Class 112 DMU about to leave Bacup station with a train for Manchester Victoria on the last day of services east of Rawtenstall, 3 December 1966.

Junction to Accrington), was listed for closure in the 'Beeching Report'. While the section from Bury to Rawtenstall was reprieved until 1972 (see Bury [Bolton Street] to Rawenstall), the steeply graded four miles east from Rawtenstall to Bacup closed completely on 5 December 1966. The line from Clifton Junction (north of Manchester Victoria) to Bury closed on the same day.

Stubbins Junction to Accrington

The 7¼-mile line between Stubbins Junction (on the Bury to Bacup railway) and Accrington was opened by the East Lancashire Railway in 1848. With gradients as steep as 1-in-38 and a summit of 771 feet above sea level near Baxenden the line was difficult to work, with double-heading of goods and excursion trains being the norm. The ELR was absorbed by the Lancashire & Yorkshire Railway in 1859.

Served by trains from Manchester Victoria via Clifton Junction and Bury, the line saw an improved frequency service and new diesel multiple units in 1956. The intermediate stations of Baxenden and Haslingden closed in 1951 and 1960 respectively although Helmshore station remained open until closure of the line. With passenger numbers on the decline, the line was

listed for closure in the 'Beeching Report'.

Complete closure came on 5 December 1966 – the last train which ran on Saturday 3 December carried the Helmshore Brass Band who played a selection of tunes including the nineteenth-century 'The Railway Excursion Train Gallop'. Following closure a railway museum was operated at Helmshore station but this was later transferred to Bury where it remains today.

Haslingden station was near the summit of the steeply graded line between Stubbins Junction and Accrington. It was photographed from a southbound train by Henry Casserley on 23 April 1954.

CLOSED
MARCH
6
1967

Northallerton to Harrogate

In its latter years an important north-south route used by Pullman trains, the 25¼-mile railway between Harrogate and Northallerton via Ripon was opened in two stages. The first railway on the scene was the Leeds & Thirsk Railway which opened throughout from Leeds to Harrogate, Ripon and Thirsk in 1849. Two years later the company changed its name to the Leeds Northern Railway and, in 1852, opened a single-track railway from Melmerby, on the Ripon to Thirsk line, to Northallerton where it met the York, Newcastle & Berwick Railway. In 1854 the LNR, YN&BR and the York & North Midland Railway became the constituent companies of the newly formed North Eastern Railway.

Until 1901 most through trains from Leeds, and beyond, to the northeast were routed via Harrogate, Ripon and Thirsk but the doubling of the Melmerby to Northallerton route in that year saw these trains taking this shorter route. These included Liverpool to Newcastle restaurant car expresses and Pullman car expresses which ran between King's Cross and Newcastle via Leeds, Harrogate

English Electric Type 4 diesel D278 crosses the viaduct over the River Ure at Ripon with a Liverpool (Lime Street) to Newcastle express in December 1966. Note the interesting selection of road vehicles bottom left.

and Ripon. From 1928 the latter train was named the 'Queen of Scots' and extended to Edinburgh and Glasgow (Queen Street). Although withdrawn during the Second World War, this famous train was reinstated in the late 1940s and continued to operate until 1964. By then passenger numbers north of Harrogate were in serious decline – the Melmerby to Thirsk line had closed completely in 1959 and all intermediate stations except Ripon and Melmerby had gone the same way – and the line was listed for closure in the 'Beeching Report'.

The end came for passenger services on 6 March 1967 with the

last Liverpool to Manchester express headed by D1998 on Saturday 4 March. Following closure on 6 March the line was temporarily reopened for a couple of days following an accident on the East Coast Main Line at the end of July but thereafter it was closed completely north of Melmerby. Goods traffic continued to serve an MoD depot at Melmerby until 1968 and to Ripon until 1969. The grand station building at Ripon has since been restored as private residences.

A Class 101 DMU heads north through Melmerby with a Harrogate to Northallerton train on 3 April 1965. The trackbed of the Marham branch line can be seen on the left.

Alnmouth to Alnwick

The three-mile branch line from Alnmouth, on the Newcastle to Berwick main line, to the historic market town of Alnwick was opened by the Newcastle & Berwick Railway in 1850, and in 1854 the N&BR became part of the new North Eastern Railway. Replacing the original station which was inconveniently situated on the town's outskirts, the NER opened a new overall-roofed terminus near the town centre on 5 September 1887. On the same day the 35½-mile railway to Coldstream was opened; serving only scattered farming communities in a sparsely populated region this line lost its passenger service as early as 1930.

The Alnwick branch was served by a regular shuttle service from the East Coast Main Line at Alnmouth with some trains remaining steam-hauled until 1966. BR Standard Class '9F' 2-10-0 No. 92099 had the honour of hauling the last steam-hauled train on 18 June that year. Surprisingly, the branch was not listed for closure in the 'Beeching Report' but, after economy measures such as singling the line and in spite of much local opposition, passenger services ceased on 30 January 1968. Goods trains continued to run until October 1969.

Today, the impressive station building (home to a secondhand book shop) at Alnwick and its overall roof survives, while the Aln Valley Railway also aims to reopen part of the line to Alnmouth as a heritage railway in the future.

BR Standard Class '9F' 2-10-0 No. 92099 operated the last day of steam services on the Alnwick branch on 18 June 1966. With a smartened-up front end, the loco is seen here from under Alnwick's fine overall-roofed station.

Eryholme to Richmond

The 9¾-mile double-track branch line from Eryholme Junction, on the East Coast Main Line south of Darlington, along Swaledale to the historic market town of Richmond was opened by the Great North of England Railway in 1846. It was leased from opening by York & Newcastle Railway, becoming part of the North Eastern Railway in 1854.

From 1911, the line was used by the NER to test a new electrically operated fog signalling system. A four-mile branch line was opened from Catterick Bridge, the final station before Richmond, to Catterick Army Camp in 1915. It closed on 26 October 1964. Eryholme Junction was closed in 1911, with all trains starting or ending their journey at Darlington. Diesel multiple units were introduced in the late 1950s and by 1961 the branch had a service of 12 return trains each weekday with two or three extra late on Saturday evenings for army personnel. A 12.30am departure from Darlington on Monday mornings was also laid on for soldiers returning after leave to Catterick Camp.

This scenic line was listed for closure in the 'Beeching Report', goods traffic withdrawn on 2 October 1967 and, following two temporary reprieves, passenger services on 3 March 1969. The line remained open for military traffic to Catterick Bridge until 1970 when the track was lifted. Today, the attractive Grade II stone terminus at Richmond has been sympathetically restored and is used for a range of commercial and community activities.

A photograph full of wonderful detail, taken when our mail was still carried by train: a Class 101 DMU waits under the overall roof of Richmond station with a train for Darlington in September 1967. Of course the railway was swept away but fortunately the station building still survives.

Class 77 electric loco No. 27002 passes Torside with a Manchester Piccadilly to Sheffield Victoria express on 18 April 1964.

Gavin Morrison's photograph of the western portal of Woodhead Tunnel was taken from the driving cab of Class 76 electric loco No. 26053 on 24 August 1968. The nineteenth-century single-bore tunnels can be seen on the left.

CLOSED
JANUARY
5
1970

Sheffield to Manchester via Woodhead

Building the 41½-mile Manchester to Sheffield railway up Longdendale and across the Pennines was a major feat for Victorian engineers and cost the lives of many men before it was completed. Opened in 1845 by the Sheffield, Ashton-under-Lyne & Manchester Railway, the railway included several viaducts and the three-mile single bore Woodhead Tunnel, then the longest railway tunnel in Britain. Linking two major industrial centres, the line was an immediate success and a second single-bore tunnel at Woodhead was opened in 1852. In the meantime the SA&MR merged with two other companies to form the Manchester, Sheffield & Lincolnshire Railway. Although carrying coal

Class 76 electric loco No. 26049 passes Torside with a van train for Manchester on 16 October 1969.

from the South Yorkshire coalfield to the industries of Manchester and Liverpool was the lifeblood of the line, passenger services were not forgotten and by 1899 through express passenger trains were using the route to and from the new London Extension to Marylebone, while in 1897 the MS&LR had changed its name to the Great Central Railway.

The Woodhead route became part of the newly-formed LNER in 1923 and the company soon looked at ways of modernising it by introducing overhead electrification and constructing a new double-track tunnel at Woodhead. Although work started on this massive project in 1936, progress was delayed by the Second World War and the project was not completed until 1954. By then the 1.5kV DC system was already out-of-date and the route remained a technological anachronism until its closure. This built-in obsolescence coupled with the decline in Britain's coal industry soon put a question mark on the line's future viability.

Despite this the line was not listed for closure in the 'Beeching Report' while the more southerly route from Manchester to Sheffield via the Hope Valley was threatened instead. In the end the rapid decline in coal traffic and the high cost of modernising the route brought about the Woodhead route's demise. Apart from the Penistone to Sheffield section which was used by Huddersfield trains until 1983, and the suburban service from Manchester to Hadfield, all passenger services ceased on 5 January 1970. Westbound coal traffic and eastbound empties continued until 17 July 1981 when the line closed completely. Today, the 6½ miles of trackbed between Hadfield and the western end of Woodhead Tunnel is a footpath and cycleway known as the Longdendale Trail.

Class 'K4' 2-6-0 No. 3442 'The Great Marquess' on its first outing in preservation heads the RCTS 'The Dalesman' Rail Tour past Earby heading for Barnoldswick on 4 May 1963.

CLOSED
FEBRUARY
2
1970

Colne to Skipton

The 17¼-mile line from Burnley to Skipton was built by two different companies. First to reach the mill town of Colne was the Leeds & Bradford Extension Railway which opened from Skipton in 1848. By that date the line had been leased to the Midland Railway which then absorbed it in 1851. In 1849 the station at Colne became an end-on junction with the East Lancashire Railway's Blackburn, Burnley, Accrington & Colne Extension – the ELR was absorbed by the Lancashire & Yorkshire Railway in 1859. Colne soon found itself in the unusual situation of being served by through trains from Liverpool and Manchester from the south and by through carriages from Leeds and, in later years, London, from the north via Skipton. For many years passengers travelling between Burnley and Skipton were forced to change trains at Colne.

Apart from the short branch line from Earby to Barnoldswick (see Earby to Barnoldswick), the Burnley to Skipton line was not listed for closure in the 'Beeching Report'. The 1962 timetable shows a healthy service of trains, many of them originating or ending their journeys at Manchester Victoria, but in reality passenger numbers were declining. Eventually the downward spiral of fewer customers and a reduced train service brought the inevitable and the line closed between Colne and Skipton on 2 February 1970. Now at the end of a single-track branch line from Burnley, Colne is still served by Northern Rail trains to and from Preston and Blackpool South.

CLOSED
JUNE
1
1970

Poulton-le-Fylde to Fleetwood

The 6¼-mile branch line across reclaimed land from Poulton-le-Fylde to Fleetwood was opened from Preston by the Preston & Wyre Railway, Harbour & Dock Company in 1840. The coming of the railway transformed what was once a small village into a busy harbour town and resort. Railway-owned steamer services to Ulverston, the Isle of Man and Ireland were introduced from Fleetwood even before the railway had opened. In 1870 the railway and steamers were taken over by a joint committee made up of the London & North Western Railway and the Lancashire & Yorkshire Railway.

Trains to Fleetwood could run either from Blackpool North or Preston via a three-way junction at Poulton and the line was kept busy not only with passengers destined for the steamer services but also with the transportation of large amounts of locally caught fish. However, by 1961 Fleetwood had lost all of its steamer services to nearby Heysham Harbour and the docks went into decline. While the 'Beeching Report' recommended closure of the Poulton to Blackpool North line, that from Preston to Fleetwood was not threatened. Despite this, the line was cut back ¾ mile to Wyre Dock in 1966 and closed to passengers on 1 June 1970. The Blackpool North line survived and freight services continued to an ICI plant at Burn Naze until 1999. The junction at Poulton still survives, as does around 1½ miles of overgrown track, and there are now proposals to reopen the branch to Fleetwood.

You can almost smell the Irish Sea – Fleetwood terminus on 19 August 1959 with BR Standard Class '4' 2-6-4T No. 80046 waiting to leave with a train for Preston.

Bolton (Trinity Street) to Bury (Knowsley Street) and Heywood North Junction

The 5¾-mile line from Bolton (Trinity Street) to Bury (Knowsley Street) was opened as part of the Liverpool and Bury Railway in 1848. Before it had opened it was absorbed by the Manchester & Leeds Railway which in turn became part of the Lancashire & Yorkshire Railway. Serving numerous collieries, the line featured an 86ft-high eight-span viaduct across the River Tonge at Darcy Lever. From the east, the M&LR had opened a branch line to Heywood from a junction with its main line south of Castleton in 1841. This was extended to Bury by the L&YR in 1848. The 10½-mile line between Bolton and Heywood

North Junction was now open and became an important route for L&YR traffic from Liverpool to Rochdale and eastwards over the Pennines via the Calder Valley.

Up to the early 1960s the passenger service consisted of fairly frequent trains running between Bolton and Rochdale with many originating or ending their journeys at Liverpool Exchange, Southport, Blackpool, Preston, and Wigan. On Sundays in 1962 a late night non-stop service from Bolton to Rochdale carried through carriages from Liverpool to York while on Saturday afternoons there was a through train from Scarborough (Londesborough Road) to Liverpool.

Following the 'Beeching

Report', Bury eventually lost all of its passenger services except the reprieved electric trains from Manchester and the line from Bolton to Rochdale. Despite it not being listed for closure, the latter route saw its last passenger train on 5 October 1970 although it continued to be used by coal trains from Heywood Junction to Rawtenstall via Bury until December 1980. However, the north and south junctions at Heywood remained in place to serve the track depot at Castleton. With this physical link to the national rail network remaining in place, the section from Heywood to Bury was reopened as a heritage railway by the East Lancashire Railway in 2003.

Down and out in Bury Knowsley Street station after closure.

CLOSED

MARCH

6

1972

Penrith to Keswick

Strongly opposed by John Ruskin, Alfred Lord Tennyson and Robert Browning, the 18¼-mile line between Penrith and Keswick was opened by the Cockermouth, Keswick & Penrith Railway in 1865. Passenger trains were worked from the outset by the London & North Western Railway. The only railway to cross the Lake District from east to west, this steeply-graded route was also used by mineral trains from northeast England via the Stainmore route to steel works at Workington until the 1920s. Served by through carriages from Euston, Manchester and Newcastle, tourist traffic to Keswick during the summer months was particularly heavy and remained so until the 1950s. Diesel multiple units were introduced for local services in 1955 but steam still clung on until 1962 hauling the summer through trains.

By then, with increased competition from road transport, both passenger and goods traffic were in decline and the entire 39¾-mile route from Penrith to Workington was listed for closure in the 'Beeching Report'. Through goods trains ceased to run on 1 June 1964 and the western section from Keswick to Workington closed completely on 18 April 1966. The Penrith to Keswick section was temporarily reprieved but despite much local opposition to closure the outlook was not good – through trains ceased to run, stations became unstaffed and Keswick was served by diesel multiple units shuttling to and from Penrith. The end came on 6 March 1972 when the line closed completely.

Since closure the station building at Keswick has been restored as part of an adjoining hotel while four miles of the trackbed and numerous bridges now form the four-mile Keswick Railway Path to Threlkeld.

Lengthened to two three-car DMU sets to cope with the demand, the 2.15pm Penrith to Keswick train leaves Threlkeld on the last day of service on this scenic line, 4 March 1972.

Class 25 diesel No. 25027 with the daily coal train at Rawtenstall on 20 July 1976.

CLOSED

JUNE

3

1972

Bury (Bolton Street) to Rawtenstall

The 8¼-mile line from Bury (Bolton Street) to Rawtenstall was opened by the East Lancashire Railway in 1846. Serving the important cotton spinning and weaving mills of the Rossendale valley, the ELR extended the line to Newchurch in 1848. A further extension to the town of Bacup (see Clifton Junction to Bury [Bolton Street] and Rawstall to Bacup) was opened in 1852. The railway was absorbed by the Lancashire & Yorkshire Railway in 1859.

Although an increased frequency of new diesel multiple units was introduced to the Bury to Bacup service as early as 1956, the route, along with the line to Accrington, was listed for closure in the 'Beeching Report'. While the section from Bury to Rawtenstall was reprieved until 1972, the steeply graded four miles of line east from Rawtenstall to Bacup closed completely on 5 December 1966. Now at the end of a branch line, Rawtenstall continued to be served by a diesel multiple unit service from Bury until 3 June 1972 when the line closed to passengers. Coal trains continued to serve Rawtenstall until 1980.

Following complete closure a preservation group started running trains from Bury to Ramsbottom in 1987. Known as the East Lancashire Railway, the mainly steam-hauled line reopened to Rawtenstall in 1991 and was extended eastwards from Bury to Heywood in 2003.

CLOSED MAY 3 1976

Haltwhistle to Alston

Built to serve lead mines in the South Tyne Valley, the 13-mile branch line from Haltwhistle, on the Newcastle to Carlisle main line, to the market town of Alston was opened by the Newcastle & Carlisle Railway in 1852. The NCR was absorbed by the North Eastern Railway in 1862. Featuring several spectacular viaducts the branch was linked to the coal-carrying Brampton Railway at Lambley; originally opened in 1775 as a horse-drawn wagonway, this 10-mile line was taken over by the National Coal Board in 1947 and closed in 1953.

In an effort to reduce operating costs, diesel multiple units were introduced in 1959, stations became unstaffed and goods trains ceased in the early 1960s. By then the line saw around seven return services each way, connecting with Newcastle to Carlisle trains at Haltwhistle. Although listed for closure in the 'Beeching Report', the Alston branch kept operating for many more years as roads to the town were not suitable for replacement bus services. Inevitably the roads were eventually improved and the line closed for good on 3 May 1976 – one of the last of the lines to be killed off by the 'Beeching Axe'. Efforts by a preservation group to reopen the branch as a heritage railway were thwarted by British Railways which lifted the track in indecent haste.

Since then, 2¼ miles of the line between Alston and Kirkhaugh has been reopened as a 2ft gauge steam railway by the South Tynedale Railway. An extension to Slaggyford is being considered.

With just over two months to go before closure of this branch line a Class 101 DMU approaches Clayton West station with a train from Huddersfield on 14 November 1982.

CLOSED JANUARY 24 1983

Shepley Junction to Clayton West

A curious survivor of the 'Beeching Axe', the four-mile branch line from Shepley, on the Huddersfield to Penistone line, to Clayton West was opened by the Lancashire & Yorkshire Railway in 1879. Although built as a single-track railway, all bridges and the 511-yard Shelley Woodhouse Tunnel were designed to accommodate double track. The branch was served by through trains to and from Huddersfield with diesel multiple units being introduced in 1959. In 1961, six return trains on weekdays plus a late night service on Saturdays sufficed to serve the few customers making use of the line. Needless to say this loss-making branch line along with the Huddersfield to Penistone service were both listed for closure in the 'Beeching Report' but, despite poor patronage, it survived another 20 years before closure on 24 January 1983. The Huddersfield to Penistone (for Barnsley) line was reprieved and is open today.

The Clayton West branch line came back to life in 1991 when the 15in gauge miniature Kirklees Light Railway was opened along the trackbed from the terminus to Cuckoo's Nest. It was extended to Skelmanthorpe in 1992 and through Shelley Woodhouse Tunnel in 1997.

A two-car Gloucester R C & W Co/Metro-Cammell DMU calls at Lambley station with the 5.40pm Haltwhistle to Alston train on 27 June 1968.

SCOTLAND

F

G

INVERNESS

2

36

34

23

8

12

35

24

11

19

ABERDEEN

26

27

13

31

18

DUNDEE

9

17

43

5

40

41

38

42

16

33

32

25

44

GLASGOW

30

29

E

1

B

28

D

EDINBURGH

27

C

4

21

37

20

39

10

3

A

7

15

39

14

6

CARLISLE

THE CASUALTIES

1. Lugton to Beith Town – 5 November 1962
2. Elgin to Lossiemouth – 6 April 1964
3. Ayr to Dalmellington – 6 April 1964
4. Hurlford to Darvel – 6 April 1964
5. Kinross to Alloa – 15 June 1964
6. Riddings Junction to Langholm – 15 June 1964
7. St Boswells to Tweedmouth via Kelso – 15 June 1964
8. Tillynaught to Banff – 6 July 1964
9. Gleneagles to Comrie – 6 July 1964
10. Lanark to Muirkirk – 5 October 1964
11. Maud Junction to Peterhead – 3 May 1965
12. Fraserburgh to St Combs – 3 May 1965
13. Ballinluig to Aberfeldy – 3 May 1965
14. Castle Douglas to Kirkcudbright – 3 May 1965
15. Dumfries to Challoch Junction via Castle Douglas – 14 June 1965
16. St Andrews to Leven – 6 September 1965
17. Dunblane to Crianlarich (Lower) – 27 September 1965
18. Killin Junction to Killin – 27 September 1965
19. Dyce to Fraserburgh – 4 October 1965
20. Haughead Junction (Hamilton) to Coalburn – 4 October 1965 (since reopened Hamilton to Larkhall)
21. Strathaven to Stonehouse – 4 October 1965
22. Crosshouse to Irvine – 11 October 1965
23. Aviemore to Forres – 18 October 1965
24. Craigellachie to Boat of Garten – 18 October 1965
25. Kilmacolm to Greenock (Princes Pier) – 30 November 1965
26. Aberdeen to Ballater – 28 February 1966
27. Connel Ferry to Ballachulish – 28 March 1966
28. Dalry to Kilmarnock – 18 April 1966*
29. Lochwinnoch Loop (Elderslie to Dalry via Lochwinnoch) – 27 June 1966
30. Arkleston Junction to Renfrew Wharf – 5 June 1967
31. Kinnaber Junction to Stanley Junction via Forfar – 4 September 1967
32. Falkirk (Grahamstown) to Grangemouth – 29 January 1968*
33. Larbert (Alloa Junction) to Alloa – 29 January 1968*
34. Craigellachie to Elgin – 6 May 1968
35. Craigellachie to Keith – 6 May 1968
36. Elgin to Cairnie Junction via Cullen – 6 May 1968
37. Ayr to Heads of Ayr – 16 September 1968*
38. Dunfermline Upper to Stirling – 7 October 1968*
39. Edinburgh to Carlisle (Waverley Route) – 6 January 1969
40. Leuchars Junction to St Andrews – 6 January 1969*
41. Wormit to Newport-on-Tay – 5 May 1969*
42. Thornton Junction to Leven – 6 October 1969*
43. Bridge of Earn to Cowdenbeath via Kinross – 5 January 1970*
44. Shields Junction to Kilmacolm –10 January 1983

Note: Dates given are for withdrawal of passenger services
* = not listed for closure in the 'Beeching Report'

THE SURVIVORS

A. Ayr to Stranraer
B. Glasgow to Kilmarnock via Barrhead
C. Kilmarnock to Barassie Junction
D. Pollokshaws West to East Kilbride
E. Glasgow to Midcalder Junction via Shotts
F. Inverness to Wick/Thurso
G. Inverness to Kyle of Lochalsh

Closed on 14 June 1965, the Dumfries to Challoch Junction line across the wilds of Galloway was the first major Beeching casualty in Scotland. Here, in happier days, the summer (SO) Newcastle to Stranraer express, double-headed by Stanier 'Black 5' 4-6-0s Nos 44789 and 45498, enters Newton Stewart on 1 July 1961.

Branching off from the Ardrossan to Largs railway, the short extension to Fairlie Pier station was opened by the Glasgow & South Western Railway in 1882. The railway pier, seen here on 11 September 1971, served ferries to Great Cumbrae and the Isle of Bute until 1 October 1971 when the last train ran, although the branch officially closed on 31 July 1972.

The closure of the Waverley route between Edinburgh and Carlisle on 6 January 1969 left vast swathes of the Borders region without any rail connections to the outside world. The last train to run over the route, the sleeper train from Edinburgh to London St Pancras, was held up by this protest at Newcastleton – on the right is MP David Steel who happened to be a passenger on the train and who later tried to calm protesters' tempers. Taken by photographer John Goss, the photo also features three characters in the foreground, from left to right: John Hunt (blowing a shunter's horn), Alan Cattle (waving a shunter's horn) and the late Paul Riley (throwing his arms wide).

Ex-LMS 0-4-4T No. 55264 waits to depart from Beith Town station with a train for Lugton on 10 September 1955.

The grand station at Lossiemouth on 25 April 1952. Ex-GNoSR Class 'D41' 4-4-0 No. 62231 waits to depart with the 8.45am train to Elgin.

CLOSED
NOVEMBER
5
1962

Lugton to Beith Town

The five-mile branch line from Lugton, on the Caledonian Railway/Glasgow & South Western Railway Joint line from Glasgow to Kilmarnock, to Beith was opened by the Glasgow, Barrhead & Kilmarnock Railway in 1873. The company was jointly taken over by the Caledonian Railway and Glasgow & South Western Railway in 1880. Although listed for closure in the 'Beeching Report', the branch line closed to passengers on 5 November 1962, nearly five months before its publication. Goods services continued to serve Beith Town until 5 October 1964 when the line was cut back to Barrmill to serve a large MoD munitions centre reached via a short connection to the former Lanarkshire & Ayrshire Railway line near Giffen. Although the last trains ran to the depot in 1996 the overgrown track is still in situ.

CLOSED
APRIL
6
1964

Elgin to Lossiemouth

The 5½-mile branch line from Elgin to the port of Lossiemouth was opened by the Morayshire Railway in 1852. Built in Glasgow, the two diminutive locomotives for the line were delivered by boat to Lossiemouth. The company also built a short-lived railway from Rothes, on its line from Elgin to Craigellachie (opened throughout in 1863, see Craigellachie to Elgin), to Orton, on the Inverness & Aberdeen Junction Railway's main line from Elgin to Keith. It opened in 1858 and was closed by 1866, although the track was not lifted until 1907. The Morayshire Railway was amalgamated with the Great North of Scotland Railway in 1880 by which time the branch was busy with herring traffic and daytrippers. Lossiemouth was also the destination of one of the longest through coach workings in Britain with a daily service to and from London (King's Cross) that lasted from 1923 until 1939. Despite the introduction of diesel multiple units in the early 1960s, the line was listed for closure in the 'Beeching Report'. Passenger services were withdrawn on 6 April 1964, and goods traffic ceased on 28 March 1966. Today, much of the trackbed is a public footpath.

CLOSED
APRIL
6
1964

Ayr to Dalmellington

The 15-mile line between Ayr and Dalmellington started life as a mineral railway serving the Dalmellington Iron Company's coal and ironstone workings. The first section along the Doon Valley to Waterside was opened by the Ayr & Dalmellington Railway in 1854. The railway was extended northwards to Falkland Junction and south to Dalmellington in 1856, the major engineering feature being the 17-arch Burnton Viaduct near Hollybush. Two years later the company was taken over by the Glasgow & South Western Railway.

Primarily a coal and iron ore-carrying line, the railway also provided a passenger service with around five return trains between Ayr and Dalmellington on weekdays with two extra provided on Saturdays. There was a connecting service from an interchange platform at Holehouse Junction to Rankinston but this ceased in 1950. Despite the introduction of cost-saving measures such as unstaffed stations and diesel railbuses, the railway was listed for closure in the 'Beeching Report'. Passenger services ceased on 6 April 1964. Coal traffic, steam-hauled by 'Crab' 2-6-0s until 1966, from Dalmellington to Ayr Harbour continued for some years – the line remains open for this traffic from an open-cast mine at Chalmerston.

CLOSED
APRIL
6
1964

Hurlford to Darvel

The 7¼-mile branch line from Hurlford (east of Kilmarnock) to Darvel has a fascinating history. The first 3½ miles to Galston was opened by the Glasgow, Paisley, Kilmarnock & Ayr Railway in 1848 and to Newmilns (seven miles from Hurlford) in 1850. In the same year the company merged with the Glasgow, Dumfries & Carlisle Railway to form the Glasgow & South Western Railway. An extension from Newmilns to Darvel was opened in 1896.

The branch line became a through line in 1905 when a new railway was opened eastwards from Darvel to Strathaven where it joined the Caledonian Railway's line from Hamilton (opened 1862). The new railway was jointly owned by the G&SWR and the CR who took it in turns to operate the line every six months. This was not a success and it was closed in 1939 with track being lifted in 1951. Listed for closure in the 'Beeching Report', the Darvel branch continued to be served by passenger trains from Kilmarnock until they were withdrawn on 6 April 1964 – in its latter years the branch was served by four-wheel diesel railbuses. Today, the impressive 26-arch viaduct at Newmilns still survives.

Swansong of the 'Crabs' on the Dalmellington branch – No. 42909 heads tender first through Patna with a loaded coal train from Waterside to Ayr Harbour on 3 August 1965.

BR Standard Class '4' 2-6-4T No. 80091 about to leave Darvel station with the 5.12pm train for Kilmarnock on 17 August 1963.

An eerily quiet Crook of Devon station on the Kinross to Alloa line on 30 March 1959.

Carlisle Kingmoor's Ivatt Class '4' 2-6-0 ('Doodlebug') No. 43011 departs from Langholm station with the 3.28pm train to Carlisle on 10 October 1963.

CLOSED

JUNE
15
1964

Kinross to Alloa

The heavily-engineered scenic 17-mile railway between Alloa and Kinross took 20 years to complete. From the west, the first 3½ miles from Alloa to Tillicoultry was opened by the Stirling & Dunfermline Railway in 1851. From the east, the 6½ miles from Kinross to Rumbling Bridge was opened by the Devon Valley Railway in 1863. The intervening section along the Devon Valley between Tillicoultry and Rumbling Bridge was beset by problems and involved the construction of two viaducts, 17 bridges, cuttings through sand and high embankments. It was opened throughout in 1871. The line was worked by the North British Railway from the outset and taken over by it in 1874, opening up a second direct railway route between Perth and Glasgow and marketed as the 'Picturesque Route'. In addition to through passenger trains the western half was also kept busy with coal traffic from Dollar.

Local passenger traffic was never heavy, with most trains from Stirling and Alloa terminating at Dollar. Diesel railbuses were introduced for this service and by 1964 there were five return trains each weekday with an additional one on Saturday evenings. By that date the line had been listed for closure in the 'Beeching Report' and there was only one through diesel service (running between Perth and Stirling) along the entire route. Closure to passengers came on 15 June 1964 although coal traffic from Dollar to Alloa continued until 1973.

CLOSED
JUNE
15
1964

Riddings Junction to Langholm

Although Langholm came close to being served by the Caledonian Railway's proposed (but never built) line from Carlisle to Hawick, the seven-mile branch line from Riddings Junction (just inside England on the Waverley Route) was eventually the town's only rail link with the outside world. It was opened by the Border Union Railway (owned by the North British Railway) in 1864 and for just over a century, apart from on Sundays, continued to serve this important woollen milling town as well as, until 1922, several collieries at Canobie. Sentinel steam railcars were used in the 1930s and the line was kept fairly busy until after the Second World War when increasing competition from road transport brought a rapid decline in passenger traffic. Inevitably the line was listed for closure in the 'Beeching Report' and passenger services, steam-hauled to the end, were withdrawn on 15 June 1964. On 26 March 1967, an enthusiasts' special hauled by Ivatt Class '4' 2-6-0 No. 43121 was the last passenger train to use the line. Goods trains continued to operate until 18 September 1967.

CLOSED
JUNE
15
1964

St Boswells to Tweedmouth via Kelso

The delightful 33¾-mile cross-border route between St Boswells and Tweedmouth was built by two separate railways. Although never completed, the first on the scene was the Berwick & Kelso Railway which was authorised as early as 1811 and abandoned in 1827. Later, George Hudson's York, Newcastle & Berwick Railway opened from Tweedmouth, on the East Coast Main Line south of Berwick, to Sprouston in 1849. From the west the North British Railway completed its branch line from St Boswells (on the Waverley Route) to Kelso in 1851. The intervening line between Kelso and Sprouston Junction was also opened by the NBR in the same year. Primarily a country byway serving rural communities, the St Boswells to Tweedmouth line was used for a short time by a passenger service between Edinburgh and Berwick via Galashiels and Kelso. This same route was used for Anglo-Scottish expresses when the East Coast Main Line north of Berwick was closed by floods in 1948 and 1950 – it must have been a strange sight to see the 'Flying Scotsman' steam through sleepy Kelso station!

While carrying livestock to and from market was the lifeblood of the line, passenger numbers were few and had declined so much that a single carriage sufficed by the early 1960s. Journey times were soporifically slow with the steam-hauled through trains from Berwick taking over 1½ hours, including a reversal at Tweedmouth. By 1964, when the line had been listed for closure in the 'Beeching Report', there were only two return trains each weekday. Steam-hauled to the end, closure to passengers came on 15 June 1964 although goods traffic continued to run until 1965; the last eastern section to remain open was from Tweedmouth to Coldstream which carried goods traffic for the Wooler branch until 29 March. Kelso remained open for goods trains from St Boswells until 29 March 1968 when the last train departed behind diesel shunter D3891.

'V3' 2-6-2T No. 67607 calls at Kelso station with the 9.58am train from Berwick to St Boswells on 14 September 1957.

Tillynaught to Banff

The six-mile branch line from Tillynaught to the fishing port of Banff was opened by the Banff, Portsoy & Strathisla Railway in 1859. At that time it formed part of that company's 'main line' from Grange, on the Great North of Scotland Railway's main line between Aberdeen and Keith, with a 2¾-mile branch line to Portsoy. The railway was not a commercial success and was taken over by the GNoSR in 1863. The latter company extended the Portsoy branch around the coastline to Elgin in three stages; its construction included the building of viaducts at Cullen and an impressive bridge across the River Spey near Garmouth. When completed in 1886 it became the GNoSR's second route for Elgin to Aberdeen trains, with Banff becoming a branch line served by connecting trains from Tillynaught Junction.

In addition to fish traffic, the branch saw around ten return passenger trains each day with the majority connecting with Elgin to Aberdeen trains at Tillynaught. Listed for closure in the 'Beeching Report', the Banff branch lost its passenger service on 6 July 1964. The last train on the previous Saturday consisted of two packed carriages hauled by BR Standard Class '2' 2-6-0 No. 78045. Goods traffic continued until 6 May 1968 when the Elgin to Cairnie Junction line also closed. Offering fine coastal views, the trackbed westwards from Banff is now a footpath and cycleway.

BR Standard Class '2MT' 2-6-0 No. 78045 waits to depart from Banff with the 2.30pm train to Tillynaught on 15 August 1963. Less than a year later this loco had the honour of working the last passenger train on this branch.

Gleneagles to Comrie

The 14¾-mile branch line from Gleneagles, on the Stirling to Perth main line, to the town of Comrie once formed part of a meandering but short-lived cross-country line that skirted Loch Earn to end at Balquhidder. First on the scene was the Crieff Junction Railway that opened its nine-mile branch line from Gleneagles to the town of Crieff in 1856. The company was taken over by the Scottish Central Railway in 1865, which in a short time was itself absorbed by the Caledonian Railway. It was many years before the railway was extended beyond Crieff by the Crieff & Comrie Railway. Opening in 1893, the 5¾-mile line was worked from the outset by the CR and taken over by that company in 1898.

The final 15¼-mile extension of the railway from Comrie to the Callander & Oban Railway at Balquhidder was opened throughout by the Lochearnhead, St Fillans & Comrie Railway in 1905, by which time it had already been taken over by the CR. Traffic on this latter scenic section was never heavy and it was closed to passengers in 1951 and to goods in 1961.

Four-wheel diesel railbuses were introduced on the remaining Gleneagles to Comrie line in 1958 and a number of small halts also opened. With passenger numbers declining the line was listed for closure in the 'Beeching Report'. In the last year of operation, steam haulage was reinstated to replace the unreliable railbuses but the axe finally fell on 6 July 1964 when the line closed completely. Crieff continued to be served by goods trains from Perth via the Almond Valley line until 1967.

Superpower for the Comrie branch train. Deputising for a failed diesel railbus, BR Standard Class '5MT' 4-6-0 approaches Gleneagles with its one-coach train on 11 May 1963.

Lanark to Muirkirk

The flourishing coal mining and iron-making town of Muirkirk was first reached from the west by the Glasgow, Paisley, Kilmarnock & Ayr Railway's line from Auchinleck which had opened in 1848. It was also reached from Lanark in the east by the Caledonian Railway in 1874. Now an east-west through route, but operated by two companies, the line saw the introduction of Ayr to Edinburgh trains in 1878. Although these were not successful the two railways flourished with coal and iron traffic until the 1930s.

Amidst rapidly declining coal and iron industries, the two lines to Muirkirk struggled on through the Second World War until 1951 when passenger services from Auchinleck were withdrawn. This line closed completely in 1969 apart from Auchinleck to Cronberry which remained open for coal traffic until 1976.

Meanwhile, taken over by diesel multiple units, the remaining Lanark to Muirkirk service carried on until listed for closure in the 'Beeching Report'. By the summer of 1964 there were only five return trains each weekday traversing the whole line with another three

The RCTS 'Three Summits' Rail Tour (via Ais Gill, Beattock and Shap) pauses at Muirkirk on 30 June 1963. The train is headed by preserved Highland Railway 'Jones Goods' 4-6-0 No. 103 and ex-Caledonian Railway 0-6-0 No. 57581. Watched by the driver of No. 103, the well-dressed enthusiasts seem to be scrambling for the best view point to take a photograph but our roving photographer Gavin Morrison has wisely taken up a position on the track!

terminating at Douglas West. The end came on 5 October 1964 when passenger services were withdrawn and the line closed completely between Ponfeigh and Muirkirk. The remaining section remained open for coal traffic for a few more years.

Just before steam was replaced by DMUs on this route, BR Standard Class '4' 2-6-4T No. 80029 storms out of Peterhead with the 12.47pm train to Aberdeen on 12 June 1959.

CLOSED
MAY
3
1965

Maud Junction
to Peterhead

The 38-mile railway between Dyce, on the GNoSR main line from Aberdeen to Elgin, to the fishing port of Peterhead was opened by the Formartine & Buchan Railway in 1862. A branch line to Peterhead Harbour was opened in 1865. From Brucklay (later renamed Maud Junction), a 16-mile branch was opened to the fishing port of Fraserburgh in 1865 (see Fraserburgh to St Combs). The F&BR was taken over by the GNoSR in 1866. A branch line from Ellon, south of Maud Junction, was opened to Boddam in 1897 – serving a railway-owned hotel at Cruden Bay, the line had a short life and was closed to passengers in 1932 and to goods in 1945.

Up until closure, goods traffic in the form of coal and agricultural produce was an important source of revenue for the line. However, this was eclipsed by the vast amounts of fresh fish carried overnight in refrigerated trains from Peterhead to Billingsgate fish market in London. Passenger traffic consisted of around five return journeys between Peterhead and Aberdeen each weekday with carriages for Fraserburgh being detached or joined at Maud Junction. Steam haulage ended in 1959 when diesel multiple units were introduced but despite this cost-cutting measure the line was listed for closure in the 'Beeching Report'. Passenger services were withdrawn between Maud Junction and Peterhead on 3 May 1965 (the Fraserburgh branch clung on until 4 October), although goods traffic continued until 7 September 1970.

The trackbed of the line now forms part of a footpath and cycleway known as the Formartine & Buchan Way while the station buildings, platforms and turntable pit at Maud Junction survive intact.

CLOSED
MAY
3
1965

Fraserburgh to St Combs

The five-mile branch line from Fraserburgh to the coastal village of St Combs was opened as a light railway by the Great North of Scotland Railway in 1903. An early trial of steam railcars was shortlived and, until the introduction of diesel multiple units in 1959, branch locos were required to be fitted with cow-catchers – one of the rules enforced on a light railway. Even as late as 1964 passengers were well-served on this delightful line with 11 return trains each weekday (plus an extra on Saturday). However, by this time it was living on borrowed time and the line was closed completely on 3 May 1965.

Scything the grass at St Combs' diminutive terminus on 11 June 1959. BR Standard Class '2MT' 2-6-0 No. 78045 (*sans* cow-catcher) simmers gently before heading off with a train to Fraserburgh.

CLOSED
MAY
3
1965

Ballinluig to Aberfeldy

The 8¾-mile branch line from Ballinluig, on the Highland main line, and the historic riverside town of Aberfeldy was opened by the Highland Railway in 1865. Heavily engineered with over 40 bridges, the railway became popular with Victorian visitors eager to discover the delights of the beautiful Tay Valley. Until 1935, when a new halt was opened at Balnaguard, the only intermediate station was at Grandtully. Passenger services, until the late 1950s in the hands of Caledonian Railway 0-4-4 tank locomotives, consisted of six return workings each day and in their latter years were hauled by powerful Type 2 diesel locomotives. A rail-connected distillery at Aberfeldy generated much of the goods traffic on this line, which was generally carried in mixed trains.

Listed for closure in the 'Beeching Report', the Aberfeldy branch lost its goods service on 25 January 1965 with passenger trains continuing until 3 May – just two months short of the centenary of its opening.

Today, the magnificent iron railway bridge (open to pedestrians, cyclists and light traffic) across the River Tay to the west of Ballinluig is a lasting reminder of this picturesque line. Some sections of the trackbed can still be walked while the station site at Grandtully with its surviving platform and bridge is now a camp site. A cosmetically restored 0-4-0 'Puggy' steam locomotive is displayed on a short length of track at Aberfeldy Distillery.

Forty-six-year-old ex-Caledonian Railway 0-4-4T No. 55218 stands at Aberfeldy station with its two-coach train for Ballinluig on 13 June 1959. You can almost smell the smoke wafting across the platform! Happy days...

CLOSED

MAY 3 1965

Castle Douglas to Kirkcudbright

The 10¼-mile single-track branch line from Castle Douglas, on the Dumfries to Stranraer line (see Dumfries to Challioch Junction via Castle Douglas), to the county town of Kirkcudbright was opened by the Kirkcudbright Railway in 1864. Featuring two viaducts across the River Dee at Tongland and Bridge of Dee, the railway was absorbed by the Glasgow & South Western Railway in 1865. Trains from Kirkcudbright terminated at a temporary station in Castle Douglas until 1867 due to protracted negotiations over the joint use of the Castle Douglas & Dumfries Railway's existing station. Also serving intermediate stations at Tarff and Bridge of Dee, the train service for many years amounted to seven trains each way on weekdays. Bridge of Dee station closed in 1949 and increased competition from road transport saw traffic decline to such an extent that by 1964 there were only three trains each weekday (plus an extra on Saturdays) to Dumfries with four in the opposite direction. By then the line had been listed for closure in the 'Beeching Report' and the end came on 3 May 1965 when it closed completely. Within a year the viaducts over the Dee had been demolished and the track lifted. Today, the station buildings at Tarff and Kirkcudbright survive albeit with different uses, while the trackbed between Castle Douglas and Bridge of Dee is a footpath.

Stanier Class '3' 2-6-2T No. 40152 prepares to leave Kirkcudbright station with a train for Castle Douglas on 1 July 1961. The station building at Kirkcudbright survives today.

CLOSED

JUNE 14 1965

Dumfries to Challoch Junction via Castle Douglas

With an eye on the all-important sea traffic to Northern Ireland, the 73¾-mile railway across the sparsely populated wilds of Galloway from Dumfries to Stranraer Harbour was built in two stages: the Castle Douglas & Dumfries Railway opened in 1859 while the Portpatrick Railway from Castle Douglas to Stranraer opened in 1861. The latter was extended to the harbour town of Portpatrick the following year.

The steeply graded line down to the small harbour at Portpatrick was not ideal and by 1874 all ferry traffic for Northern Ireland had been moved to a new harbour at Stranraer. Facing an uncertain financial future, the Portpatrick Railway was rescued by four major railway companies eager to keep the link with Stranraer open: in 1885, the London & North Western Railway, the Midland Railway, the Caledonian Railway and the Glasgow & South Western Railway took over the line (and a branch from Newton Stewart to Whithorn) which was then run jointly as the Portpatrick & Wigtownshire Joint Railway.

Meanwhile, the Castle Douglas & Dumfries Railway had been absorbed by the G&SWR in 1865. The through route between Dumfries and Stranraer remained an important link for Anglo-Irish traffic until after the Second World War; despite little intermediate traffic, the line (single track from Castle Douglas to Challoch Junction) was heavily used by

A Dumfries to Stranraer Harbour service headed by Stanier 'Black 5' 4-6-0 No. 44885 crosses the Big Water of Fleet Viaduct near Gatehouse of Fleet on 1 July 1961. The imposing 20-arch viaduct survives intact today.

CLOSED
SEPTEMBER
6
1965

St Andrews to Leven

What became a 39-mile through route serving small fishing villages and towns along the Fife coast, began life in 1852 when the St Andrews Railway opened between the latter station and St Andrews. Absorbed by the North British Railway in 1877, it remained a branch line for another ten years. From the west, the Leven Railway opened from Thornton Junction to Leven in 1854 and in 1857 was extended to Kilconquhar by the East of Fife Railway. These two companies merged in 1861 to become the Leven & East Fife Railway which then extended the coastal route to Anstruther in 1863. The final section between St Andrews and Anstruther was opened by the Anstruther & St Andrews Railway in 1887 and within ten years the entire coastal route had been taken over by the NBR.

Meanwhile the opening of the Forth Bridge in 1890 had seen the Fife Coast become a popular destination for holidaymakers from Glasgow and Edinburgh. During the summer, through trains from these cities were a regular feature along the Fife Coast line until the 1960s and remained steam-hauled by 'B1' 4-6-0s until closure. With traffic declining the route between St Andrews and Leven was listed for closure in the 'Beeching Report'. The end came at the end of the summer timetable on 6 September 1965 when all passenger services were withdrawn. The western section from Thornton Junction to Leven remained open for passengers until 6 October 1969 and for coal traffic to Methil Power Station and to the Diageo distillery at Cameron Bridge until the 1990s, at which point the track was mothballed.

troop trains, cattle trains and an overnight sleeping car train from Euston. During the summer there was an additional service from Newcastle to Stranraer on Saturdays. The Portpatrick branch closed in 1950 by which time traffic on the 'main line' from Dumfries was in serious decline. Listed for closure in the 'Beeching Report', the railway struggled on with just the overnight sleeper service and three return stopping trains each weekday until 14 June 1965 when these (steam-hauled to the end) were withdrawn. Stranraer continued to be served by trains from Glasgow and Ayr (this route having been saved from closure).

Discussing the planned closure of the railways to Stranraer, Lord Stonham in his House of Lords speech in May 1963 said: 'But about the Stranraer line, Mr Marples said, "So the people there need not worry that there will not be consultation before it is closed down." That is the kind of consultation that a condemned man gets when they ask him what he wants for breakfast before they hang him.'

Today much of the route of this scenic railway can still be followed. Of note is the rusting steel bridge over Loch Ken and the impressive viaducts at Gatehouse of Fleet and Glenluce. Two sections of trackbed – north of Creetown and between New Galloway and Gatehouse of Fleet – are now footpaths and cycleways.

With less than a month to go before closure of the Fife coastal route, 'B1' Class 4-6-0 No. 61099 departs from Crail with the 12.30pm train to Edinburgh Waverley on 7 August 1965.

27
1965

Dunblane to Crianlarich (Lower)

The 40¼-mile railway between Dunblane and Crianlarich once formed part of the Caledonian Railway's scenic route from Glasgow (Buchanan Street) to Oban. It took many years to complete with the first section from Dunblane and Callander being opened in 1858 by the Dunblane, Doune & Callander Railway. This railway was leased to the Scottish Central Railway which was then taken over by the CR in 1865.

Passing through difficult terrain, the remaining route to Oban was not so easy to build – financially backed by the CR, the Callander & Oban Railway opened in stages: to Tyndrum in 1873, to Dalmally in 1877 and to Oban in 1880. A five-mile branch from an interchange

platform at Killin Junction to Killin and Loch Tay opened in 1886 (see Killin Junction to Killin). Crianlarich was also reached by the West Highland Railway's line from Glasgow to Fort William in 1894 – at Crianlarich the latter served Upper station while the C&OR served Lower station.

Along with the Killin branch, the Dunblane to Crianlarich section was listed for closure in the 'Beeching Report' but even as late as the summer of 1964 there was still a through sleeping car service between London (Euston) and Oban and four other through trains between Glasgow and Oban – one of these included a miniature buffet and an observation car. Although closure was planned for 1 November 1965, when Oban trains were to be diverted via the

West Highland Line to Crianlarich, the end came sooner when a landslide in Glen Ogle prematurely closed the line from Callander to Crianlarich (Lower) on 27 September. Callander continued to be served by trains from Dunblane until the official closure date of 1 November.

Today, much of the trackbed of the railway from Callendar alongside Loch Lubnaig and up Glen Ogle to Killin is a popular footpath and cycleway.

By 1961 the unreliable North British Locomotive Company's Type 2 diesels had taken over many of the steam workings on the Oban line. Here, D6102 (1,000hp) and D6123 (1,100hp) climb up through spectacular Glen Ogle with the combined 12 noon ex-Glasgow (Buchanan St) and 11.40am ex-Edinburgh (Princes Street) train to Oban.

CLOSED
SEPTEMBER
27
1965

Killin Junction to Killin

The five-mile branch line from an interchange platform at Killin Junction to the village of Killin and a pier on Loch Tay was opened by the Callander & Oban Railway in 1886. The coming of the railway transformed the loch into a major tourist attraction with daytrippers travelling from Glasgow before taking a cruise aboard the *Lady of the Lake* steamer. Passenger services between Killin and Loch Tay ceased at the outbreak of war in 1939, never to return. However, the diminutive engine shed at Loch Tay remained open with services between Killin Junction and Killin remaining steam-hauled until closure. Along with the Dunblane to Crianlarich line (see Dunblane to Crianlarich [Lower]), the Killin branch was listed for closure in the 'Beeching Report'. Scheduled for 1 November 1965, closure came earlier when the 'main line' was blocked by a landslide in Glen Ogle on 27 September. Today, much of the trackbed between Killin Junction and Killin may be walked or cycled.

BR Standard Class '4' 2-6-4T No. 80093 prepares for a day's work on the Killin branch at the diminutive engine shed at Loch Tay in August 1965. Just over a month later this delightful branch line closed for good.

Kittybrewster's BR Standard Class '4' 2-6-4T No. 80112 prepares to leave Maud Junction with an Aberdeen to Fraserburgh train on 12 June 1959. Steam haulage on the line was replaced by diesel shortly after this.

CLOSED
OCTOBER
4
1965

Dyce to Fraserburgh

While the railway from Dyce to Peterhead had opened in 1862 (see Maud Junction to Peterhead), the Formartine & Buchan Railway's 16-mile branch from Brucklay (later renamed Maud Junction) to Fraserburgh opened in 1865. A year later the railway was taken over by the Great North of Scotland Railway. Up until closure, goods traffic in the form of coal and agricultural produce was an important source of revenue for the line but this was eclipsed by the vast amounts of fresh fish carried overnight in refrigerated trains from Fraserburgh to Billingsgate fish market in London. Passenger traffic consisted of around five return journeys between Fraserburgh and Aberdeen each weekday with carriages for Peterhead being detached or joined at Maud Junction. Steam haulage ended in 1959 when diesel multiple units were introduced but despite this cost-cutting measure the line was listed for closure in the 'Beeching Report'. Passenger services were withdrawn between Maud Junction and Fraserburgh on 4 October 1965 (the Peterhead branch had already closed to passengers on 3 May) although goods traffic continued until 8 October 1979. A hoped-for revival of the railway during the boom years of North Sea oil platform construction failed to materialise. Today, the trackbed of the line forms part of a footpath and cycleway known as the Formartine & Buchan Way.

CLOSED
OCTOBER
4
1965

Haughead Junction (Hamilton) to Coalburn and Stonehouse to Strathaven

Serving an important coalfield, the 18¼-mile railway between Hamilton (reached from Glasgow in 1849) and the isolated village of Coalburn was opened as far as Lesmahagow by the Caledonian Railway-backed Lesmahagow Railway in 1856. Passenger services commenced in 1868 and the line was later extended to Coalburn as part of an unfinished route to Muirkirk. The railway was absorbed by the CR in 1881.

Along with passenger services between Stonehouse and Strathaven, the Coalburn branch had been threatened in the early 1950s but managed to survive until being listed for closure in the 'Beeching Report'. By the summer of 1964 there were only two through trains running from Glasgow Central to Coalburn on weekdays with only one in the opposite direction and an additional Saturday service which needed a change at Hamilton. Strathaven via Stonehouse was similarly served. This minimal service

ended altogether on 4 October 1965 although coal traffic continued to use the line until 16 September 1968. The section from Hamilton to Larkhall was reopened to passengers as part of the electrified Argyle Line from Glasgow on 12 December 2005. An extension to Stonehouse and Strathaven is under consideration.

No. 57630 waits patiently in the evening sunshine at Lesmahagow station while Henry Casserley photographs the 7.05pm Coalburn to Hamilton train on 4 July 1957.

CLOSED
OCTOBER
11
1965

Crosshouse to Irvine

The 5½-mile railway between Crosshouse, west of Kilmarnock, to Irvine was opened by the Glasgow, Paisley, Kilmarnock & Ayr Railway in 1848. The company amalgamated with the Glasgow, Dumfries & Carlisle Railway in 1850 to form the Glasgow & South Western Railway. Serving several collieries around Springside, the line was also used by Kilmarnock to Ardossan excursion trains until complete closure on 11 October 1965.

Ex-LMS 'Class '2P' 4-4-0 No. 40687 stands at Irvine on 6 July 1957 with the 10.15am train to Kilmarnock via Crosshouse.

CLOSED
OCTOBER
18
1965

Aviemore to Forres

The 36-mile railway between Aviemore and Forres was opened as part of the ambitious Inverness & Perth Junction Railway in 1863. The following year the company absorbed the Perth & Dunkeld Railway and in 1865 combined with the Inverness & Aberdeen Junction Railway to form the Highland Railway. The section from Aviemore to Forres became a secondary route when the HR opened its more direct line from Aviemore to Inverness via Slochd Summit in 1898.

With five intermediate stations at Boat of Garten, Broomhill, Grantown-on-Spey, Dava and Dunphail, the line from Aviemore to Forres was served on weekdays by through trains to and from Inverness. By 1964, when the line was already threatened with closure, there were six northbound services each weekday with one originating in Glasgow; southbound, there were only four including one that only ran on Saturdays. Curiously in 1964, there were two through trains in each direction on Sundays, one a Glasgow/Edinburgh to Inverness service and the other an Inverness to London (Euston) sleeping car train. This all came to an end on 18 October 1965 when the line closed.

Since 1972, the 8¼-mile section from Aviemore to Broomhill has been reopened as a heritage railway by the Strathspey Railway. An extension to Grantown-on-Spey is under construction.

Trouble on the line – Birmingham R C & W Co. Type 2 diesel D5335 rumbles through Grantown-on-Spey (West) station with a breakdown train on a snowy 23 February 1963.

Craigellachie to Boat of Garten

The 33-mile railway along the meandering Spey Valley from Craigellachie to Boat of Garten was opened as far as Abernethy (Nethy Bridge) by the Strathspey Railway in 1863. This was an extension of their line from Dufftown which had already been reached by the Keith & Dufftown Railway the year before. Beyond Abernethy the completion of the railway to Boat of Garten was held up until 1866 by an acrimonious dispute with the newly opened Inverness & Perth Junction Railway over a proposed junction – in the end the SR (by now taken over by the Great North of Scotland Railway) built its own dedicated track to run alongside the I&PJR into Boat of Garten.

Heavily engineered with numerous bridges across the Spey, this scenic line became an important lifeline for the numerous whisky distilleries scattered along the valley. Whisky distilleries at Dailuaine and Cromdale even had their own branch lines, while timber traffic also became important during the Second World War.

Diesel railbuses were introduced in 1958 when four new halts were also opened. Passenger traffic was always light and by 1964 was catered for by three return services on weekdays plus an extra train on Saturday evenings. Listed for closure in the 'Beeching Report', the line lost its meagre passenger service on 18 October 1965. Distilleries between Boat of Garten and Aberlour continued to be rail-served until 4 November 1968, and the last section from Aberlour to Craigellachie and Dufftown finally closed on 15 November 1971.

Today, much of the trackbed along this scenic route is now a footpath and cycleway known as the Speyside Way. The latticed girder bridge over the Spey at Ballindalloch and the majority of the stations between Boat of Garten and Dufftown still survive in all their restored glory – some provide holiday accommodation for fishing enthusiasts while Aberlour station is a tea room and Ballindalloch is a hostel.

Shiny Park Royal diesel railbus SC79970 waits for passengers at Craigellachie before heading off up the Spey Valley to Aviemore, July 1960.

High above Port Glasgow, two Stanier 'Black 5' 4-6-0s tender-to-tender (No. 45476 leading) haul an empty boat train from Princes Pier back to Glasgow St Enoch station in May 1964. By then the line from Kilmacolm had been singled and its days were numbered.

CLOSED
NOVEMBER
30
1965

Kilmacolm to Greenock (Princes Pier)

What was eventually to become the Glasgow & South Western Railway's route from Glasgow (St Enoch) to Greenock (Princes Pier) started life as a short branch line from Johnstone to Bridge of Weir which was opened by the Bridge of Weir Railway in 1864. A year later it was taken over by the G&SWR. The important and growing port of Greenock on the River Clyde was already served by the Caledonian Railway on its Greenock & Wemyss Bay line but the G&SWR also wanted a slice of this cake. To achieve this aim and despite much opposition from the CR, the G&SWR-backed Greenock & Ayrshire Railway was opened between Bridge of Weir and Princes Pier in Greenock in 1869.

The opening of the line saw an all-out price war for Glasgow to Greenock traffic between the two rival companies. Fares were reduced to a ridiculously low level but the G&SWR eventually won as their trains connected directly with Clyde steamers at Princes Pier while the CR had no similar direct connection to its Custom House Quay. Neither service was profitable so in the end the two companies agreed to fix their fares and share the revenue. The G&AR was taken over by the G&SWR in 1872.

Stiff competition for Greenock passenger traffic continued until the formation of British Railways in 1948. Clyde steamer traffic was then withdrawn from Princes Pier although the station still served ocean liner traffic with special trains from St Enoch. Local trains between Kilmacolm and Princes Pier were withdrawn in 1959 but the steam-hauled and double-headed ocean-liner specials continued until 30 November 1965. Goods traffic was withdrawn from the eight-mile line on 29 September 1966. Despite also being listed for closure in the 'Beeching Report', Kilmacolm continued to be served by passenger trains until 1983 (see Shields Junction to Kilmacolm).

Today, the trackbed of the line between Kilmacolm and Greenock forms part of a footpath and cycleway known as the Paisley & Clyde Railway Path.

Aberdeen to Ballater

The 43½-mile railway up the Dee Valley from Aberdeen to Ballater was built in three stages. First was the Deeside Railway that opened from Guild Street station in Aberdeen to Banchory in 1853. A westward extension up the valley to Aboyne was opened by the Deeside Extension Railway in 1859. The two railways were leased by the Great North of Scotland Railway in 1866 and from 1867 trains for Aboyne left the new joint station in Aberdeen. The final section came in 1866 when the Aboyne & Braemar Railway opened as far as Ballater. Despite Braemar being the final goal the section beyond Ballater was never completed due to pressure from Queen Victoria. All three railways were absorbed by the GNoSR in 1875.

The line was regularly used by royal trains bringing the royal family and their guests to Balmoral Castle – the first recorded visit was in 1866 and the last on 15 October 1965. However, by the 1950s competition from cars, buses and lorries had brought a steady decline in rail traffic along the Dee Valley and the line was listed for closure in the 'Beeching Report'. Despite its royal patronage and strong local protests the Ballater branch closed to passengers on 28 February 1966. Goods trains continued to serve Ballater until 18 July when the line was cut back to Culter. This last section from Ferryhill Junction continued to be served by goods trains until 2 January 1967.

Today, much of the trackbed is a footpath and cycleway known as the Deeside Way. The Royal Deeside Railway now runs trains for over a mile along relaid track between Milton of Crathes and Banchory.

Connel Ferry to Ballachulish

The 27-mile branch line from Connel Ferry to Ballachulish was opened by the Callander & Oban Railway in 1903. Built to serve slate quarries at Ballachulish, the line featured substantial bridges over Loch Creran at Creagan and over Loch Etive at Connel Ferry. When built, the latter was the second-largest cantilever bridge in the world (after the Forth Bridge) and initially only carried rail traffic. A roadway was added in 1914 although vehicles had to pay a toll to the railway until the line closed.

The railway was worked from the outset by the Caledonian Railway and remained the stamping ground of that company's veteran 0-4-4 tanks until a few years before closure when diesel locomotives were introduced. By 1964 the line had been listed for closure in the 'Beeching Report' and by then the train service consisted of four return trains (the majority originating or ending their journeys at Oban) each weekday. Goods traffic was withdrawn on 14 June 1965 although the passenger service struggled on until 28 March 1966.

Today, much of the trackbed alongside Loch Linnhe has been reopened as a footpath and cycleway while the station building and platform at Creagan has been lovingly restored as a private residence. Other station buildings at Duro, Kentallen and Ballachulish have found other uses. The bridge over Loch Creran at Creagan has been rebuilt to take the realigned A828 although the original structure survived for 30 years after the line's closure and was often used by locals taking a short cut! However, the main feature of the line is still the magnificent bridge at Connel Ferry.

Rusting rails and no customers in sight – a sad end to the once-busy royal station at Ballater on 2 June 1965 as a two-car DMU departs along the Dee Valley to Aberdeen.

Ivatt Class '2MT' 2-6-0 No. 46460 trundles off the road/rail cantilever bridge at Connel Ferry with a train from Ballachulish in June 1962.

Stanier 'Black 5' 4-6-0 No. 44901 leaves Crosshouse station with a Glasgow (St Enoch) to Kilmarnock service on 2 August 1965.

CLOSED
APRIL
18
1966

Dalry to Kilmarnock

The 11¼-mile line from Dalry to Kilmarnock via Crosshouse was opened by the Glasgow, Paisley, Kilmarnock & Ayr Railway in 1843 – this company became the Glasgow & South Western Railway in 1850. A line from Crosshouse to Irvine, providing a through route for trains between Ardrossan and Kilmarnock, was opened in 1848 (see Crosshouse to Irvine). Although mainly used as a through route for G&SWR trains between Glasgow (St Enoch) and Kilmarnock, the Dalry line also carried local livestock and coal traffic. The intermediate stations at Cunninghamhead and Montgreenan closed in 1955 although the junction station at Crosshouse remained open until 1966. Despite it not being listed for complete closure in the 'Beeching Report', the line closed to passenger trains on 18 April 1966. Freight trains and diverted passenger trains continued along the line until 23 October 1973 when it closed completely.

BR Standard Class '4MT' 2-6-0 No. 76094 passes through the closed Kilbarchan station with the 6.22am Kilmarnock to Glasgow (St Enoch) train on 2 August 1965.

CLOSED
JUNE
27
1966
Lochwinnoch Loop (Elderslie to Dalry via Lochwinnoch)

By the beginning of the twentieth century the Glasgow & South Western Railway's main line between Glasgow and Ayr was stretched to capacity. Quadrupling the line was not possible due to the confines of the valleys and lochs so a 13-mile relief loop line was built on the western side of the valley from Elderslie Junction, west of Paisley, to Brownhill Junction, north of Dalry. Serving the intermediate stations of Kilbarchan, Lochwinnoch and Kilburnie the double-track line opened in 1905.

The stations were built in a distinctive style with island platforms reached via a subway from the road below. Passenger services along the line consisted of through trains running between Glasgow St Enoch and Ayr, Largs or Kilmarnock – Lochwinnoch was a popular destination for daytrippers from Glasgow on summer weekends. While diesel multiple units were introduced in the early 1960s the line was listed for closure in the 'Beeching Report'. Passenger trains were withdrawn on 27 June 1966 although goods trains continued until 1971 when the line north of Kilbirnie was completely closed. The southern section from Brownhills Junction remained open to Glengarnock steelworks until 1977.

Today, the majority of the trackbed alongside the lochs between Johnstone and Kilbirnie is a footpath and cycleway.

CLOSED
JUNE
5
1967
Arkleston Junction to Renfrew Wharf

The three-mile branch line from Arkleston Junction to Renfrew Wharf was opened by the Paisley & Renfrew Railway in 1837. Built to a gauge of 4ft 6in, it was worked by steam locomotives until 1842 when they were replaced by horses. Although taken over by the Glasgow & South Western Railway in 1852, its non-standard gauge led to the line being let privately. In 1866 it was regauged to standard and doubled with a connection made to the Glasgow & Paisley Joint Railway at Arkleston Junction. Steam haulage was reintroduced in the same year. The branch also served two shipyards at Renfrew until the early 1960s.

By 1964 passenger traffic on the line had dwindled to one workmen's train each way on weekdays; the 7.18am from St Enoch arrived at Renfrew Wharf at 7.58 while the return service left Renfrew Fulbar Street at 4.58pm. The discrepancy for the different stations at Renfrew lies in the fact that by then there was no run-round loop at Wharf station – the morning train was propelled backwards to the yard where the loco ran round and took the train to Fulbar Street station to await the afternoon departure. We may never know why the train was not propelled back into Wharf station! Needless to say, this loss-making line was closed to passengers on 5 June 1967. The short section from Arkleston Junction to Sandyford remained open for goods traffic until 1981. Much of the trackbed is now a footpath and cycle route.

Only one train a day from St Enoch and nothing back – that was the sad situation at Renfrew Wharf station in the last few years preceding closure. Here, on 25 July 1966, BR Standard Class '4MT' 2-6-0 No. 76046 has just arrived at the semi-derelict and overgrown station with the 7.18am from Glasgow Central.

CLOSED
SEPTEMBER
4
1967

Kinnaber Junction to Stanley Junction via Forfar

What eventually became part of the Caledonian Railway's trunk route between Glasgow and Aberdeen started life in 1839 when the 5ft 6in gauge Arbroath & Forfar Railway opened. It was converted to standard gauge in 1847 and leased to the Aberdeen Railway a year later, the section from Guthrie to Forfar becoming part of that company's line to Aberdeen.

Completed in 1848, the next section to open was the Scottish Midland Junction Railway's route from Perth to Forfar. The final link in the chain was the Aberdeen Railway's line between Guthrie and Aberdeen Ferryhill via Bridge of Dun which opened throughout in 1850. In 1856 the AR and the SMJR merged to form the Scottish North Eastern Railway which, in turn, was absorbed by the Caledonian Railway in 1866.

At Kinnaber Junction the CR's line to Aberdeen was met by the North British Railway's route from Edinburgh. This was the finishing post for the famous 'Railway Races to the North' in the late nineteenth century when trains from King's Cross and Euston would compete for the fastest journey time to Aberdeen. The railway proved to be a race track once again when rejuvenated 'A4' Pacifics were introduced on the three-hour expresses between Glasgow and Aberdeen in 1962.

However, the A4's swan song ended on 3 September 1966 when diesels took over. By then the line between Stanley Junction, north of Perth, and Kinnaber Junction was living on borrowed time as it had been listed for closure in the 'Beeching Report'. The end came for passenger services on 4 September 1967 when all trains between Aberdeen and Glasgow were rerouted via Dundee – Glasgow Buchanan Street station had already closed on 7 November 1966 with trains diverted to Queen Street station. The last southbound train on Sunday 3 September was the 5.30pm from Aberdeen to Glasgow worked as far as Perth by NBL No. D6106. Goods trains continued to operate from Kinnaber Junction to Bridge of Dun and the Brechin branch until May 1981 and between Stanley Junction and Forfar until June 1982. Today, Bridge of Dun station is the southern terminus of the CR's heritage railway from Brechin.

Gresley's 'A4' 4-6-2s performed their swansong on the Glasgow-Aberdeen three-hour expresses until 3 September 1966. Here, No. 60007 'Sir Nigel Gresley' (since preserved) speeds through closed Auldbar Road station with the 1.10pm Aberdeen to Glasgow express on 5 August 1965.

CLOSED
JANUARY 29 1968

Falkirk (Grahamstown) to Grangemouth

Established as an important port by the Forth & Clyde Navigation Company, Grangemouth is reached along a three-mile branch line from Grangemouth Junction, east of Falkirk. The Grangemouth Railway was built by the canal company and opened in 1860 – it was initially worked by the North British Railway. However both the canal company and the railway were taken over by the NBR's rival, the Caledonian Railway, in 1867.

Grangemouth prospered as a port and for a while both companies ran passenger trains from Glasgow. Although the branch line's lifeblood was (and still is) freight, especially after the opening of the enormous oil refinery in 1924, passenger trains continued to run until they were withdrawn on 29 January 1968 (despite not being listed for closure in the 'Beeching Report'). Today, the line remains very busy with traffic from the oil refinery and a major container terminal and there are proposals to reintroduce passenger trains.

CLOSED
JANUARY 29 1968

Larbert (Alloa Junction) to Alloa

The 5½-mile line between Alloa Junction, north of Larbert, and Alloa started life in 1850 when the Scottish Central Railway opened a branch line from the junction of the Stirling line to the south bank of the River Forth opposite the harbour town of Alloa. Passengers and goods were transferred across the river by ferry until the Alloa Railway opened its 20-span swing bridge in 1885, by which time the railway had been taken over by the Caledonian Railway.

Diesel railbuses were introduced in the early 1960s and by 1964 the passenger service consisted of four return journeys on weekdays with two extra on Saturdays (one of these still steam-hauled). Although the line was not listed for closure in the 'Beeching Report' the cost of maintaining the 1,600 foot long swing bridge over the Forth was no doubt the deciding factor that led to its demise. Passenger services were withdrawn on 29 January 1968 and the swing bridge was demolished in 1971. The remaining section from Throsk southwards to Alloa Junction remained open for goods until 1 April 1978.

Park Royal four-wheel diesel railbus SC79973 emerges from the gloom of Grangemouth station to roll up the hill to Falkirk in March 1967.

After crossing Alloa swing bridge with a goods train, Clayton Type 1 diesel D8580 halts at Throsk while the driver hands over the single line tablet to the signalman on a day in May 1967.

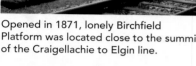

Opened in 1871, lonely Birchfield Platform was located close to the summit of the Craigellachie to Elgin line.

English Electric Type 1 diesel D8032 with a short van train at Craigellachie on 29 June 1966.

CLOSED
MAY
6
1968

Craigellachie to Elgin

The 12½-mile line between Elgin and Craigellachie was opened by the Morayshire Railway in 1863. From 1866 it was worked by the Great North of Scotland Railway and amalgamated with that company in 1880. A branch from Rothes to Orton (on the Inverness & Aberdeen Junction Railway's main line from Inverness to Keith) opened in 1858 but was closed in 1866. At Craigellachie, the MR's line from Elgin met the Strathspey Railway's new route from Abernethy and the Keith & Dufftown Railway's line from Keith. Serving numerous distilleries, these three railways converging on Craigellachie were all worked by and eventually taken over by the GNoSR.

For many years the GNoSR was forced to use the route via Keith and Craigellachie for its Aberdeen to Elgin trains. The more direct route via the Highland Railway from Keith to Inverness was the subject of years of feuding between the two companies and was only resolved in 1897, after which the two GNoSR routes (the coastal route from Cairnie Junction to Elgin had opened in 1886) effectively became secondary routes.

By 1964 the railway from Elgin to Craigellachie had been listed for closure in the 'Beeching Report' – diesel multiple units had already been introduced and the majority of the five or six trains that ran on weekdays connected with trains to and from Elgin via the coastal route at Cairnie Junction Exchange Platform to the east of Keith. Closure to passengers came on 6 May 1968 although goods trains continued to use the line until 4 November.

Today, only the station buildings at Elgin East and Longmorn survive, while the site of Craigellachie station is now a car park for the Speyside Way long distance path.

CLOSED
MAY
6
1968

Craigellachie to Keith

The 14½-mile line from Keith to Craigellachie was built in two stages. Built to serve distilleries in the Spey Valley, the Keith & Dufftown Railway opened in 1862. The railway was extended northwards to Craigellachie and then down the Spey Valley to Abernethy by the Strathspey Railway in 1863 (see Craigellachie to Boat of Garten). Both railways were worked by the Great North of Scotland Railway and were taken over by that firm in 1866. The line between Keith and Craigellachie was used as part of the GNoSR's secondary route for trains between Aberdeen and Elgin and these continued to operate through to British Railways' days when diesel multiple units were introduced.

By 1964, with closure looming for most of the former GNoSR lines north of Aberdeen, the passenger service between Keith and Craigellachie was handled mainly by trains running from Cairnie Junction Exchange Platform (for the alternative coastal route to Elgin), east of Keith, through to Elgin. These were withdrawn on 6 May 1968, a black day for the railways in this region. The section from Dufftown and Craigellachie continued to see goods traffic for distilleries at Aberlour until 15 November 1971. The Glenfiddich Distillery at Dufftown remained rail-served for goods traffic and luxury charter trains until May 1985 when the line was mothballed.

Taken over by a group of volunteers in 2000, the 11-mile section between Keith Town and Dufftown was reopened as a heritage railway on 18 August 2001. Known as the Keith & Dufftown Heritage Railway it currently operates a diesel multiple unit service between the two towns at weekends.

Elgin to Cairnie Junction via Cullen

What was to become the Great North of Scotland Railway's coastal route from Cairnie Junction to Elgin started life in 1859 when the Banff, Portsoy & Strathisla Railway opened from Grange (Cairnie Junction) to Banff (see Tillynaught to Banff). At the same time the company also opened a 2¾-mile branch from Tillynaught to Portsoy. The BP&SR was taken over by the GNoSR in 1863 and the Portsoy branch was then extended along the coastline via Cullen and Buckie to Elgin, opening throughout in 1886. This scenic route involved the construction of two large viaducts at Cullen (complete with far-reaching sea views) and an impressive steel-arched bridge over the River Spey at Spey Bay. When completed, this route became the GNoSR's second route for trains between Aberdeen and Elgin – the other was via Craigellachie.

For many years the line's lifeblood was fish traffic from the port of Buckie but by the 1950s much of this had been lost to road transport. With increasing competition from buses, passenger traffic also shrank at the same time. Even so, a service of six passenger trains (dieselised by 1960) ran each weekday between Elgin and Aberdeen until closure. Along with the majority of former GNoSR lines in the region, the coastal route was listed for closure in the 'Beeching Report'. The line closed completely on 6 May 1968.

Lord Stonham offered the following views on replacement bus services in Scotland in 1963: 'On Tuesday in another place the Minister of Transport, knowing that 15,000 square miles of Scotland would be entirely without railways, said that the situation could be met with 100 extra buses. This is in Hansard. How can one respect the judgement of a Minister who is so manifestly out of touch with the situation and talks such utter nonsense?'

Today much of the trackbed along the coast from Garmouth to Portsoy is a footpath and cycleway forming part of the Speyside Way long distance path, whose notable features along this route still include the massive bridge and viaducts.

One of the two BR Standard Class '4' 2-6-4Ts to be allocated to Keith shed at this time was No. 80121. It is seen here at Tillynaught Junction with the 3.45pm Aberdeen to Elgin train on 12 June 1959. The branch train for Banff can be seen behind the station building.

CLOSED
SEPTEMBER
16
1968

Ayr to Heads of Ayr

The four-mile branch line from Alloway Junction, south of Ayr, to Heads of Ayr started life in 1906 when the Maidens & Dunure Light Railway opened along the Ayrshire coast via Turnberry to Girvan. Built to serve the Glasgow & South Western Railway-owned hotel and golf course at Turnberry, this scenic line was never a financial success and was closed between Alloway Junction and Turnberry in 1930. At the southern end the Girvan to Turnberry section closed to passengers in 1942 and to goods traffic in 1955.

Meanwhile the northern section from Alloway Junction to Heads of Ayr was reopened in 1932 to serve a new holiday camp. This closed prematurely in 1933 but was reopened in 1947 in conjunction with a new Butlin's holiday camp. Although not listed for closure in the 'Beeching Report', passenger services along the short branch line from Ayr were withdrawn on 16 September 1968.

In pouring rain 'Crab' 5MT 2-6-0 No. 42861 approaches Alloway Junction with the 9.20am Heads of Ayr to Edinburgh Princes Street train on 31 July 1965.

Class 'J38' 0-6-0 No. 65921 passes through Alloa with a freight for Kincardine Power Station on 9 August 1965.

CLOSED
OCTOBER
7
1968

Dunfermline Upper to Stirling

The 20¼-mile line between Dunfermline Upper and Stirling was built by the Stirling & Dunfermline Railway in two stages. First to open in 1850 was the section from Dunfermline to Alloa, followed by Alloa to Stirling in 1852. The railway's primary source of revenue came from the numerous coalfields in West Fife which were connected to the 'main line' by short branches. Double track throughout, it had intermediate stations at Oakley, East Grange, Bogside, Forest Mill, Alloa, Cambus and Causewayhead. The S&DR was absorbed by the Edinburgh & Glasgow Railway in 1858 which was then taken over by the North British Railway in 1865.

While coal was the lifeblood of the line, passengers were well catered for with a fairly frequent service of trains running between Stirling and Edinburgh right up until closure. It was therefore no surprise that the line was not threatened with closure in the 'Beeching Report'. By then diesel multiple units had been introduced although goods trains remained steam-hauled until the very end. The announcement of closure came as a shock to users of the line, who saw their passenger service withdrawn on 7 October 1968; goods trains continued until the 1980s, with the last section from Dunfermline to Comrie Colliery closing in 1986.

Since closure the railway has sprung back to life in two very different ways: the trackbed from Dunfermline Upper to Clackmannan is a footpath and cycleway known as the West Fife Cycleway; and the line from Stirling to Alloa reopened for passengers and for merry-go-round coal traffic to Longannet Power Station in 2008.

Edinburgh to Carlisle (Waverley Route)

Known as the Waverley Route, the 98¼-mile railway from Edinburgh to Carlisle had its beginnings in the Edinburgh & Dalkeith Railway which opened in 1838 as a horse-drawn tramway between Leith Docks and collieries to the southeast of Edinburgh. Part of the route of this tramway was rebuilt by the Edinburgh & Hawick Railway (taken over by the North British Railway in 1845) which opened from South Esk to Hawick in 1849. With Carlisle now in its sights, the NBR-sponsored Border Union Railway was opened across sparsely populated and desolate country from Hawick to Carlisle in 1862. Despite this achievement the NBR still had problems at Carlisle where disputes with the incumbent London & North Western Railway and Caledonian Railway continued for some years. The Waverley Route only made

financial sense once the Midland Railway had reached Carlisle from Settle in 1876, and for the first time passengers between London and Scotland had a third choice for an Anglo-Scottish route.

Apart from locally generated livestock traffic, business from intermediate stations was never heavy. However, the double-track railway remained an important trunk route for Anglo-Scottish freight traffic until the 1960s. By 1964, passenger services consisted of three stopping trains between Carlisle and Edinburgh on weekdays plus two Edinburgh-Hawick all stations (plus an extra on Saturday) and one Carlisle to Hawick all stations. Two other through trains also operated – these were 'The Waverley' express and an overnight sleeper train, both between London St Pancras and Edinburgh. 'The Waverley' had its origins in the 1927 'Thames-Forth Express' and continued to run, apart

Preceded by Clayton Type 1 diesel D8606, train 1M82 had arrived at Newcastleton at around 12.45am on 6 January. There the level crossing had been blocked by a vociferous crowd of protesters and the police had unsuccessfully intervened to clear the way ahead for the train. Tempers became frayed and Liberal MP David Steel (a passenger on the train) addressed the crowd in an attempt to restore order. Eventually the train left at 1.50am and the 'Battle of Newcastleton' was over but the Waverley Route was dead!

D60 'Lytham St Annes' of Leeds Holbeck shed waits to depart from a cold Edinburgh Waverley station with train 1M82, the 9.55pm to London St Pancras, on 5 January 1969.

The scene at Hawick station on the night of 5 January 1969 – even at this late hour the platform is thronged with local people witnessing the last train to travel over the Waverley Route.

from a break during the Second World War, until September 1968.

The cross-border railway was also served by branch lines from Langholm to Riddings Junction, Bellingham to Riccarton Junction, Berwick, Kelso and Jedburgh to St Boswells, Selkirk and Peebles to Galashiels and Lauder to Fountainhall Junction. By the 1960s the steady closure of these vital feeder lines had, inevitably, brought the Waverley Route to its knees and the entire route was listed for closure in the 'Beeching Report'. Despite strong objections from local MPs (including David Steel) and the public, closure was set for 15 July 1968. This date came and went without closure due to the difficulties in arranging alternative bus services, but finally the dreaded day came on 5 January 1969. That weekend special enthusiasts' trains were

run and the local services were (unusually) filled to bursting with people witnessing the last rites.

Famously, the final train to traverse the route, the 9.55pm Edinburgh to St Pancras sleeper service headed by D60 'Lytham St Annes', was halted in its tracks at Newcastleton by protesters blocking the level crossing gates. Tempers were running high, police were called in and Borders Liberal MP David Steel got out of the train to address the assembled throng. Finally peace was restored and the train got going again, but not before the clock had ticked past the appointed closing time of midnight.

With nearly all of its infrastructure still intact the northern section from Edinburgh to Galashiels and Tweedbank is due to be reopened in 2014 – 45 years after closure. South of Hawick the impressive curving 15-arch viaduct at Shankend still stands in all its glory, while at Whitrope the Waverley Route Heritage Association is bringing the line back to life again. The walk from here along the trackbed to the eerily quiet site of Riccarton Junction station is a poignant pilgrimage for railway enthusiasts.

Last train over the Waverley Route, tickets please! Ticket inspection at Edinburgh Waverley for the 9.55pm sleeper train to London St Pancras on 5 January 1969.

CLOSED JANUARY 6 1969

Leuchars Junction to St Andrews

The first part of what was to become the North British Railway's scenic route along the East Fife coastline was opened between Leuchars Junction and St Andrews by the St Andrews Railway in 1852. Although the five-mile railway was absorbed by the NBR in 1877 the rest of the route around the coast to Thornton Junction was only completed in 1887. Starting life as a branch line, the Leuchars Junction to St Andrews section reverted back to this status when the rest of the route closed in 1965 (see St Andrews to Leven). Despite not being listed for closure in the 'Beeching Report', the branch line closed completely on 6 January 1969. There are currently proposals to reopen the railway to this historic town.

Ex-NBR Class 'D30/2' 4-4-0 No. 62418 'The Pirate' waits to leave St Andrews station with the 2.17pm train from Dundee to Thornton Junction on 8 September 1955.

CLOSED MAY 5 1969

Wormit to Newport-on-Tay

The first railway to reach Tayport was opened by the Edinburgh, Perth & Dundee Railway via Leuchars in 1850. Until the building of the Tay and Forth bridges this line linked ferry services across both of the estuaries. The opening of the Tay Bridge in 1878 should have seen the railway's demise but the bridge's dramatic collapse the following year brought it back to life. The second Tay Bridge opened in 1887 and the line went into obscurity, closing in 1956. Meanwhile the 4¾-mile Newport Railway had opened from Wormit, south of the Tay Bridge, to Tayport in 1879. Served by trains over the Tay Bridge from Dundee, Tayport lost its passenger service on 23 May 1966 when the Tay Road Bridge opened. The line was then cut back to Newport-on-Tay which lost its passenger service on 5 May 1969.

A two-car DMU waits to depart from neatly tended Tayport station with a train for Arbroath on 30 September 1965.

CLOSED OCTOBER 6 1969

Thornton Junction to Leven

Following the closure of the Leuchars Junction to St Andrews branch line on 6 January, the branch line from Thornton Junction to Leven became the only remaining section of what was once a 39-mile through route along the Fife coast. Although Thornton Junction to Leven was not listed for closure in the 'Beeching Report' it was closed to passengers on 6 October 1969. Coal traffic to Methil Power Station and freight to and from the Diageo distillery at Cameron Bridge continued until the 1990s when the track was mothballed. There are currently proposals to reopen this section of line both for freight and passenger traffic.

'B1' 4-6-0 No. 61330 enters Cameron Bridge station with the two-coach 2.42pm Crail to Thornton Junction train on 6 August 1965. Although closed to passengers on 6 October 1969, the Leven branch saw freight traffic to and from the Diageo distillery at Cameron Bridge until the 1990s.

Class 'J38' 0-6-0 No. 65910 storms up Glenfarg Bank with a Perth to Thornton Junction coal empties train on 6 August 1965.

BR Standard Class '4' 2-6-4T No. 80112 leaves Bridge of Weir station with the 6.45am Glasgow (St Enoch) to Kilmacolm train on 2 August 1965.

CLOSED
JANUARY 5 1970
Bridge of Earn to Cowdenbeath via Kinross

Although not listed for closure in the 'Beeching Report', the death of this once-important main line deserves mention in this book as it was once the direct route for trains between Perth and Edinburgh, but was sacrificed for the building of the M90 motorway. Serving collieries at its southern end, the line was opened from Cowdenbeath to Kinross by the Kinross-shire Railway in 1860. This was absorbed by the Edinburgh, Perth & Dundee Railway in 1861. Meanwhile, Kinross had already been reached by the Fife & Kinross Railway from Ladybank, in the east, via Mawcarse in 1857. The F&KR was amalgamated with the EP&DR in 1862 before being absorbed by the North British Railway in the same year.

To the north, the Edinburgh & Northern Railway had reached Hilton Junction at Perth from Ladybank via Abernethy and Bridge of Earn as early as 1848 but it took another 42 years before the NBR opened its line southwards from Bridge of Earn over Glenfarg Summit to join the Ladybank to Kinross line at Mawcarse. Therefore it was not until 1890, when the Forth Bridge was opened, that the NBR had completed its shorter route from Edinburgh to Perth.

By the 1960s motorways were seen, rather short-sightedly in the author's opinion, as the answer to Britain's transport needs. The M90 motorway from Edinburgh to Perth was one of these schemes and much of it was built along the course of the railway from Cowdenbeath to Bridge of Earn. To make way for the motorway, the entire route closed to passengers and for goods between Bridge of Earn and Kinross on 5 January 1970. Goods traffic continued from Cowdenbeath to Kinross until 4 May 1970. Trains between Edinburgh and Perth now operate by a much longer route via Ladybank and Hilton Junction.

CLOSED
JANUARY 10 1983
Shields Junction to Kilmacolm

What was eventually to become the Glasgow & South Western Railway's route from St Enoch to Greenock (Princes Pier) started life as a short branch line from Johnstone to Bridge of Weir opened by the Bridge of Weir Railway in 1864. A year later it was taken over by the G&SWR. It was later extended for eight miles to Kilmacolm and Greenock (Princes Pier) by the G&SWR in 1869.

The Paisley Canal line from St Enoch joined the Bridge of Weir and Kilmacolm line at Elderlsie Junction. Much of this railway ran along the course of the Glasgow, Paisley & Johnstone Canal which had been bought by the G&SWR in 1869 – the company closed it in 1881 and opened the railway across the 1811-built canal aqueduct over the River Cart in 1885.

The line north of Kilmacolm closed to ocean-liner specials from St Enoch on 30 November 1965 and to goods on 29 September 1966, leaving Kilmacolm at the end of a long branch line – St Enoch station closed on 7 June 1966 after which trains were rerouted via Shields Junction to Central station. While the entire route to Princes Pier had been listed for closure in the 'Beeching Report', the line from Shields Junction to Kilmacolm was reprieved until it, too, closed to passengers on 10 January 1983. However the line between Shields Junction and Elderslie Junction remained open for heavy freight traffic until 1985 after which the track was lifted.

The section from Shields Junction to Paisley Canal via Corkerhill reopened to passenger trains from Central station in 1990. There are proposals to electrify the line and extend it to Elderslie. Today, the trackbed from Paisley to Bridge of Weir and Kilmacolm forms a footpath and cycleway known as the Paisley & Clyde Railway Path.

INDEX

Note: Page numbers in **bold** refer to information contained in captions.

PHOTO CREDITS

A DAVID & CHARLES BOOK
© F&W Media International, Ltd 2013

David & Charles is an imprint of F&W Media International, Ltd
Brunel House, Forde Close, Newton Abbot, TQ12 4PU, UK

F&W Media International, Ltd is a subsidiary of
F+W Media, Inc
10151 Carver Road, Suite #200, Blue Ash, OH 45242, USA

First published in the UK in 2013

Text copyright ©Julian Holland 2013
Photographs copyright © see above

Julian Holland has asserted his right to be identified as author of this work in accordance with the Copyright, Designs and Patents Act, 1988.

A catalogue record for this book is available from the British Library.

ISBN-13: 978-1-4463-0267-5
ISBN-10: 1-4463-0267-9

Printed in the UK by Butler Tanner & Dennis Ltd, for F&W Media International, Brunel House, Newton Abbot, Devon

10 9 8 7 6 5 4 3

Community Leader Judith Harvey
Junior Acquisitions Editor Verity Graves-Morris
Design Manager Sarah Clark
Designer Marieclare Mayne
Production Manager Beverley Richardson

F+W Media publish high quality books on a wide range of subjects.
For more great book titles visit: www.fwmedia.co.uk